Lecture Notes in Co

Founding Editors

Gerhard Goos
Juris Hartmanis

Editorial Board Members

Elisa Bertino, *Purdue University, West Lafayette, IN, USA*
Wen Gao, *Peking University, Beijing, China*
Bernhard Steffen ⓘ, *TU Dortmund University, Dortmund, Germany*
Moti Yung ⓘ, *Columbia University, New York, NY, USA*

The series Lecture Notes in Computer Science (LNCS), including its subseries Lecture Notes in Artificial Intelligence (LNAI) and Lecture Notes in Bioinformatics (LNBI), has established itself as a medium for the publication of new developments in computer science and information technology research, teaching, and education.

LNCS enjoys close cooperation with the computer science R & D community, the series counts many renowned academics among its volume editors and paper authors, and collaborates with prestigious societies. Its mission is to serve this international community by providing an invaluable service, mainly focused on the publication of conference and workshop proceedings and postproceedings. LNCS commenced publication in 1973.

Zsuzsa Pluhár · Bence Gaál
Editors

Informatics in Schools

Innovative Approaches to Computer
Science Teaching and Learning

17th International Conference on Informatics in Schools:
Situation, Evolution, and Perspectives, ISSEP 2024
Budapest, Hungary, October 28–30, 2024
Proceedings

Editors
Zsuzsa Pluhár ⓘ
Eötvös Loránd University
Budapest, Hungary

Bence Gaál ⓘ
Eötvös Loránd University
Budapest, Hungary

ISSN 0302-9743   ISSN 1611-3349 (electronic)
Lecture Notes in Computer Science
ISBN 978-3-031-73473-1   ISBN 978-3-031-73474-8 (eBook)
https://doi.org/10.1007/978-3-031-73474-8

© The Editor(s) (if applicable) and The Author(s), under exclusive license to Springer Nature Switzerland AG 2025

This work is subject to copyright. All rights are solely and exclusively licensed by the Publisher, whether the whole or part of the material is concerned, specifically the rights of translation, reprinting, reuse of illustrations, recitation, broadcasting, reproduction on microfilms or in any other physical way, and transmission or information storage and retrieval, electronic adaptation, computer software, or by similar or dissimilar methodology now known or hereafter developed.
The use of general descriptive names, registered names, trademarks, service marks, etc. in this publication does not imply, even in the absence of a specific statement, that such names are exempt from the relevant protective laws and regulations and therefore free for general use.
The publisher, the authors and the editors are safe to assume that the advice and information in this book are believed to be true and accurate at the date of publication. Neither the publisher nor the authors or the editors give a warranty, expressed or implied, with respect to the material contained herein or for any errors or omissions that may have been made. The publisher remains neutral with regard to jurisdictional claims in published maps and institutional affiliations.

This Springer imprint is published by the registered company Springer Nature Switzerland AG
The registered company address is: Gewerbestrasse 11, 6330 Cham, Switzerland

If disposing of this product, please recycle the paper.

Preface

This volume contains selected papers presented at the 17th International Conference on Informatics in Schools: Situation, Evolution, and Perspectives (ISSEP 2024). The conference was hosted by Eötvös Loránd University, Faculty of Informatics, in Hungary, Budapest, during 28–30 October.

ISSEP serves as a vital forum for researchers, educators, and practitioners dedicated to the advancement of informatics education in primary and secondary schools. This conference offers a unique opportunity for the exchange of ideas and the development of innovative approaches to teaching and learning in the field of informatics. Since its inception in 2005 in Klagenfurt, Austria, the ISSEP conference has grown and evolved, with previous editions held in cities such as Vilnius (2006), Torun (2008), Zürich (2010), Bratislava (2011), Oldenburg (2013), Istanbul (2014), Ljubljana (2015), Münster (2016), Helsinki (2017), St. Petersburg (2018), Larnaca (2019), Tallinn (2020), Nijmegen (2021), Vienna (2022), and Lausanne (2023). Each conference contributed to the ongoing dialogue and development in the field of informatics education.

The conference continues to strongly support young researchers through the Doctoral Consortium, held the day before the main conference, as was successfully done in Lausanne and Vienna in the past 2 years. On October 27, 2024, several doctoral students presented and discussed their research, benefiting from the guidance of international experts and infusing their work with new perspectives.

On the first day of the event, local teachers participated in practical workshops and lectures as part of the memorial conference honoring László Zsakó, a key figure in Hungarian informatics education. This initiative fosters closer interaction between teachers and researchers, ensuring classroom relevance and providing teachers with insights into the latest developments in the field.

The ISSEP 2024 Program Committee received 42 paper submissions. Based on 3–5 blind reviews, 14 full papers were included in the conference publication this year, corresponding to a 33% acceptance rate. We express our sincere thanks to the reviewers for their dedicated and timely work. The entire submission, review, and selection process was done using the EasyChair conference management system.

Based on the papers submitted and accepted, the themes of the conference were thus defined as follows:

- Curricula and Computer Science Concepts
- Teacher's Perspective
- Problem Solving, Algorithms, and Programming

We would like to sincerely thank the Program Committee for their diligent review of submissions and invaluable feedback to authors. Thanks also go to the authors for their numerous high-quality contributions. Finally, we are grateful to our colleagues and the local organizing committee for managing the logistics of the physical conference, as well as to our institution, the Eötvös Loránd University and the John von Neumann Computer Society for providing funding and supporting the conference.

August 2024

Zsuzsa Pluhár
Bence Gaál

Organization

Conference Chairs

Zsuzsa Pluhár — Eötvös Loránd University, Hungary
Ágnes Erdősné Németh — Eötvös Loránd University, Hungary

Steering Committee

Erik Barendsen — Radboud University and Open University, the Netherlands
Andreas Bollin — University of Klagenfurt, Austria
Valentina Dagienė — Vilnius University, Lithuania
Gerald Futschek — TU Wien, Austria
Yasemin Gülbahar — Teachers College, Columbia University, USA
Juraj Hromkovič — ETH Zürich, Switzerland
Ivan Kalaš — Comenius University, Slovakia
Mart Laanpere — Tallinn University, Estonia
Gabriel Parriaux — University of Teacher Education, Lausanne, Switzerland
Jean-Philippe Pellet — University of Teacher Education, Lausanne, Switzerland
Zsuzsa Pluhár — Eötvös Loránd University, Hungary
Sergei Pozdniakov — Saint Petersburg Electrotechnical University, Russia

Program Committee

Andreas Bollin — University of Klagenfurt, Austria
Andrej Brodnik — University of Ljubljana, Slovenia
Špela Cerar — University of Ljubljana, Slovenia
Christian Datzko — Gymnasium Liestal, Switzerland
Monica Divitini — Norwegian University of Science and Technology, Norway
Ágnes Erdősné Németh — Eötvös Loránd University, Hungary
Gerald Futschek — TU Wien, Austria
Bence Gaál — Eötvös Loránd University, Hungary

Yasemin Gülbahar	Teachers College, Columbia University, USA
Micha Hersch	University of Teacher Education, Lausanne, Switzerland
Juraj Hromkovič	ETH Zürich, Switzerland
Corinna Hörmann	Johannes-Kepler-Universität Linz, Austria
Ivan Kalaš	Comenius University, Slovakia
Kaido Kikkas	Tallinn University of Technology, Estonia
Dennis Komm	ETH Zürich, Switzerland
Martina Landman	TU Wien, Austria
Peter Larsson	University of Turku, Finland
Lukas Lehner	TU Wien, Austria
Nina Angela Lobnig	University of Klagenfurt, Austria
Birgy Lorenz	Tallinn University of Technology, Estonia
Tilman Michaeli	TU Munich, Germany
Mattia Monga	Università degli Studi di Milano, Italy
Stefan Pasterk	University of Klagenfurt, Austria
Gabriel Parriaux	University of Teacher Education, Lausanne, Switzerland
Jean-Philippe Pellet	University of Teacher Education, Lausanne, Switzerland
Zsuzsa Pluhár	Eötvös Loránd University, Hungary
Giovanni Serafini	ETH Zürich, Switzerland
Vipul Shah	ACM India, India
Jacqueline Staub	Trier University, Germany
Gabrielė Stupurienė	Vilnius University, Lithuania
Maciej Sysło	Warsaw School of Computer Science, Poland
Michael Weigend	University of Münster, Germany
Markus Wieser	University of Klagenfurt

Additional Reviewers

Smitha Balakrishanan
Ľudmila Jašková
Lisa Kuka
Karolína Miková
Michal Winczer

Contents

Curricula and Computer Science Concepts

Secondary Teachers' Self-perceived AI Competences in Relation
to Renowned European Digital Competence Frameworks 3
    Michael Jemetz, Dominik Dolezal, and Renate Motschnig

Effect of New Computing Curriculum: Results from Incoming High
School Freshmen 18
    Greg Lee, Yi-Ling Wu, and Jia-Yi Chen

K-8 Digital Literacy Curriculum in the Netherlands 30
    Nataša Grgurina and Jos Tolboom

Implementing Informatics Core Curriculum in Early School Education
in Poland 44
    Maciej M. Sysło

Problem Solving, Algorithms and Programming

Mastering Control Structures in Secondary Education: Student
Observations and Descriptions of Program Logic 61
    *Corinna Mößlacher, Katharina Brugger, Tatjana Angermann,
    and Andreas Bollin*

From Guesswork to Game Plan: Exploring Problem-Solving-Strategies
in a Machine Learning Game 73
    Clemens Witt, Thiemo Leonhardt, Erik Marx, and Nadine Bergner

A Learning Environment to Promote the Computational Thinker: A Bebras
Perspective Evaluation 85
    *Oliver Kastner-Hauler, Karin Tengler, Barbara Sabitzer,
    and Zsolt Lavicza*

Programming Tasks in the Bebras Challenge: Are They a Good Idea
in Terms of the Contestants' Workload? 99
    Václav Šimandl, Václav Dobiáš, and Jiří Vaníček

Teaching Task Specification Efficiently in Introductory Programming
Courses in Higher Education 111
    Győző Horváth

Teacher's Perspective

A Glimpse Into Primary and Secondary Teachers' Knowledge to Teach
Informatics 125
    Gabriel Parriaux, Jean-Philippe Pellet, and Vassilis Komis

Exploring Transformative Professional Development Within K-12
Computing Education 139
    Sue Sentance, Robert Whyte, and Diana Kirby

Teachers' Motivation to Engage with Students in a Computer Science
and Computational Thinking Challenge: Does Motivation Conform
to a 'One-Size-Fits-All' Model? 152
    Lidia Feklistova, Tatjana Jevsikova, Bence Gaál, and Zsuzsa Pluhár

Analyzing Teachers' Diagnostic and Intervention Processes in Debugging
Using Video Vignettes 167
    Heike Wachter and Tilman Michaeli

Role-Playing of Misconceptions in Teacher Training: Enhancing
Pre-service Teachers' Understanding of Students' Programming Processes 180
    Martin Weinert and Hendrik Krone

Author Index 195

Curricula and Computer Science Concepts

Secondary Teachers' Self-perceived AI Competences in Relation to Renowned European Digital Competence Frameworks

Michael Jemetz[1,2,3](✉), Dominik Dolezal[1,4,5], and Renate Motschnig[1]

[1] Faculty of Computer Science, University of Vienna, Vienna, Austria
{michael.jemetz,dominik.dolezal,renate.motschnig}@univie.ac.at
[2] Doctoral School Computer Science (DoCS), University of Vienna, Vienna, Austria
[3] HTL Pinkafeld, Pinkafeld, Austria
[4] University of Applied Sciences Technikum Wien, Vienna, Austria
[5] TGM - Vienna Institute of Technology, Vienna, Austria

Abstract. The fast-paced developments in GenAI technology have begun to change school realities. The aim of this study is to identify what competences teachers of technical subjects are relying on when managing AI use in the classroom and to what degree these competences are covered in the DigComp framework. This study used a qualitative research approach utilizing semi-structured interviews. Nine educators from two vocational upper secondary schools in Austria were interviewed and a thematic analysis of the interviews was conducted to identify competences which were then mapped to DigComp2.2. Results show that several of the AI-related competences identified, such as information literacy and privacy can smoothly be mapped to DigComp2.2. However, other competences such as prompting, and the reflected goal-oriented use of GenAI tools appear not to fit in well and hence point to the necessity of adapting DigComp2.2. Furthermore, the importance of interpersonal skills and a well-founded subject knowledge were highlighted as crucial. This research is targeted at curriculum designers, educators, educational researchers, and administrators. It will also speak to teachers who wish to better deal with and prosper from the emergence of GenAI in schools. Future work will address key factors in developing educators' and students' AI literacy.

Keywords: digital competence · generative AI · AI literacy · information competence · vocational education · DigComp2.2 · DigCompEdu

1 Introduction

Recent developments in the field of generative artificial intelligence (GenAI) and large language models (LLM) demonstrated how quickly disruptive technologies can gain popularity, even though many aspects of their usage - especially regarding the responsible, ethical, and reflective use - are still unclear. Since their application will bring both great opportunities as well as high risks for individuals and organizations in the future, the authors therefore endeavor to promote the active and reflective integration of GenAI into modern education.

The formulation of educators' competence profiles has been a focus of education research long before these developments and has become even more relevant with the advent of GenAI tools. However, the integration of these newly emerging competences into existing frameworks for digital competences has not been covered widely yet. The European DigComp2.2 framework [1], which is one of the most established in the field, yet not specific to educators, is one of the few efforts made in this direction to date.

The goal of this paper is to investigate to what extent this prominent current framework covers the responsible use of GenAI in education and to identify concrete competences that may be valuable additions. Based on a literature review and interviews with nine teachers from two different vocational upper secondary schools, we mapped emerging competencies reported by our interviewees to DigComp2.2 [1] to explore overlaps and identify possible short-comings.

2 Background

2.1 Digital Competence

It is beyond dispute that digitalization, which goes hand in hand with the 21st century, has lastingly changed the skills required in today's digital world, which naturally include digital literacy skills [3]. The digital competences relevant in modern life are defined by several national and international frameworks. One of the most well-established competence models is the DigComp framework developed by the European Commission, which has been continuously refined over the last years. In the newest version of the framework, DigComp2.2 [1], AI competencies are addressed, however, merely in form of scenarios mapped to existing digital skills. Notably, the DigComp 2.2 framework was developed before the general rise of generative AI, which raises the question whether recent developments in this field create the need for a new or an updated framework.

Digital Competence in Teaching Practice. It is clear that teachers' digital competence should go beyond the mere ability to use technology and rather extend to the pedagogical usage of technology [1,4] to be capable of fostering their learners' digital skills. The concept of digital competences has grown more and more central in education over the last decades. There are several different models that formalize the digital skills needed in this specific context. Amongst the most prominent are the TPACK [4] and DigCompEdu [2] models.

The TPACK framework specifically deals with the overlap between the different areas of expertise expected from educators working in a digitally enhanced environment [4]. The model defines the areas of technical, pedagogical and content knowledge and highlights their interplay [4].

DigCompEdu, which is part of the larger DigComp framework and presents the didactic application dimension of digital skills, is closely linked to the general competence model and can be seen as an extension thereof [1,2]. The main aspects modeled are the professional and pedagogical competences of educators and the fostering of learners' digital competencies.

2.2 AI Literacy

AI pervades more and more areas of daily life, such as customer service [5] and psychotherapy [6]; recent literature even uses the term "Human-AI interaction (HAII)" [7]. Current research also highlights its potential in climate research [8]; experts even estimate that AI may facilitate the accomplishment of 134 of the 169 targets of the Sustainable Development Goals (SDG) [9]. Similarly, AI has also found entry into the field of education: Current applications and approaches include the usage of AI tools to foster academic writing [10], tracking students' wellbeing [11], and AI-supported learning platforms [12]. However, due to missing technical knowledge and accelerated by media coverage, students may perceive AI as dangerous and even fear it [13] or may overly rely on the new technology to the point that they lose learning opportunities [14], which is why it should be addressed at school and in teacher education (TE) programs [13].

A number of frameworks and models to describe skills needed for work with generative AI have been developed over the last two years [15]. A common theme here is that these skills are considered in isolation and not integrated into a wider range of digital skills such as presented in the competence models described above. Brauner et al. developed a competence framework for AI professionals based on job advertisements and probabilistic topic modeling, defining the five competence areas: Data science, AI software development, AI product development and management, AI client servicing, as well as AI research [16]. Long and Magerko approached the concept from a wider perspective and formulated a list of competences defining general AI literacy for learners at K12 level [17]. Based on a literature review, Ng et al. extended the DigCompEdu framework as well as the P21 Framework for 21st Century Learning to include the use of AI technology [18], proposing four processes to foster students' AI competence. This work added a broad frame of reference, which in an abstract manner integrates AI literacy into the similarly high-level model of DigCompEdu, which is mainly focused on the application of digital competences rather than knowledge and skills directly [2]. The construct developed by Ng et al. therefore provides an overview of where AI competence is relevant and how it relates to teacher's tasks [18]. A similar, larger-scale effort was made by Bekiaridis and Attwell [19].

As these two models [18,19] contextualize their findings within DigCompEdu [2], the competences presented there occur within specific application contexts. With this modeling of competences – we believe – the focus is placed more on the professional tasks they are required for than the competences themselves. This research project therefore aims to more concretely analyze the basic competences required of teachers rather than the specific applications thereof.

2.3 Research Questions

The aim of this project is to answer the following three questions:

1. What competences do teachers from vocational secondary schools identify as important in their work with students in a time where GenAI has become widely accessible and utilized among them?
2. What competences do teachers from vocational secondary schools identify as important when making use of GenAI in their professional work themselves?
3. In how far are these AI-related competencies covered by the DigComp2.2 framework?

3 Methodology

3.1 Research Design

The research project presented in this paper employed a series of semi-structured expert interviews for data collection. A thematic analysis was conducted on the data gathered in these interviews.

3.2 Expert Interviews

Participants and their Recruitment. The nine participants, who were recruited via the authors' social contacts, were all employed at technical, vocational upper secondary schools – two of them in an urban one and seven in a rural area – at the time of data collection. They all have teaching experience in technical subjects such as data science and artificial intelligence, programming, database systems, network technologies, media technologies, and construction.

They range from relative beginners with only a few months of teaching experience to practitioners who have been teaching Computer Science (CS) for over two decades at the time of data collection. Detailed information on the individual participants can be found in Table 5.

Structured Interviews - Guide and Process. Topics covered in the data collection included learners' GenAI use and how the educators approach it, how they encourage their students to utilize GenAI and to what extent. The educators' own utilization of the new technology for professional tasks and potential new challenges they expect were also discussed. For description of the relevant sections of the interview guide, see Table 7. Other topics like the educators' strategies for developing their AI literacy were also covered in the interviews and are going to be followed up in further research.

The interviews were planned and conducted in accordance with the guidelines provided by McGrath et al. [20] and Denirici [21]. Pre-interview talks were held with all participants to build rapport and to clarify the purpose of the research and what to expect from the interviews. Furthermore, declaration of consent forms were designed to offer privacy options to participants and discussed with each interviewee during the meeting.

An interview guide (see Table 5 in the appendix) was created based on our research interests and used as a loose outline for the interviews. While all questions were asked in all conversations, topics and examples brought up during answers were further explored when the interviewer found them to likely be relevant to the research interest. Furthermore, participants were given the chance to go on tangents and to add anything they had on their mind.

The active listening technique as described by Rogers and Farson [22] was utilized during the interviews as a first instrument for participant validation [20]. Further checking was done by sending transcripts out to those willing to review them. All participants were available for follow-up questions.

3.3 Data Analysis

After an AI-aided transcription [23–25] of the conducted interviews, a thematic analysis was performed. This process was guided by the method proposed by Nowell et al. [26]. In accordance with the authors' recommendations, an audit trail was carefully constructed. The interviewer took reflective notes during and after the meetings with the participants [26]. Based on the insights gained, the preliminary coding framework, which was deductively generated based on DigComp2.2 [1] was further developed and complemented with inductively generated categories. All transcripts were stored in standardized documents with a header containing meta-information on the participants and the interview settings.

These full transcriptions were screened by the first author and then filtered according to the research questions from approximately 48.000 to 15.000 words before the analysis was conducted by two members of the team. This initial screening also served as a second information source for inductive category generation and as an indicator of theoretical saturation as described in Grounded Theory [27]. As only one of the last three interviews contained any new information adjacent to the research interests, the nine interviews were deemed sufficient and data collection was concluded.

In preparation of the coding process, a meeting was held, where the coding framework was discussed, and minor adjustments were made. The first author did a preliminary pass over the data that informed further refinement of the framework, which was then consulted with and used by two authors in the analysis. Team members then coded the data individually before the codes were merged by the first author and another meeting for code verification was held. Finally, themes were summarized by the first author and reviewed by the team.

4 Results and Interpretation

From the interviewees' responses, various competences needed in their teaching contexts could be identified. As can be seen in Table 1, these are not limited to what was already defined in DigComp2.2. Furthermore, educators indicated that some issues cannot be individual teachers' responsibilities but need to be approached on a systematic level, speculated on potential uses of GenAI in and outside of school settings and related the competences to the vocational context they are preparing learners for.

Table 1. Top-level category system of competences identified in the data

theme	description
digital competences	the competences described in DigComp2.2 [1] and DigCompEdu [2]
other competences	anything not covered by the DigComp2.2 [1] framework and related to educators' skills and knowledge
existing organizational or didactic strategies	handling AI usage with didactic strategies that don't directly require new competences from the teacher
systemic issue	issues that cannot be addressed by individual teachers alone
business applications	identifying where AI might be useful in commercial contexts and how learners may benefit from being proficient in using it
future potential	aspects of AI usage that might only become relevant or useful later

4.1 Competences Identified as Important by Educators

Outside of general digital competences as defined in DigComp2.2, the competences identified by educators can be grouped into three major categories described in Table 2. Specifically, these are interpersonal and didactic skills, competences related to the subject taught and AI literacy.

Table 2. Sub-category system for 'other competences'

theme	description
general interpersonal or didactic skills	communication, building relationships with learners, supporting learning, etc. (outside of digital channels)
proficiency in one's subject	competences related to subject-specific tasks, awareness for task complexity and relevance
AI literacy	competences needed to utilize AI that are not modeled in DigComp2.2

Since the field of AI literacy was the main focus of this project, a more finely grained perspective on the aspects of the concept was adapted during analysis. As can be seen in Table 3, the main aspects identified were a technical understanding of the GenAI systems in question, an ethical approach, legal awareness and application competence in the widest sense. Yet, basic application competence is not enough, rather a goal-oriented approach to GenAI usage, prompting and the ability to recognize and evaluate output generated by such systems are required.

Table 3. Sub-category system for 'AI literacy'

theme	description
technical understanding	knowledge related to the inner workings of a modern AI, its capabilities and limitations, the underlying data, biases, hallucinations, etc.
ethics	ethical considerations of AI use, responsible use, critical perspective
basic application competence	being able to access and utilize an AI model on a basic level
reflected, goal-oriented use	formulate a goal which one strives to reach through the work with AI tools and finding strategies for achieving that goal
prompting	formulating inputs for an AI tool so that outcomes are likely to be useful
(recognizing and) evaluating output	review the output generated by an AI and determine if it is useful and correct based on the input and fitting for one's needs, critical thinking
legal boundaries	utilizing AI content in a legally sound manner

Competences Needed for Managing Learners' AI Usage. Based on the data collected, educators need a variety of competences to appropriately deal with learners' usage of GenAI tools and to be able to facilitate the development of good practices. Firstly, it is important for educators to be able to ensure learning goals are met by learners. Educators partially rely on pre-existing strategies such as submission-talks, presentations or pen-and-paper tests for assessment and prohibiting AI use for certain tasks. The main argument for these practices being that learners need to be equipped with some fundamental knowledge in the subjects for them to become proficient enough to critically utilize GenAI tools. Therefore, a strong awareness for which subject-specific competences are so fundamental to their domain that it must be known by someone who wishes to work in it is required of educators. However, it has been noted that defining this fundamental knowledge as well as assessment practices need to be addressed not just at the individual but rather at a systematic level. Furthermore, educators need to be able to detect when an artefact is likely generated by an AI to be able to react to students' use of the tool. Here, a basic understanding of the inner workings of GenAI tools and a well-founded knowledge of the subject taught have proven beneficial. In addition to recognizing AI use, it is important for educators to be able to judge whether the usage is reasonable in the context it occurred in from a didactic and subject-specific standpoint. In other words, educators need to be able to judge if learning goals were met and the end product fulfills quality expectations. Again, subject knowledge is needed here.

Competences Needed for Utilizing AI for Teaching and Other Professional Tasks. However, a reflective and goal-oriented use of GenAI tools is seen as highly important by the educators – especially because it is likely going to enable learners in their future careers. Here it was noted that learners need to develop an understanding for GenAI as a tool. In order to facilitate learners' competences in effectively using GenAI tools, educators, again, need to have an understanding of the technical backgrounds of these tools, a well-founded subject knowledge, but also need to be knowledgeable in prompting as well as being able to guide learners in clearly defining their goals when using the tool and supporting them in working towards them reflectively. To motivate learners to reasonably work with GenAI rather than using it as a "shortcut" (participant 03) and for "avoiding learning" (participant 09), educators need to be able to argue for the importance of fundamental knowledge and design meaningful and complex learning tasks. This requires not only subject knowledge but also social and didactic skills. Soft skills in general are also seen as growing in importance in the context of GenAI developments with knowledge generation and automatization of menial tasks becoming more widespread among educators and learners.

Additionally, educators need to be able to foster the learners' output-evaluation skills – which is strongly linked to critical thinking and information literacy – and raise awareness for ethical considerations regarding the application of GenAI tools and the utilization of generated output. Data bias, worldviews represented in the data and the unreliable nature of generative AI were mentioned in this context that was often linked to technical understanding. Additionally, an awareness for legal aspects comes into play here. Learners need to be aware that GenAI usage cannot substitute human reasoning and must not be used in certain critical contexts such as decision making or tasks that require certain certifications of those performing them. Furthermore, learners need to develop transparency in their usage and properly declare it according to guidelines. A consideration of data security when using GenAI also needs to be fostered.

The effective usage of GenAI for teaching – e.g. as a tool for research tasks or material creation but also for proposed future use cases such as a tool for diagnostics – and professional engagement – such as developing one's subject-knowledge – requires largely the same competences as the ones for fostering learners AI literacy. Teaching in general, however, starts to require some competences more in the context of AI-literate learners. On the one hand, educators need to be even more aware of new developments in technology and keep themselves updated. On the other hand, educators' interpersonal and emotional skills will become more relevant, as due to the availability of information in easily accessible form through GenAI tools, they will need to be more coach than knowledge provider. This includes motivating learners and providing them with guidance. Yet, a well-founded knowledge of the subject will still be required.

Additionally, educators need to be aware that different models can vary heavily in terms of output quality and are often not free to be used. Further, they need to find available, fitting GenAI tools for the needs of their learners and ideally find ways of lessening inequalities arising from limited availability as far as possible. Again, institutional support would be needed in this regard.

4.2 Coverage of the Competences in DigComp

Many of the competences identified from the interviews can be mapped to DigComp2.2. Information competence and the critical evaluation of digital artefacts needed for evaluating outputs and reflective use of GenAI are defined in the framework. The evaluation of AI outputs, however, also requires an understanding for the inner workings and unreliability of GenAI models beyond what is described in DigComp2.2. A technical understanding of capabilities and limitations of GenAI technology also is not included in the competence descriptions.

Digital content creation is covered in DigComp2.2, however, prompting as a central technique in working with text-based GenAI is not mentioned. Data security and ethical considerations are mentioned in scenarios. This is also true for copyright and licenses when using AI-generated content. Legal boundaries, however, are not covered beyond that. The identification of available and useful AI tools corresponds to the identification of needs and responses, however, the creative use competence only touches upon goal-orientation in scenarios.

4.3 Suggested Additions to DigComp

Based on these findings, we suggest some concrete additions to the DigComp framework described in Table 4.

Table 4. Suggested additions to DigComp and DigCompEdu and possible integrations

addition	within DigComp2.2 [1]
critical evaluation of generative AI output informed by basic technical knowledge	"information and data literacy"
AI ethics	"safety"
awareness for AI systems' capabilities and their limitations	"needs and responses"
awareness for legal boundaries impacting AI use	"digital content creation"
goal setting and orientation skills	"creative use"
prompting strategies to support goal-oriented AI use	"digital content creation" or "problem solving"

Regarding DigCompEdu [2], the complements to accommodate AI competence would mainly concern the necessity of teachers' professional development in the field of AI-competence. This being covered, teachers need to apply their competence to facilitate learners' competences to understand, apply, adapt and create AI technology for constructive progress in different areas. Overall, the additions identified here all are relevant in each of the three areas of DigCompEdu [2].

5 Discussion

5.1 Limitations

The two main limitations of this study are that all schools under investigation are from one nation with teachers sharing the same cultural context and that – due to space limitations given in this format – the investigation is focused on the relation of the relevant competencies just to the DigComp model family. However, we believe that the results of this study are representative of trends within the wider target group of educators and can be a basis for further research.

5.2 Findings and Implications

Findings. Concerning the first two research questions, educators reported the importance of goal-oriented, critical, and reflected usage of GenAI, a basic underlying understanding of the technology as well as the consideration of ethical and legal questions arising from using these tools for both being able to manage learners GenAI use as well as for their own professional utilization of this new technology. Subject-knowledge as well as interpersonal and didactic abilities were also highlighted. In regard to the third research question: The DigComp2.2 framework models most of the identified competences, such as information literacy, ethical and legal aspects to some degree, however, does not capture their full range. Furthermore, the technique of prompting and the technical understanding of GenAI systems and their capabilities are not covered by DigComp2.2.

Implications. Consistent with the findings of Ng et al. [18] and Bekiaridis and Attwell [19], all dimensions of DigCompEdu [2] have been discussed in relation to AI literacy and the aspects thereof identified in the interviews are largely coherent with those found by Long and Magerko [17]. This provides a boost to the validity of the current empirical study. While all research questions were responded to in Sect. 4, the broader implications of the work points to the fact that DigComp2.2 will need adaptations to more specifically and comprehensively accommodate competencies needed for a goal-oriented, responsible, and learning-supportive use of GenAI tools by both teachers and learners. The findings also point towards institutional support being needed in competence development and the identification of available and useful GenAI tools for teaching. Intriguingly, our research moreover strengthens the crucial importance of the human potential in terms of advanced soft- or professional skills to deal with the new situation brought about by the disruptive contribution of GenAI technologies.

6 Conclusion

The analysis of the nine expert interviews conducted in this project identified critical thinking and technical knowledge in the AI domain as well as social and didactic skills as central competences for educators in a time where GenAI tools are easily available. While most of these competences are covered to some degree by DigComp2.2, technical knowledge of GenAI systems and skills needed for the reflected, critical usage of these tools would be promising additions.

An analysis of the competence development strategies of the educators interviewed in this project as well as a second series of interviews with a broader group of teachers with more varied backgrounds are planned in the near future. In addition to including teachers with more varied cultural backgrounds, quantitative research methods could help further define general competence needs.

Acknowledgments. This work was supported by the Austrian Ministry of Education under the projects M795001: "Teaching Digital Thinking" and B3-16: "dig!doc - Gelingensbedingungen einer Digitalen (Grund-)Bildung". We sincerely thank the Bundesministerium für Bildung, Wissenschaft und Forschung, directorates of education and the participating schools and teachers. We also thank the dig!doc consortium for their valuable input and F. Laschober and R. Jemetz for their help with the transcription.

Disclosure of Interests. The authors have no conflicting interests to declare.

A Appendix

A.1 Additional Information on the Participants

Table 5. Biographic information on the participants

ID	gender	subjects	years active	region
1	male	Programming, Data Science & AI, Project Management	6 years	rural
2	male	Database Systems, Applied Computer Science, Computer Architecture*, Game Development & VR+, Programming	6 years	rural
3	male	Construction, Applied Computer Science|	<1 year	rural
4	male	Programming, Web- and Mobile Programming, Geography*	7 years	rural
5	female	Data Science and AI, Mathematics, Project Management	10 years	urban
6	male	Media Technology, Project Management	6 years	urban
7	male	Foundations of Computer Science, Network Technology, Computer Architecture*	21 years	rural
8	male	Applied Computer Science, Computer Architecture, Game Development, Foundations of Computer Science, Network Technology, Database Systems, History	4 years	rural
9	female	Programming, Web and Mobile Programming, Media Technology, Computer Architecture*	9 years	rural

In Table 5 the subjects the participants taught in the past are marked with a *, subjects they plan to teach and are involved in preparing are marked with a +, and subjects they were not formally trained for with a |.

Table 6. GenAI tool usage as reported by the participants

ID	reported (in-class or own) GenAI tool usage	training own models
1	ChatGPT	yes
2	ChatGPT, GitHub-Copilot, image generators	yes
3	ChatGPT	no
4	ChatGPT, GitHub-Copilot	no
5	ChatGPT, GitHub-Copilot, MS Copilot, LLMs, image generators	yes
6	ChatGPT, GitHub-Copilot, image generators	no
7	ChatGPT, image recognition	no
8	ChatGPT, GitHub-Copilot, IDE plug-ins, MS Copilot, search engines	no
9	ChatGPT, GitHub-Copilot, IDE plug-ins, Auto-Correct, MS Copilot, image generators	no

A.2   Additional Information on the Interview Process

Table 7. Interview questions connected to this paper's research questions

ID	question
Q01	Do you think AI is a disruptive technology? To what extent do you think this label is warranted?
Q02	How many years have you been teaching so far?
Q03	What subjects are you teaching?
Q04	Did you notice that your students are using AI in the classroom? What are they using it for? Do you know the tools they are using?
Q05	How do you manage this? How do you respond to that?
Q06	Are your students allowed to use AI in your classroom/for your subject? To what extent? Why or why not?
Q07	Do you encourage your students to use AI? Why or why not?
Q08	Do you use AI for your professional tasks? Why or why not? Which tools do you use? What tasks do you use them for?
Q09	Did you notice that your colleagues use AI for other tasks?
Q10	Are there any new challenges in the school system that emerged due to the developments in AI?
Q11	Do you think that AI adds or subtracts value to the teaching profession? Did you notice any other changes? How do you feel about that?

The interviews were conducted in German and all questions presented in Table 7 were translated from German into English for this paper. The average duration of the interviews was 47 min with the longest taking one hour and seven minutes and the shortest taking 32 min. Audio recordings of the interviews were made by the interviewer given the participants' consent. One interview was not recorded but rather transcribed live in order to make the situation less threatening for the participant.

Rationale for Question Choice. The questions presented in Table 7 were chosen for a number of different reasons. While Q02 and Q03 were simply intended to record biographic information on the participants, Q04 to Q09 were derived from research questions RQ1 and RQ2. Q01, Q10 and Q11 were intended to get participants talking about the topic in a broad manner and to allow for them to address different points they think are important. This was done as the authors felt that such explorations of the topic would also yield interesting insights into RQ1 and RQ2.

Note on the Use of the Term 'AI' During the Interviews. The term 'AI' was used during all interviews (rather than 'GenAI', 'LLM', etc.) and elaborated by the interviewer when necessary. This was done to elicit as wide a range of responses as possible. For all interviewees, the tools they refered to were elicited (see Table 6) and the research focus was clarified if needed.

References

1. Vuorikari, R., Kluzer, S., Punie, Y.: DigComp 2.2, The Digital Competence framework for citizens. With new examples of knowledge, skills and attitudes. EUR, vol. 31006. Publications Office of the EU, Luxembourg (2022). https://doi.org/10.2760/115376
2. Redecker, C., Punie, Y.: European Framework for the Digital Competence of Educators: DigCompEdu. Publications Office of the EU, Luxembourg (2017). https://doi.org/10.2760/159770
3. Trilling, B., Fadel, C.: 21st Century Skills. Learning for Life in our Times. Jossey-Bass, San Francisco (2012)
4. Mishra, P., Koehler, M.J.: Technological pedagogical content knowledge: a framework for teacher knowledge. Teach. Coll. Rec. (2006). https://doi.org/10.1111/j.1467-9620.2006.00684.x
5. Yang, C., Hu, J.: When do consumers prefer AI-enabled customer service? The interaction effect of brand personality and service provision type on brand attitudes and purchase intentions. J. Brand Manag. (2022). https://doi.org/10.1057/s41262-021-00261-7
6. Lee, J., Lee, D.: User perception and self-disclosure towards an AI psychotherapy chatbot according to the anthropomorphism of its profile picture. Telematics Inform. (2023). https://doi.org/10.1016/j.tele.2023.102052
7. Sundar, S.S.: Rise of machine agency: a framework for studying the psychology of human-AI interaction (HAII). JCMC (2020). https://doi.org/10.1093/jcmc/zmz026

8. Larosa, F., Hoyas, S., García-Martínez, J., Conejero, J.A., Fuso Nerini, F., Vinuesa, R.: Halting generative AI advancements may slow down progress in climate research. Nat. Clim. Chang. (2023). https://doi.org/10.1038/s41558-023-01686-5
9. Vinuesa, R., et al.: The role of artificial intelligence in achieving the sustainable development goals. Nat. Commun. (2020). https://doi.org/10.1038/s41467-019-14108-y
10. Meyer, E., Weßels, D.: Natural language processing im akademischen Schreibprozess - mehr Motivation durch Inspiration? In: Schmohl, T., Watanabe, A., Schelling, K. (eds.) Künstliche Intelligenz in der Hochschulbildung. Chancen und Grenzen des KI-gestützten Lernens und Lehrens, pp. 227-251. transcript, Bielefeld (2023). https://doi.org/10.14361/9783839457696
11. Tang, X., Upadyaya, K., Toyama, H., Kasanen, M., Salmela-Aro, K.: Assessing and tracking students' wellbeing through an automated scoring system: school day wellbeing model. In: Niemi, H., Pea, R.D., Lu, Y. (eds.) AI in Learning: Designing the Future, pp. 55–71. Springer, Cham (2023). https://doi.org/10.1007/978-3-031-09687-7_4
12. Niu, S.J., Li, X., Luo, J.: Multiple users' experiences of an AI-aided educational platform for teaching and learning. In: Niemi, H., Pea, R.D., Lu, Y. (eds.) AI in Learning: Designing the Future, pp. 215–231. Springer, Cham (2023). https://doi.org/10.3390/educsci12120858
13. Lindner, A., Berges, M., Lechner, M.: KI im Toaster? Schüler:innenvorstellungen zu künstlicher Intelligenz. In: Humbert, L. (ed.) Informatik - Bildung von Lehrkräften in allen Phasen. 19. GI-Fachtagung Informatik und Schule. LNI, pp. 133-142. Gesellschaft für Informatik, Bonn (2021). https://doi.org/10.18420/infos2021_f199
14. Memarian, B., Doleck, T.: ChatGPT in education: methods, potentials, and limitations. Comput. Hum. Behav. Artif. Hum. **1**(2), 1000222 (2023). https://doi.org/10.1016/j.chbah.2023.100022
15. Mikeladze, T., Meijer, P.C., Vorheff, R.P.: A comprehensive exploration of artificial intelligence competence frameworks for educators: a critical review. Eur. J. Educ. (2024). https://doi.org/10.1111/ejed.12663
16. Brauner, S., Murawski, M., Bick, M.: The development of a competence framework for artificial intelligence professionals using probabilistic topic modelling. JEIM (2023). https://doi.org/10.1108/JEIM-09-2022-0341
17. Long, D., Magerko, B.: What is AI Literacy? Competencies and Design Considerations. CHI (2020). https://doi.org/10.1145/3313831.3376727
18. Ng, D.T.K., Leung, J.K.L., Su, J., Ng, R.C.W., Chu, S.K.W.: Teachers' AI digital competencies and twenty-first century skills in the post-pandemic world. ETRD (2023). https://doi.org/10.1007/s11423-023-10203-6
19. Bekiaridis, G., Attwell, G.: Supplement to the DigCompEDU Framework: Outlining the Skills and Competences of Educators Related to AI in Education. University of Bremen, Institute Technology and Education, Bremen (2024)
20. McGrath, C., Palmgren, P.J., Liljedahl, M.: Twelve tips for conducting qualitative research interviews. Med. Teach. **41**(9), 1002–1006 (2018). https://doi.org/10.1080/0142159X.2018.1497149
21. Denirici, J.R.: About research: conducting better qualitative interviews. J. Hum. Lact. **40**(1), 21–24 (2024). https://doi.org/10.1177/08903344231213651
22. Rogers, C., Farson, R.E.: Active listening. In: Danzinger, M.A., Cohen, M. (eds.) Communicating in Business Today. Lexington, D.C. Heath & Company (1987)
23. Bian, M., Huh, J., Han, T., Zissermann, A.: WhisperX: Time-Accurate Speech Transcritpion of Long-Form Audio (2023). https://github.com/m-bain/whisper

24. Systran: Faster whisper (2023). http://huggingface.co/Systran/faster-whisper-large-v3
25. Plaquet, A., Bredin, H.: Powerset multi-class entropy loss for neural speaker diarization (2023). http://huggingface.co/pyannote/speaker-diarization-3.1
26. Nowell, L.S., Norris, J.M., White, D.E., Moules, N.J.: Thematic analysis: striving to meet the trustworthiness criteria. Int J Qual Methods **16**, 1–13 (2017). https://doi.org/10.1177/1609406917733847
27. Strübing, J.: Was ist grounded theory? In: Strübing, J. (ed.) Grounded Theory. QS, pp. 9–37. Springer, Wiesbaden (2021). https://doi.org/10.1007/978-3-658-24425-5_2

Effect of New Computing Curriculum: Results from Incoming High School Freshmen

Greg Lee[✉][iD], Yi-Ling Wu[iD], and Jia-Yi Chen[iD]

National Taiwan Normal University, Taipei, Taiwan
{leeg,ylwu}@csie.ntnu.edu.tw, 81147002S@ntnu.edu.tw

Abstract. In 2019, a new education curriculum was enacted in Taiwan, where the Information Technology (IT) education curriculum was also revamped. The focus of the new curriculum is computational thinking (CT) and problem-solving through programming. To understand students' learning achievements, a new problem-solving assessment, the Chippy Challenge, was developed. Tasks in the challenge are taken from real-life scenarios, requiring students to use their problem-solving, analytical, and programming skills to solve. By analyzing the results from the Chippy Challenge, we can assess students' CT and programming skills, and offer insights into students' learning achievement. This paper examines and reports the change in students' CT and programming skills before and after the new IT curriculum went into effect. This study included 9,735 participants, comparing achievements from 4,421 students to 5,314 students from before and after the new curriculum. Research methods include independent sample t-tests to analyze the differences in students' CT and programming skills performance between the two groups. The results showed that students who went through the new curriculum had significantly better problem-solving skills compared to the other group. Furthermore, students from the urban schools performed significantly better than students from the rural schools. The results show that the new curriculum has a positive effect on students' CT and programming problem-solving skills. However, the results are also alarming in that the majority of students still have lower-than-expected achievements.

Keywords: Information Technology Education · Computational Thinking · CS education

1 Introduction

In this digital age, the importance of Information Technology (IT) education has been widely recognized. Many countries have revised their IT curriculum to incorporate Computational Thinking (CT) into the curriculum [1,2]. In Taiwan, the new IT curriculum, implemented in 2019, mandates that students in grades

7–9 receive at least one hour of IT instruction per week throughout the three academic years. Unlike the previous curriculum, which stressed the use of IT as a tool and integration of IT into other subjects' teaching and learning, the new curriculum has IT taught as a subject where the focus is on developing students' CT and problem-solving skills through programming. These changes aim to cultivate higher-order thinking to facilitate CT, critical thinking, and problem-solving skills [3].

Before the new curriculum, the IT learning contents were software application and knowledge-replicative based. Although some teachers would teach Scratch [4] programming, it was without a specific learning outcome as the goal. Therefore, students' programming skills or problem-solving skills were often not found. It is important to transform traditional knowledge-replicative learning toward developing CT and programming skills for problem-solving. Therefore, in contrast to the previous curriculum, the new curriculum supports a knowledge-generative learning method that encourages students to learn through practice for problem-solving [5].

In [6], we have conducted a baseline study that assesses students's programming for problem-solving skills when learning under the previous curriculum. With the goal of understanding the impact of the new curriculum on IT education, this study used the same assessment tool to test the first group of grade 7–9 students who had gone through the new IT curriculum. The results are reported and compared to the baseline study in [6].

2 Programming Assessment

There was some research in the literature on evaluating the effectiveness of IT education. In particular, teaching, learning, and evaluation of CT and programming skills have often been studied. Various methodologies can be found in the literature for the assessment of CT skills. In [7], Araujo et al.. tried to analyze students' CT abilities using results from the Bebras Challenge. It was concluded that multiple CT skills are necessary for solving real-life problems. However, the Bebras tasks could not be independently used to assess the various components of CT. In [8], Chen et al.. developed an instrument to assess students' CT, contextualized for coding in robotics and reasoning in everyday events. The instrument has good psychometric properties and can reveal student learning challenges and growth in CT. In [9], Román-González et al.. assessed CT using a multiple-choice test that measures students' understanding of CT concepts. This test involves the ability to formulate and solve problems by relying on fundamental computing concepts and the logic-syntax of programming languages, including basic sequences, loops, iteration, conditionals, functions, and variables.

On the other hand, some programming assessment tools were developed to assess students' programming proficiency. In [10], Aziz et al.. introduced Web-CAT, a versatile automatic scoring system tailored for programming courses. This tool accommodates various programming languages and seamlessly integrates with other resources to improve code clarity and error detection. Offering detailed feedback and assessing code quality, it facilitates large-scale automated evaluation of students' programming abilities. Sendjaja et al.. [11] investigated the use of a control-flow graph (CFG) algorithm for evaluating student programming submissions against instructor reference codes. This approach seeks a more comprehensive assessment beyond output comparison, emphasizing fairness in grading based on code structure. The experiment demonstrated that CFG comparison can advantage students with minor errors, thereby enhancing their scores. In summary, various programming assessment tools have been developed to comprehensively evaluate students' programming proficiency, emphasizing code clarity, fairness in grading, and the identification of errors. These tools facilitate large-scale automated assessment and provide insights into students' programming abilities and solution characteristics. Through automated evaluation functionalities, these tools enable large-scale automatic assessment of students' programming abilities.

For this study, we use the same in-house Chippy Challenge assessment tool as in [6]. The Chippy Challenge tool consists of two types of tasks: goal-based and problem-based tasks. The goal-based tasks provide animated task descriptions and challenge students to identify the solution patterns (often repetitive patterns) en route to reaching the final goal in the given task. Students need to devise algorithms and write Scratch or Blockly programs to perform the same task. On the other hand, problem-based tasks are text-based tasks that require students to exhibit good abstraction, problem decomposition, algorithmic thinking, and evaluation skills, as well as programming skills in Scratch or Blockly, to correctly solve all different problem instances (test cases). One significant difference of the Chippy Challenge tool is that it offers students immediate feedback on program execution. For the goal-based tasks, students' program executions are visually shown with task animation. For the problem-based tasks, feedback with text-based hints to incorrectly or yet unconsidered problem instances are provided to the students. For novice programmers, the visual feedback and hints afford students to concentrate more on the algorithmic design aspect of problem-solving [8].

3 Research Setup

3.1 Participants

For this study, we called for high school IT teachers to participate in this study in 2021 and 2022. Incoming high school students in 2021 went through the old IT curriculum in their middle school years, whereas incoming high school students in 2022 went through the new IT curriculum in middle school. Participating high school IT teachers registered and had their IT class students participate in the Chippy Challenge within the first four weeks of the new school semester. Over the two-year period, a total of 57 schools with 305 classes for a total of 9,735 students participated in this study. The breakdown is shown in Table 1.

Table 1. Number of participating schools, classes and students.

New Curriculum	Location	No. of Schools	No. of Classes	No. of Students
Before	Urban	12	105	3,628
	Rural	5	25	793
After	Urban	28	121	4,106
	Rural	12	54	1,208

This study categorized schools into urban and rural areas based on their location. Urban areas, with a population of 1.25 million, offer more comprehensive educational resources as schools have more enrolling students, The average number of students in urban schools compared to rural schools was 1,352.32 vs. 727.67 in 2021 and 1,761.08 vs. 932.00 in 2022, respectively.

3.2 Procedure

The participating teachers use one class period within the first four weeks of the new school year to conduct the Chippy Challenge. The assessment was conducted before additional programming lessons in high school. Teachers were instructed to use the first 5 min of the class to introduce the assessment tool to students. Subsequently, students were given 45 min to work on the four tasks mentioned above. While teachers were allowed to provide assistance in understanding the tasks, students were required to independently conceptualize, think, write, and debug programs. Each student's program for each task was evaluated instantly and allowed students to ascertain whether they had completed tasks correctly. The same four tasks were used in the two years of the study to ensure no change in task difficulties.

3.3 Tasks for the Assessment

The same four tasks are used for both year's tests and are fully explained in [12]. The four tasks are shown in Fig. 1(a). The two goal-based tasks are Light and Robot Vacuum. The Light task repetitively projects different colored light onto the stage. Students must watch the animation, observe the repetitive projected light color pattern, and write a program to automatically control the light switches. For the Robot Vacuum task, the robot goes around the classroom to clean dust off the floor. Students are to recognize and program a strategy to move the vacuum around the classroom to complete the task. The program codes for both tasks are quite simple as shown in Fig. 1(b).

The two problem-based tasks are Cake Promotion and Drink Orders. The Cake Promotion task asks students to take orders, calculate the discount and the shipping fee, and then output the total price. Students need to have good abstraction (use of variables), decomposition, and algorithmic thinking (breaking problem into 3 subtasks) skills to properly design algorithms to solve this

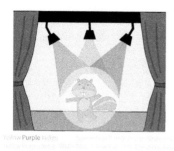
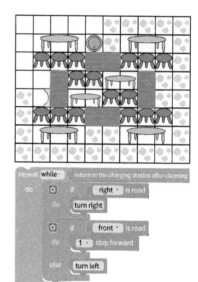
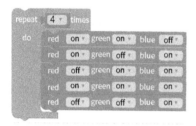

(a)   (b)

In order to celebrate the 1ˢᵗ anniversary of store opening, Chippy Cake Shop decided to hold a promotion on its official website. The original price of all cakes in the store is NT$300, and the shipping fee for each order is NT$80. The promotion rules are as follows:
1) Buy 1 to 5 cakes to enjoy a 10% discount.
2) Buy 6 to 10 cakes to enjoy a 20% discount.
3) Buy 11 to 15 cakes to enjoy a 30% discount.
4) Buy 16 cakes and above to enjoy a 40% discount.
Customers who spend more than NT$1,200 after the discount will get free shipping. Please design a pricing program for this promotion. The program will need to output the total order amount and price after each user enters the quantity of cakes to be purchased.

Chippy often found the need for handling drink orders in his class. To make things easier, he decided to write a program that allows his classmates to place orders and calculate the price right away. There are 5 different drinks available in the beverage store in collaboration with the school. The drink options are as follows:
1) Pearl Milk Tea (NT$45/cup).
2) Earl Grey Tea (NT$25/cup).
3) Oolong Green Tea (NT$30/cup).
4) Sijichun Tea (NT$40/cup).
5) Pearl Fresh Milk Tea (NT$60/cup).
His classmates will have to enter the number corresponding to the drink options, and enter "-1" to complete an order. The program will then perform calculations by summing up the total order amount and price, and output the results.

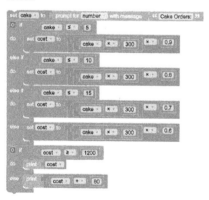
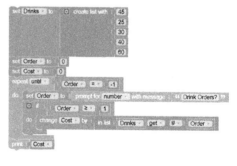

(c)   (d)

Fig. 1. The Chippy Assessment Tasks: (a) Light, (b) Robot Vacuum, (c) Cake Promotion, (d) Drink Orders. [6]

task. The Drink Orders task is similar to the Cake Promotion task but has the added requirement to use a list/array data structure to save all orders. Both problem-based tasks require students to demonstrate good abstraction, problem decomposition, and algorithmic design skills. The two tasks each have 5 and 6 test cases, respectively. Possible correct programs for the two tasks are shown in Fig. 1(c) and (d).

3.4 Assessment Scale

There are only four tasks used in the assessment. As Cortina [13] pointed out, when the number of items in a unidimensional test is too small, Cronbach's Alpha coefficient tends to be lower. Specifically, he found that with six items, the Cronbach's Alpha was about .72. Therefore, to ensure content validity, all four tasks were reviewed by CT experts to ensure that the tasks cover some CT skills and can comprehensively assess students' CT skills as shown in Table 2.

Table 2. The CT skills used in each task. [6]

Tasks	Skills			
	Pattern Recognition	Abstraction	Decomposition	Algorithm Design
Light	✓			
Robot Vacuum	✓			✓
Cake Promotion		✓	✓	✓
Drink Orders		✓	✓	✓

The assessment test was scored objectively, with each task having a maximum score of 100, totaling 400 points. In the two goal-based tasks, students can visually observe program execution through task animation. The task is either correctly solved (score of 100) or not correctly solved (score of 0). For the two problem-based tasks, scores were awarded based on the number of test cases that the programs could pass. Thus the scores can range from 0 to 100.

3.5 Data Collection and Analysis

Although students taking the Chippy challenge in the two years are different, the same tool and tasks were all the same. The tests were all taken by the incoming high school students (grade 10). The data collected for the two-year study includes school type (urban or rural schools), attempted tasks (lights, vacuum, cake, drinks), and task scores (0 to 100×4). T-test will be used to compare and see if there is a significant difference between the means of the assessment results between two groups of students, including the before and after of the new curriculum groups and the rural and urban groups.

3.6 Expected Performance

Upon finishing the new IT curriculum in the junior high school (7th to 9th grades), it is anticipated that high school freshmen (10th grade) will have the ability to complete the two goal-based tasks and at least one of the two problem-based tasks within 45 min. The average student should easily solve the two problem-based tasks and have ample time to attempt one problem-based task. Students with more practice may potentially complete all four tasks. Assessment scores are classified into four categories, as illustrated in Table 3. An **Average** (or on-par) programming for problem-solving skill set is having a score in the 251 to 350 range, which is equivalent to solving both two goal-based tasks and partially solving one problem-based task (a.k.a., solving 2+ tasks). An **Excellent** skill set is having a score surpassing 351, exhibiting outstanding CT and programming skills, and solving almost all four tasks. On the other hand, scores ranging from 151 to 250 indicate a **Subpar** skill set, as at most the two goal-based tasks are solved. A score below 150 indicates an **Inadequate** skill set, as at most one goal-based task can be solved.

Table 3. The programming for problem-solving skill set categories.

Task Completed	Score Range	Skill set relative to the new IT curriculum
3+	351–400	**Excellent** CT and programming skills.
2+	251–350	**Average** CT and programming skills.
1+	151–250	**Subpar** CT or programming skills.
0+	0–150	**Inadequate** CT and programming skills.

4 Results and Discussion

4.1 Overall Analysis

The descriptive statistics of students' performance in the two years are depicted in Table 4, showing a breakdown of the percentage of students in each of the four programming for problem-solving categories. Figure 2 shows the 2021–2022 student score histogram and probability density plots. The distribution indicates that the student scores follow a normal distribution. Therefore, a t-test will be used for the subsequent analysis. Students before the new curriculum and after the new curriculum had average scores of 200.22 (s.d. = 76.66) and 209.56 (s.d. = 62.21), respectively. The average improvement in score of nearly 10 points is significant, as the standard deviation is also more compact. Furthermore, the percentage of students having **Inadequate** skills is relatively the same in the two groups (15.5% vs. 16.9%). However, the percentage of students having **Average** or **Excellent** skills rose by 7.2%, from 12.4% to 19.6%. This shows that the implementation of the new curriculum helped more students become knowledgeable about problem-solving with programming. Finally, although 63.6% of students still have **Subpar** skills, there are reasons to believe that as teachers gain more experience in conducting CT and programming lessons, more students will improve their assessment scores in future years of study.

Table 4. Number of students and percentage of students in each score range.

New Curriculum	Mean Scores	s.d.	CT/Prog. Skill Set (Score range)			
			Inadequate (0–150)	Subpar (151–250)	Average (251–350)	Excellent (351–400)
Before	200.22	76.66	681 (15.5%)	3193 (72.2%)	392 (8.9%)	155 (3.5%)
After	209.56	62.21	895 (16.9%)	3380 (63.6%)	664 (12.5%)	375 (7.1%)

Fig. 2. Score distribution plot for 2021-2022.

4.2 Analysis of Scores that Meet or Exceed Expected Scores

We used t-test to analyze the mean scores of the given two groups of students for both the Average and the Excellent categories. The results are depicted in Table 5. From Table 5, if the Average and the Excellent categories were seen as one category, the after curriculum group had a significantly better score than the before curriculum group, with mean scores of 334.56 to 324.84 and $t = 3.82$

($p < .001$). Furthermore, if the Average and Excellent mean scores were analyzed separately, the after curriculum group also had a significantly better score than the before curriculum group (average score of 297.99 vs. 296.69 and 399.33 vs. 396.04) with $t = 2.12$ ($p < .05$) and $t = 6.13$ ($p < .001$), respectively. In addition, the after curriculum group in all three tests all have had much lower standard deviations. In all, these results show that implementation of the new curriculum had a very positive effect on students' problem-solving skills.

Table 5. Results of the independent t-test of mean scores for different skill levels.

Level	New Curriculum	No. of Students(%)	Mean Scores	s.d.	t
Excellent+Average	Before	547 (12.4%)	324.84	45.81	3.82***
	After	1,039 (19.6%)	334.56	49.32	
Excellent	Before	155 (3.5%)	396.04	7.76	6.13***
	After	375 (7.1%)	399.33	4.44	
Average	Before	392 (8.9%)	296.69	10.16	2.12*
	After	664 (12.5%)	297.99	9.25	
Subpar	Before	3,193 (72.22%)	200.79	17.31	3.77***
	After	3,380 (63.61%)	201.32	22.59	
Inadequate	Before	681 (15.40%)	97.47	4.66	-1.85
	After	895 (16.84%)	95.55	6.50	

*$p < .05$, **$p < .01$, ***$p < .001$.

4.3 Analysis of Performance of Students in Rural Vs Urban Schools

With extra resources and funding channeled to rural schools in recent years, it is of interest to compare students' learning achievements in rural and urban schools. Again, the independent t-test is used to test the mean scores of the students from rural and urban schools and the results are shown in Table 6. Whether before or after the new curriculum implementation, urban school students had significantly better scores than rural school students (average scores of 193.59 vs. 201.67 and 198.18 vs. 212.90) with $t = 3.32$ ($p < .01$) and $t = 6.09$ ($p < .001$), respectively. The mean scores increased after the curriculum implementation for both rural and urban students, but the increase was more pronounced for urban students. Further investigation into the specific factors contributing to these differences and how resources are being utilized could provide deeper insights into improving educational outcomes for rural students.

In Table 7, for the students who had Average skills, the before and after group average scores were 292.67 and 298.82, respectively. The improvement is significant with $t = 3.22$ ($p < .01$). And for the students who had Excellent skills, the before and after group average scores are 394.33 and 400.00, respectively. The improvement is also significant with $t = 5.31$ ($p < .001$). More importantly, the

Table 6. Results of the independent t-test of mean scores for rural and urban school students.

New Curriculum	Location	No. of Students(%)	Mean Scores	s.d.	t
Before	Rural	793 (6.43%)	193.59	53.05	3.32**
	Urban	3,628 (10.02%)	201.67	63.95	
After	Rural	1,208 (1.51%)	198.18	72.75	6.09***
	Urban	4,106 (4.80%)	212.90	77.46	

*$p < .05$, **$p < .01$, ***$p < .001$.

percentage of students who achieved those higher scores also increased significantly (from 6.43% to 10.02% and from 1.51% to 4.80%).

Independent t-test analysis is also applied to scores of students from urban schools. For the Average skill category, there was no significant change in the average scores of the before and after curriculum groups (297.29 vs. 297.80). However, there is significant improvement among the Excellent category (396.18 vs. 399.21) with $t = 5.11$ ($p < .001$).

These results are very encouraging as the implementation of the new curriculum also had a positive impact on rural schools. Furthermore, the percentage of students that achieved Expected or Excellent scores in both the rural and urban schools increased significantly.

Table 7. Results of the independent t-test of mean scores for rural (top) and urban (bottom) school students.

Rural	New Curriculum	No. of Students(%)	Mean Scores	s.d.	t
Average	Before	51 (6.43%)	292.67	11.86	3.22**
	After	121 (10.02%)	298.82	10.38	
Excellent	Before	12 (1.51%)	394.33	8.37	5.31***
	After	58 (4.80%)	400.00	0.00	

Urban	New Curriculum	No. of Students(%)	Mean Scores	s.d.	t
Average	Before	341 (9.40%)	297.29	9.76	0.78
	After	543 (13.22%)	297.80	8.98	
Excellent	Before	143 (3.94%)	396.18	7.72	5.11***
	After	317 (7.72%)	399.21	4.83	

*$p < .05$, **$p < .01$, ***$p < .001$.

5 Conclusions

The global trend of revamping IT curriculum to focus on programming and AI education reflects the evolution of the digital era in many countries [14]. As informatic education curriculum changes over time, assessment tools are needed to help evaluate student learning outcomes under th enew curriculum. The Chippy Challenge was created as a tool for assessing students' computational thinking skills in solving problems. This two-year study compared the incoming high freshmen (Grade 10) in the year before and after the new IT curriculum were implemented so as to reflect the impact the new curriculum has on students' programming for problem solving abilities. Our study shows that the newly implemented IT curriculum is helpful for students to learn programming for problem solving. Not only are the achievement scores improved significantly, but an even higher percentage of students can achieve the expected or better scores. Even more encouraging is the new curriculum also has the same positive impact for students in the rural schools as those in the urban schools.

Overall, the additional resources and the implementation of the new curriculum have had a positive impact on both rural and urban schools. Although urban schools continue to perform better, the academic achievements of rural students have significantly improved, especially in the proportion of students with excellent scores. These results suggest that ongoing attention and support for the balanced distribution of educational resources are crucial to narrowing the gap between rural and urban schools.

Given the importance of school learning environments to the affective characteristics of students, the current findings suggest that transforming traditional knowledge-replicative learning environments into knowledge-generative computer science learning ones will render students more likely to value learning experiences. The results from our study suggest shifting from the old curriculum to the new curriculum is a good step to motivate and to help students to learn programming for problem-solving. We shall continue to collect and analyze results from incoming freshmen in the coming years. We are optimistics that the positive improvements shown by the first group of students that received the new curriculum will continue to be observed in future freshmen classes.

Acknowledgments. This work was partially supported by the National Science and Technology Council, Taiwan, ROC under grant no. 109-2511-H-003-025-MY4.

References

1. Barr, V., Stephenson, C.: Bringing computational thinking to k-12: what is involved and what is the role of the computer science education community? ACM Inroads **2**(1), 48–54 (2011). https://doi.org/10.1145/1929887.1929905
2. So, H.J., Jong, M.S.Y., Liu, C.C.: Computational thinking education in the Asian Pacific region. Asia-Pacific Edu. Res. **29**, 1–2 (2020). https://doi.org/10.1007/s40299-019-00494-w
3. Taiwan Ministry of Education. Curriculum guidelines of 12-year basic education (2024). https://www.naer.edu.tw/
4. Moreno-León, J., Robles, G.Dr.: Scratch: a web tool to automatically evaluate scratch projects. In: Proceedings of the Workshop in Primary and Secondary Computing Education, no. 2 in WiPSCE '15, pp. 13–133. Association for Computing Machinery, New York (2015). https://doi.org/10.1145/2818314.2818338

5. Bae, Y., Fulmer, G.W., Hand, B.M.: Developing latent constructs of dialogic interaction to examine the epistemic climate: rasch modeling. Sch. Sci. Math. **121**(3), 164–174 (2021). https://doi.org/10.1111/ssm.12460
6. Lee, G.C., Chen, J.Y., Yang, Y.W.: Computational thinking readiness of incoming high school students in Taiwan. In: 16th International Conference on Informatics in Schools, ISSEP 2023, Local Proceedings, Lausanne, Switzerland. Zenodo (2023). https://doi.org/10.5281/zenodo.8431959
7. Araujo, A.L.S.O., Andrade, W.L., Guerrero, D.D., et al.: How many abilities can we measure in computational thinking? a study on bebras challenge. In: Proceedings of the 50th ACM Technical Symposium on Computer Science Education, no. 7 in SIGCSE 2019, pp. 545–551. Association for Computing Machinery, New York (2019). https://doi.org/10.1145/3287324.3287405
8. Chen, G., Shen, J., Barth-Cohen, L., et al.: Assessing elementary students' computational thinking in everyday reasoning and robotics programming. Comput. Educ. **109**, 162–175 (2017). https://doi.org/10.1016/j.compedu.2017.03.001
9. Román González, M., Pérez-González, J.-C., Jiménez-Fernández, C.: Which cognitive abilities underlie computational thinking? criterion validity of the computational thinking test. Comput. Human Behav. **72**, 678–691 (2017). https://doi.org/10.1016/j.chb.2016.08.047
10. Aziz, M., Chi, H., Tibrewal, A., et al.: Auto-grading for parallel programs. In: Proceedings of the Workshop on Education for High-Performance Computing, no. 8 in EduHPC 2015. Association for Computing Machinery, New York (2015). https://doi.org/10.1145/2831425.2831427
11. Sendjaja, K., Rukmono, S.A., Perdana, R.S.: Evaluating control-flow graph similarity for grading programming exercises. In: 2021 International Conference on Data and Software Engineering (ICoDSE), pp. 1–6 (2021). https://doi.org/10.1109/ICoDSE53690.2021.9648464
12. Kane, D., Williams, J., Cappuccini-Ansfield, G.: Student satisfaction surveys: the value in taking an historical perspective. Qual. High. Educ. **14**(2), 135–155 (2008). https://doi.org/10.1080/13538320802278347
13. Cortina, J.M.: What is coefficient alpha? an examination of theory and applications. J. Appl. Psychol. **78**(1), 98–104 (1993). https://doi.org/10.1037/0021-9010.78.1.98
14. Heintz, F., Mannila, L., Färnqvist, T.: A review of models for introducing computational thinking, computer science and computing in k-12 education. In: 2016 IEEE Frontiers in Education Conference (FIE), pp. 1–9 (2016). https://doi.org/10.1109/FIE.2016.7757410

K-8 Digital Literacy Curriculum in the Netherlands

Nataša Grgurina[1,2(✉)] and Jos Tolboom[1]

[1] SLO, Amersfoort, The Netherlands
`n.grgurina@rug.nl, j.tolboom@slo.nl`
[2] University of Groningen, Groningen, The Netherlands

Abstract. So far, in the Netherlands there has been no compulsory education in digital literacy or informatics in primary or secondary education. In 2022, the Dutch Ministry of Education, Culture and Science tasked the Netherlands Institute for Curriculum Development (SLO) to develop the curriculum (i.e., the core objectives) for digital literacy for primary and lower secondary education. SLO formed a team including elementary and lower secondary education teachers, education specialists and teacher educators, and SLO curriculum specialists. Over a course of fifteen months, this team organized several meetings. They reviewed Dutch and international curricula and frameworks on digital literacy, informatics, etc., and consulted more than twenty experts. Following the standardized curriculum development procedure, the team formulated their vision on digital literacy in the context of Dutch situation yielding a document called *characteristic*, and then the core objectives constituting the curriculum were formulated. During this iterative development process, the team consulted the internal SLO monitoring team and the external advisory board consisting of representatives of stakeholder organizations involved or invested in digital literacy education. In March 2024, the digital literacy curriculum was finalized. It consists of nine core objectives grouped in three domains: (A) Practical knowledge and skills, (B) Designing and making, and (C) Interaction between digital, technology, digital, media, people and the society. This paper describes the curriculum development process and presents the resulting core objectives. The question leading this paper is: which aspects of the curriculum development process were beneficial for carrying out the necessary steps leading to the results?

Keywords: Digital literacy · informatics · curriculum development · learning standards · The Netherlands

1 Towards a Digital Literacy Curriculum

Every curriculum reform has to be initiated by a certain political consensus. Regarding digital literacy (DL), in The Netherlands, it took quite some time to reach this consensus. So far, DL in the Netherlands has not been compulsory in K-12 education, despite the introduction of an elective informatics course for grades 10 through 12 in 1998 [2, 11, 12]. However, tertiary education and society cannot rely on the knowledge students acquire during this course, since it is just an elective subject and only for two upper secondary education school types (senior secondary education and pre-university education) and thus not a part of the compulsory core curriculum. For an overview of the Dutch primary and secondary education system, see Fig. 1. The compulsory core objectives are for the primary and lower secondary education—the shaded areas in the figure. The upper secondary curricula are called programs of examination, and they are not discussed in this paper.

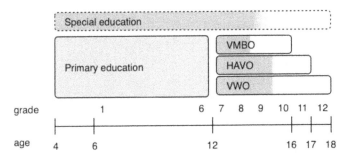

Fig. 1. Primary and secondary education in the Netherlands. The secondary education includes pre-vocational education VMBO (in Dutch: voorbereidend middelbaar beroepsonderwijs), senior secondary education HAVO (in Dutch: hoger algemeen vormend onderwijs), and pre-university education VWO (in Dutch: voorbereidend wetenschappelijk onderwijs). For students with special needs, there is special education.

Since 2012, there has been increasing pressure on the Dutch Ministry of Education, Culture and Science to reform the curriculum in such a way that all students would be trained in DL. In 2012, The Royal Netherlands Academy of Arts and Sciences published a report expressing their concerns about teaching informatics and recommended to introduce a new compulsory subject *Information and communication* in the lower grades of secondary education [14]. In 2014, The Netherlands Institute for Curriculum Development (In Dutch: Stichting Leerplanontwikkeling, SLO) was tasked to explore the relation between DL and 21st century skills. The resulting report defined DL in terms of four elements: Practical ICT skills, Media literacy, Computational thinking, and Digital information skills [20]. To meet the demand from numerous schools, SLO elaborated these elements into learning objectives [29], but the schools were not required to teach DL. In the meantime, the curriculum.nu initiative was launched to overhaul all of the primary and lower secondary curriculum, including the introduction of DL as a learning area in its own right [27]. Due to various reasons, the resulting curricula were not put to practice. In 2022, the ministry tasked SLO to develop the curriculum (i.e., the core objectives) for DL for primary and lower secondary education. In March 2024, the curriculum for digital literacy was handed over to the minister of education.

Simultaneously with the development of the DL curriculum, the existing curricula for all other learning areas for primary education and lower secondary education are being reformed as well. This entails the curricula for the Dutch language, mathematics, humanities, science, arts and culture, English and other modern foreign languages, and physical education. Additionally, the learning area of civics is being introduced and its curriculum developed. While the design of the curriculum development process is the same for all learning areas, this paper focuses on DL exclusively. We describe the assignment, the process of development between November 2022 and March 2024, the requirements that were to be met, and the resulting curriculum. We remark that regarding the level of the curriculum, SLO restricts itself to the level of the intended curriculum [9], consisting of the ideal curriculum— as represented by the *characteristic*—and the formal curriculum—as represented by the *core objectives*. In the Dutch educational tradition, the curricular assignment for SLO only concerns the *what* of the learning process, i.e., the intended curriculum, sometimes referred to as standards. The *how* of the learning process— i.e., the enacted curriculum or the pedagogy and the teaching approach—is to be designed by the schools and teachers themselves.

2 Curriculum Development

2.1 Point of Departure

SLO charted the situation and developments within educational policy, research, educational practice and society relevant to DL, thus laying a solid foundation for the curriculum development work [13]. The resulting report described the current situation of DL education: many teachers and schools acknowledged the importance of DL, and yet students still have problems with elementary things such as logging in, saving files in a searchable manner or presenting information. There was (and still is) a great variation in what is taught and how, and not much is known about the students' learning outcomes. These issues were related to the fact that there was no compulsory curriculum and that the views on DL varied greatly—even to include questionable beliefs such as equating DL to the use of digital technology or to programming. The report goes on to emphasize the role of compulsory DL education in creating equality of opportunity and inclusivity for all students regardless of their socio-economic situation. Regarding the (recent) developments in society, the report points to the human-machine relationship, ethics, artificial intelligence, value of data, the use of algorithms on various platforms to influence users' behavior, and the consequent changes in professional practices. These developments cause a number of challenges, such as dealing with digital information, interacting with each other in the digital world, privacy in the digital world, and searching for a digital balance. The subsequent process of the curriculum development faces a number of challenges as well: arguably the biggest one is to define the learning content, since, "It is a challenge to carefully determine this for a new learning area, with attention to skills, knowledge and attitude."[13] Furthermore, this new curriculum needs to connect to upper secondary education in a continuous learning path (thus, realize *vertical coherence* in the curriculum) and to align with curricula of other learning areas (*horizontal coherence*). The specific challenges regard the question of the extent or depth of core objectives: there is a whole spectrum between having experienced something and possessing a mastery of it. Finally, formulating core objectives is a challenge in its own right: with no tradition to rely on for inspiration, these need to be built up from scratch.

2.2 Curriculum Development Requirements

The curriculum development process was guided by a detailed set of instructions listing all the requirements the curriculum needs to meet, as well as all deliverables during the process. The deliverables include two products: a *characteristic* which is a short document describing the vision of DL, and the core objectives themselves. Other deliverables are process documents which are produced after each development session and contain (depending on the process schedule) the current iteration of the products, development process description, explanation on how the (current version of the) curriculum meets the requirements, and any advice the team wishes to get from the advisory board.

The instructions are meant to support the production of deliverables and to ensure they meet the specified quality criteria. For *characteristic*, this entails including a description of specific features of the particular learning area and explaining how it contributes to the attainment of the three aims of education according to Biesta: qualification, socialization and subjectification [4]. Furthermore, the *characteristic* should describe the vertical and horizontal coherence of a particular learning area with the whole of the primary and secondary curriculum, and in particular with the learning areas of the Dutch language, mathematics and civics. For the core objectives themselves, the requirements are extensive. To start with, there are generic quality criteria related to respecting the diversity in society (diversification) concerned with the choice of contents and perspectives on those contents and the formulation/use of concepts in core objectives, to literacy and numeracy, professional orientation, horizontal and vertical coherence, specific skills, and civics. The core objectives are formulated on two levels: for the end of primary education, and for the end of lower secondary education. Finally, the teaching time is specified. The schools are expected to allocate 70% of all teaching time to the compulsory core curriculum and are free to dedicate the remaining time to the issues of their choice. For DL, 7% of the core curriculum time is allocated, meaning there should be six to eight core objectives [15].

The form of the core objectives is specified as well: following the ABC principle [16], each core objective should be stated as one sentence stating the (A) audience, (B) behavior, and (C) content. The audience can be either the student or the school. The behavior is described as thinking activities and/or behaviors expressed in verbs specifying observable actions, and for each learning area a list of suggested verbs is supplied—to help prevent proliferation of various verbs which might lead to confusion and misunderstanding, and to contribute to coherence across various learning areas. The content describes learning content, i.e., knowledge, skills and/or attitude; context, sources to be used, and complicating or simplifying factors. The behavior and content of each learning goal should be further elaborated with detailed description in no more than five points. That sentence and elaboration together form a logical, consistent and well-defined whole specifying a particular core objective. Such a core objective is then a part of compulsory curriculum[1]. Additionally, up to five examples are added to each core objective to illustrate it and provide examples for school practice. Chapter 3 and the Appendix list core objectives, but without examples [10].

---

[1] A curriculum is only compulsory after the necessary legislation is passed.

2.3 Curriculum Development Process

In November 2022, the curriculum development team was formed. It consisted of five primary school teachers and three secondary school teachers—all having affinity or experience with DL education—and furthermore four education specialists or teacher trainers, four SLO curriculum experts and a process coordinator. The curriculum development process lasted 15 months and entailed eight two-day development sessions, three day-long sessions and several online meetings. During this period, the team regularly consulted internal SLO curriculum monitoring experts who checked whether the deliverables met the formal curriculum quality requirements. Additionally, the external advisory board consisting of experts and stakeholders regularly advised the team about the DL content of the deliverables.

Here we describe the method used and the milestones achieved during the development process. The milestones do not necessarily correspond to the deliverables, and we stress that the process was iterative and not straightforward.

The point of departure for the development process can best be described by a quote by Voogt et al., after having reviewed reported research and a number of curricula and frameworks: "In conclusion, it can be said that both the literature study and the analyzed reference frameworks show that there is still no consensus on what exactly the concept of digital literacy entails." [21]. For the team this meant a curse and a blessing, and they interpreted this situation as starting with a clean slate but having a lot of resources available to draw inspiration from. The team reviewed a number of Dutch [2, 27, 29] and international curricula and frameworks on informatics, computing, digital citizenship, AI, Medienpädagogik or any other topics deemed relevant [1, 3, 5, 7, 8, 17–19, 22, 23, 25, 26, 28, 30, 31]. While the team's task was to develop the core objectives only—thus the intended curriculum, they had to keep in mind what the implemented curriculum would look like and therefore the resources consulted included those related to (informatics) pedagogy as well. During various phases of the curriculum development process, the team consulted more than twenty experts to learn more about information skills, programming, media (use), data, AI and interaction with it, and about identity, resilience and appropriate (online) conduct. Last but not least, they relied on their own expertise of not only (DL) education, but also of the specific Dutch context of both education and society as a whole.

First, the team reached an agreement on the purpose of DL education, thus answered the question of what it means for a student and a citizen to be digitally literate. The answer is: being digitally literate means that students can actively participate in digital processes, that they have a basic knowledge of digital technology, communicate effectively, are creative, change perspectives and take responsibility for (digital) behavior. The team set out to formulate a concrete interpretation of this idea. Through many cycles of qualitative analysis of various literature (see Fig. 2 for an illustration of an early stage of the development process), and consulting experts, internal SLO monitoring and the external advisory board, by applying Delphi process [6], the team formulated the guiding principles for the DL curriculum. These are:

1 The learning area has specific knowledge and skills.
2 The learning area offers opportunities for expression and creative design.
3 The learning area has a reflective component.

4 The relationship between people and digital technology is reciprocal.
5 Digital literacy is intertwined with other learning areas.

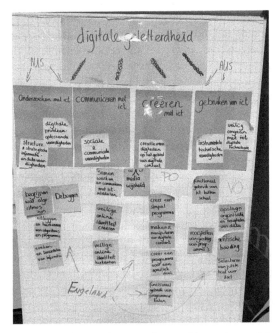

Fig. 2. Illustration of an early stage of researching and organizing ideas

During the analysis of existing frameworks and curricula, the team identified eleven often occurring themes: digital systems, software, digital information, data, communication and collaboration, artificial intelligence, digital security and privacy, creating digital content, computer programming, digital problem solving, and finally, the influence of digital technology on people and society. While the decision was unanimously made that all these topics need to be included into the Dutch DL curriculum, the challenges remained: what topics to assign priority, what are relevant details and what is a desired balance among them. During successive development sessions, several versions of draft curricula were produced. Initially, the accent lay primarily on determining and organizing the content with little attention to formulating core objectives in the required format (see Fig. 2 for illustration). Over time, after several cycles of consulting the SLO monitoring experts, external experts, student representatives, special needs experts, various stakeholders and the advisory board, the team reached the consensus on content that not only satisfied all formal requirements, but also aligned with the team's vision of DL and the guiding principles. From then on, again through several iterations, the team formulated nine core objectives and the *characteristic* which constitute the DL curriculum. The core objectives are listed in chapter 3 and the Appendix.

These core objectives are organized in a framework with three domains. The domains correspond to the first three guiding principles and reflect the three perspectives described in the Dagstuhl triangle [24]: the technological, the application-related, and the social-cultural perspective of DL. The fourth guiding principle—stating the reciprocal relationship between people and digital technology—emphasizes the agency of the users of digital technology and digital media. The last guiding principle expresses the nature of the learning area as perceived by the team: not as an isolated discipline, but in connection and supporting other learning areas. These last two guiding principles can be found throughout all core objectives of this curriculum.

The first domain approaches DL from the technological perspective and deals with the discipline-specific knowledge and skills. The first core objective, *Digital systems*, focuses on digital equipment and software and emphasizes their interdependence. It addresses the knowledge and skills required to function effectively when using digital equipment and software. Communication and collaboration in a digital environment are addressed as well, and maintenance and management, and solving technical problems are also discussed. *Digital media and Information* focuses on the digital component of the process of searching and processing information. This core objective is complementary to the related core objective in the learning area Dutch language, which deals with researching sources. There is explicit attention for information that media users encounter even without having searched for it, as is often the case with social media. *Security and privacy* addresses the vulnerability of the digital devices, digital infrastructure, data and privacy. It highlights both the technical aspects and safe behavior of users. The core objective *Data* reflect the fact that digital technology has dramatically increased the amount of data in the world. This is also the case with the possibilities to process and use data to make decisions or improve services. The aim is to introduce students to the principles of data processing. They also work with data themselves and discover how data is used in their environment and in society. *Artificial intelligence* discusses the functioning and use of artificial intelligence, which demonstrates growing possibilities and the rapid spread of its use. As a system technology, AI might fundamentally change society. Therefore, AI literacy, which includes knowledge, insight and ability to deal critically and thoughtfully with AI, is considered to be an integral part of DL.

The second domain approaches DL from the application-oriented perspective, focusing on creation and design using digital technology and digital media. The core objective *Creating with digital technology* addresses various aspects of digital content creation, including creating to express feelings, thoughts and ideas. It addresses the use of various types of software, whether or not in combination with each other, and to convey information and messages. It also addresses designing digital products and solving problems using digital tools and therefore appeals on students' computational thinking strategies. This core objective is linked to several other core objectives (1, 2, 3, 7) and enables connection with other learning areas, for example in design and problem solving using digital technology. *Programming* involves students becoming acquainted with instructing computers, deploying computational thinking strategies by acting logically and iteratively and using specific programming concepts. It teaches students how people control technology and that experimenting with programming is fun.

The third domain approaches DL from the social-cultural perspective with content that is reflective in nature and addresses the interaction between digital technology, digital media, people and society. Core objective *Digital technology, yourself and others* addresses the influence and interaction of digital technology with people, and the way in which people interact with each other in the digital world. Finally, *Digital technology, society and the world* deals with the influence and interaction of digital technology with the world. It discusses the various consequences of digital technology on society using current examples. [10].

2.4 Next Steps

SLO has developed the DL core curriculum and handed it over to the ministry. However, few more steps need to be taken before it comes into effect. First, in the fall of 2024, a testing phase is planned to ascertain whether schools and teachers understand this intended curriculum and are able to implement it into their school practice. Their feedback could lead to (minor) adjustments. From then on, it is up to the politics to pass the necessary legislature to make it compulsory. In the meantime, schools, teachers, textbook publishers, teacher educators, researchers and other stakeholders are not waiting for the legislature and are preparing the implementation. Simultaneously, an upper secondary curriculum (program of examination) for DL is to be developed as well.

3 Primary DL Core Objectives

3.1 Domain A: Practical Knowledge and Skills

1. **Digital systems.** The student uses digital systems effectively. This concerns:

   - describing the components and operation of digital systems in terms of input-processing-output;
   - using the basic capabilities of software for communication, collaboration, drawing, arithmetic, word processing, presenting and image, sound and video editing;
   - managing files in digital environments by organizing, storing and retrieving them in a structured manner;
   - recognizing commonly used digital systems;
   - maintaining and adapting digital systems and solving problems with them.

2. **Digital media and information**. The student navigates purposefully in the landscape of digital media and information for acquiring and processing information. This concerns:

   - mapping various media and sources, their reliability and usability;
   - using a suitable search strategy, search tool and search query;
   - assessing the information provided and found for reliability and usability;
   - describing how creators of digital media attract, hold and influence users' attention with coloring and directing techniques;
   - identifying factors that influence the method of offering and the visibility of search results.

3. **Security and Privacy**. The student handles digital systems, data and privacy of themselves and others safely. This concerns:
   - recognizing security risks when using digital systems and data;
   - using digital systems, data and information safely, and taking appropriate technical measures to protect them;
   - weighing dilemmas when sharing your own data, personal data, information and digital content and that of others;
   - adequately dealing with inappropriate content, inappropriate behavior and security risks in digital environments.

4. **Data**. The student explores the use of data and data processing. This concerns:
   - describing how information is created by collecting, structuring and processing data in a purposeful manner;
   - explaining how the results of data processing depend on the origin, accuracy and completeness of the dataset used;
   - using a dataset to answer a question;
   - describing the use of data in your own environment;
   - reflecting on the fact that the user of digital technology consciously and unconsciously leaves data behind and that these can be used by others.

5. **Artificial Intelligence**. The student explores how AI systems work. This concerns:
   - describing elements of an AI system and how the behavior of AI systems resembles human behavior;
   - recognizing common AI systems and their applications in your own environment;
   - interacting purposefully, responsibly and critically with an AI system.

3.2 Domain B: Designing and Making

6. **Creating with Digital Technology.** The student uses appropriate strategies when creating and using different types of digital products. This concerns:
   - experimenting with digital means to express thoughts, ideas or feelings;
   - sharing information and conveying a message;
   - using computational thinking strategies when designing a digital product;
   - designing a digital product based on the design requirements in an iterative process;
   - taking copyrights, licenses and source and name attribution into account when creating digital products.

7. **Programming.** The student programs a computer program using computational thinking strategies. This concerns:
   - experimenting with code;
   - describing the task and purpose of a computer program;
   - designing and schematically representing the algorithm associated with a task;
   - using programming concepts: input and output, variables, operators, repetition and control structures;
   - testing and adjusting your own computer program or a computer program from others.

3.3 Domain C: Interaction Between Digital Technology, Digital Media, the People and Society

8. **Digital technology, yourself and others.** The student makes well-considered choices when using digital technology and digital media. This concerns:

   - communicating and behaving online in a respectful and responsible manner;
   - evaluating the influence of digital technology and digital media on your own thinking and behavior and on the interaction with others;
   - paying attention to your own physical and mental health;
   - reflecting on one's own online identity and how it is created;
   - exploring interest in the development of digital technology and digital media.

9. **Digital technology, society, and the world.** The student explores how digital technology, digital media, and society mutually influence each other. This concerns:

   - exploring the influence of people on the development of digital technology and digital media and vice versa;
   - exploring how digital technology and media influence social well-being and social inclusion;
   - reasoning about the opportunities and risks of using digital technology in the immediate environment;
   - exploring the effects of digital technology on ecology [10].

4 Conclusion and Discussion

This paper describes the development of the curriculum for digital literacy in primary and lower secondary education: the requirements, the process and the results. First, we reflect on the quality of this curriculum. Based on the interactions taking place during the trajectory, and on the cyclic evaluations that were built in into the process, we conclude that the team has succeeded in developing a consistent, state-of-the-art curriculum. We are especially pleased with the fact that this has been accomplished within a period of year-and-a-half after accepting the assignment.

Second, we recall the developmental question leading this trajectory: which aspects of the curriculum development process were beneficial for carrying out the necessary steps leading to this result? We look at two main components of the process: the requirements, and the interaction between the team and others involved. The requirements gave the team a clear format to work with, which took a lot of guessing out of the development process. At the same time, the allocated number of six to eight core objectives was impossible to attain if all the content considered relevant were to be given the proper attention. Finalizing the core objectives and choosing appropriate verbs was a precarious balancing act. Yet, the first reactions are by and large positive, which affirms that the team has made the right choices with respect to the DL curriculum. The interactions with external stakeholders served two main goals: to learn about the topics relevant for this curriculum, and to gain feedback and advice about deliverables produced. The former allowed the team to utilize specific expertise it lacked itself or to gain new perspectives. The latter helped to modify and fine-tune the products, but it caused some frustration along the way as well. The team did not always feel the other party understood the specific DL content well, or shared the understanding of the roles of those involved. Nevertheless, applying the old Dutch saying *no shine without friction*, the team considered carefully all of the received feedback and is pleased with the resulting DL curriculum.

Appendix—Secondary DL Core Objectives

1. **Digital systems.** The student uses digital systems effectively. This concerns:
   - describing what is technically required to make digital systems work and communicate in a network;
   - describing how the internet works and the place of smart devices in it;
   - using the advanced capabilities of software for communication, collaboration, and creating and editing different types of files;
   - recognizing digital systems that are used in companies, in the world of media and by government to perform tasks or solve problems;
   - keeping track of new technological developments and their possibilities and limits.

2. **Digital media and information**. The student navigates purposefully in the landscape of digital media and information for acquiring and processing information. This concerns:
   - combining appropriate searching tools, searching queries and searching strategies;
   - assessing information—both found and stumbled upon—for reliability and usefulness, taking into account the properties of sources, search tools and media used;
   - reflecting on the suitability of used searching strategies, searching tools and searching queries for obtaining the desired result;
   - describing how social media work and attract, hold and influence users' attention;
   - reflecting on how one's own knowledge, views and preferences influence the interpretation of digital information.

3. **Security and Privacy**. The student handles digital systems, data and privacy of themselves and others safely. This concerns:
   - knowing about the rights and obligations of individuals and institutions with regard to the protection of personal data, data and privacy;
   - recognizing security risks when using digital systems of companies, institutions and governments;
   - protecting against weaknesses in digital systems and networks used;
   - recognizing how others handle privacy and the security of data they collect or store;
   - adequately dealing with inappropriate content, inappropriate behavior and security risks in digital environments.

4. **Data**. The student explores the use of data and data processing. This concerns:
   - explaining that a dataset provides a limited picture of reality;

- conducting research with a data set to answer a question, perform a task or solve a problem;
- describing the use of data by companies, institutions and governments;
- describing the increasing possibilities for data-driven work;
- reflecting on the use of AI in data processing.

5. **Artificial Intelligence**. The student explores the possibilities and limitations of AI. This concerns:
   - describing the role and influence of data on the operation of AI systems;
   - recognizing common AI systems and their use by companies, institutions and governments;
   - describing the difference between AI systems and other types of systems;
   - interacting purposefully, responsibly and critically with an AI system;
   - experimenting with training AI systems.

6. **Creating with Digital Technology.** The student uses appropriate strategies when creating and using different types of digital products. This concerns:
   - experimenting with development and editing software to express thoughts, ideas or feelings;
   - developing and sharing a digital product to inform, persuade or influence others;
   - using computational thinking strategies, consider whether, and, if so, to what extent the goal can be achieved with a digital product;
   - designing and making a product based on design requirements in an iterative process, and reflecting on the product and process;
   - taking copyrights, licenses and source and name attribution into account when creating digital products

7. **Programming.** The student programs a computer program using computational thinking strategies. This concerns:
   - describing the task and purpose of a computer program;
   - designing and schematically represent the algorithm associated with a task;
   - using programming concepts: events, data structures and combinations of logical operators; (In K-6: input and output, variables, operators, repetition and control structures)
   - documenting, testing and adjusting your own computer program or a computer program of others;
   - tackling a problem or task in such a way that programming can be used to solve it.

8. **Digital technology, yourself and others.** The student makes well-considered choices when using digital technology and digital media. This concerns:
   - communicating and acting online in a respectful and responsible manner;
   - evaluating the influence of digital technology and digital media on your own thinking and behavior and on the interaction with others;
   - paying attention to your own physical and mental health and that of others;
   - reflecting on and shaping one's own online identity in relation to others;

- exploring one's own interest in digital technology and digital media in relation to studies and professions.

9. **Digital technology, society and the world.** The student analyzes how digital technology, digital media and society mutually influence each other and explores future scenarios. This concerns:

   - exploring the possibilities to use digital technology and media to shape social involvement;
   - exploring options to guide and regulate the development of digital technology and digital media and thereby protect human and democratic values;
   - reasoning about opportunities and risks of the use of digital technology in society from an ethical, social, economic and ecological perspective;
   - analyzing how societies depend on digital technology and big technology companies;
   - describing ethical dilemmas when making choices for the future [10].

References

1. AI4K12: Five big ideas in artificial intelligence. https://ai4k12.org
2. Barendsen, E., Tolboom, J.: Advisory report (intended) curriculum for informatics for upper secondary education. SLO (2016)
3. Benaya, T., et al.: Computer science high school curriculum in Israel and Lithuania – comparison and teachers' views. Balt. J. Mod. Comput. **5**, 164–182 (2017). https://doi.org/10.22364/bjmc.2017.5.2.02
4. Biesta, G.: Good education in an age of measurement: On the need to reconnect with the question of purpose in education. Educ. Assess. Eval. Account. Former. J. Pers. Eval. Educ. **21**(1), 33–46 (2009)
5. Caspersen, M.E., et al.: Informatics Reference Framework for School. National Science Foundation, United States (2022). https://doi.org/10.1145/3592625
6. Cohen, L., et al.: Research Methods in Education, 6th edn. Routledge, London, United Kingdom (2007)
7. Coleman, G.: The Big Book of Computing Content. Raspberry Pi Foundation, Cambridge (2022)
8. CSTA Standards Task Force: K-12 Computer Science Standards, Revised 2017 (2017)
9. Goodlad, J.I., et al.: Curriculum Inquiry: The Study of Curriculum Practice (1979)
10. Grgurina, N., et al.: Kerndoelen Digitale geletterdheid (Digital Literacy Core Curriculum). SLO, Amersfoort (2024)
11. Grgurina, N., et al.: The second decade of informatics in Dutch secondary education. In: Pozdniakov, S.N., Dagienė, V. (eds.) Informatics in Schools. Fundamentals of Computer Science and Software Engineering, pp. 271–282. Springer, Cham (2018). https://doi.org/10.1007/978-3-030-02750-6_21
12. Grgurina, N., Tolboom, J.: The first decade of informatics in Dutch high schools. Inform. Educ. **7**(1), 55–74 (2008)
13. Klein Tank, M., Spronk, J.: Startnotitie kerndoelen Digitale geletterdheid. SLO, Amersfoort (2022)
14. KNAW: Digitale geletterdheid in het voortgezet onderwijs. Koninklijke Nederlandse Akademie van Wetenschappen (2012)

15. Koopmans - van Noorel, A., Bron, J.: The Netherlands: fact box. In: The Core Curriculum (2023)
16. Mager, R.F.: Preparing Instructional Objectives: A Critical Tool in the Development of Effective Instruction. 3rd The Center for Effective Performance, Atlanta, GA (1997)
17. Pijpers, R.: Digitale geletterdheid in Zweden: dit kan Nederland leren van de Zweden. https://www.kennisnet.nl/artikel/6814/digitale-geletterdheid-in-zweden-dit-kan-nederland-leren-van-de-zweden/. Accessed 17 July 2023
18. Puentedura, R.R.: Learning, Technology, and the SAMR Model: Goals, Processes, and Practice (2014). http://www.hippasus.com/rrpweblog/archives/2014/06/29/LearningTechnologySAMRModel.pdf
19. Svendsen, A.M., Svendsen, J.T.: Digital directions: curricular goals relating to digital literacy and digital competences in the Gymnasium (stx) in Denmark. Nord. J. Digit. Lit. **16**(1), 6–20 (2021)
20. Thijs, A.M., et al.: Digitale geletterdheid en 21e eeuwse vaardigheden in het funderend onderwijs: een conceptueel kader (draft). SLO (2014)
21. Voogt, J., et al.: Review digitale geletterdheid (2019)
22. Vuorikari, R., et al.: DigComp 2.2: The Digital Competence Framework for Citizens - with New Examples of Knowledge, Skills and Attitudes. Publications Office of the European Union (2022). https://doi.org/10.2760/115376
23. Computing - A Curriculum for Schools: https://www.computingatschool.org.uk/resources/2009/march/computing-a-curriculum-for-schools. Accessed 22 June 2023
24. Brinda, T., et al.: Dagstuhl-Erklärung: Bildung in der digitalen vernetzten Welt (2016)
25. Data Big Ideas: https://www.youcubed.org/data-big-ideas/. Accessed 29 May 2024
26. Digital Technologies: https://www.australiancurriculum.edu.au/f-10-curriculum/technologies/digital-technologies/. Accessed 22 June 2023
27. Digitale geletterdheid – Curriculum.nu: https://www.curriculum.nu/voorstellen/digitale-geletterdheid/. Accessed 17 Aug 2020
28. Digitales Kompetenzmodell für Österreich. https://www.fit4internet.at/view/verstehen-das-modell/%26lang%3DEN. Accessed 22 June 2023
29. Inhoudslijnen digitale geletterdheid. https://www.slo.nl/sectoren/po/inhoudslijnen-po/inhoudslijnen-digitale-geletterdheid/. Accessed 22 June 2023
30. Mediawijsheid Competentiemodel. Netwerk Mediawijsheid (2021)
31. The Digital Humanism Initiative. https://caiml.org/dighum/. Accessed 29 May 2024

Implementing Informatics Core Curriculum in Early School Education in Poland

Maciej M. Sysło

Warsaw School of Computer Science, Warsaw, Poland
syslo@ii.uni.wroc.pl

> children learn by doing and thinking about what they do
> [Papert, 1970]

Abstract. The article discusses the most important aspects of implementing the computer science curriculum for early school education (grades 1–3) in Poland. The emphasis is on the spiral development of students' computational thinking and knowledge and skills through the use of various physical and mental tools and environments provided by different stakeholders, as well as through the use of computers and computers in the background. The proposed approach is used in professional development courses for teachers of grades K-3 offered by several universities, and then teachers introduce this approach to their classes. The preliminary results of the effectiveness of the presented proposal are encouraging and will be published elsewhere.

Keywords: Informatics in K-3 · Spiral curriculum implementation · Computational thinking

1 Introduction

Informatics (computer science) education has a long history in Poland (Sysło, 2023). The term "informatics education" refers, to any use of computers, informatics, and ICT in education as educational tools and methods. To distinguish from any use of computers in education, another term "computer science education" (pl. *Kształcenie informatyczne*) has been introduced and it refers to learning and teaching of rigorous computer science. This paper mainly concerns early school education in our system, i.e. grades 1–3 (ages 7–9), which is intended to be fully integrated education. That's why all subjects at this level are called "education", hence we have informatics education in grades 1–3 and to simplify the presentation in this paper, we refer to informatics education but in the sense that it concerns rigorous computer science.

The current informatics core curriculum was introduced to K-8 (primary education) in September 2017 and to high schools in September 2019. Informatics is now the compulsory subject in all grades of K-12 for at least 1 h a week.

The current informatics core curriculum draws largely on our experience in teaching informatics in schools in Poland for over 30 years (Sysło, Kwiatkowska 2015). Fortunately, when the decision was made in 2017 to provide compulsory informatics education to all students, the education system in Poland was, in a sense, "ready" for the new core curriculum. There were computer-related subjects at every school level (grade) and there were teachers teaching these subjects, hence all we had to do was standardize, modify and expand the curriculum content. Needless to say, it would otherwise be very difficult to convince our politicians that the core curriculum needs such changes in an area that was not a top priority on the political agenda. The new 2017 informatics core curriculum unified the names of all separate computer-related subjects as rigorous informatics and focused teachers on the professional development necessary to implement the new curriculum.

This paper is devoted to informatics education in early school education, which, in our approach is the most important stage of informatics education. In the next Section, we briefly describe the informatics core curriculum and strongly emphasize its most important feature – the **spiral nature** of education, which guarantees the incremental cognitive development of students throughout all years at school. On the foundations of students' knowledge and skills built during early school education, they will build and develop knowledge and skills at each subsequent stage of school education, as well as in future education and professional work.

In the next Section, we first refer to the general structure of the informatics core curriculum and explain the spiral approach. Then we focus on some parts of the informatics core curriculum for grades 1–3 and provide the list of important students' achievements in some areas of informatics and the list of concepts from these areas, they develop during their class activities.

In Sect. 3, we draw attention to the most important approaches in informatics education, especially in early school education – computational thinking and unplugged activities. In Sect. 4, some informatics teaching and learning environments for early school education are characterized, and in Sect. 5 our approach is illustrated with selected examples of students' activities in these environments.

The new informatics core curriculum from 2017 introduced significant changes in the teaching of informatics in early school education. Before 2017, there was the subject "Computer Classes" in grades 1–3, during which students learned how to use a computer and some of its applications from the area of ICT. Such classes did not require any additional preparation from teachers of early school education, the knowledge and skills acquired during the ICT course at the university were sufficient. The new informatics curriculum for grades 1–3 (see Sect. 2) introduced elements of rigorous informatics. This put these teachers in a difficult situation. In many schools, the practice of teaching informatics in grades 1–3 by upper-class informatics teachers has become common. Such classes are held in computer labs isolated from environments enabling the integration of informatics with other educations. To counteract such a situation and give early school education teachers a chance to prepare to teaching informatics, in 2021 the Ministry of National Education (MEN) started financing in-service postgraduate studies for this group of teachers. Such a 120-h course was established in 6 universities according to the syllabus developed by a team led by the author of this article. A detailed description of this study will be the subject of another article. This article outlines the concepts and methodology of preparing early school teachers to teach informatics in environments integrating various educations.

2 Informatics Core Curriculum

The current informatics core curriculum consists of separate documents for each school level (primary: grades 1–3, 4–6, 7–8; high: 9–11/12.). However, **Unified aims**, which define 5 knowledge areas in the form of general requirements, are the same in all these curricula. The most important are the first two aims and their order in the curricula[1]: (I) **Understanding and analysis of problems**... and (II) **Programming and problem solving by using computers** and other digital devices... The content of each aim, defined adequately to the school level, consists of detailed **Attainment targets**. Thus, learning objectives are defined that identify the informatics concepts and skills students should develop and achieve in a spiral fashion through the four levels of K-12 of their education. We now briefly refer to the spiral approach and then move on to present the informatics core curriculum for early school education.

The concept of a **spiral curriculum** was put forward originally by Bruner (Bruner, 1960) based on his cognitive theory in which he distinguished tree stages: manipulating and interacting with real objects, then manipulating images of the objects or phenomena, and finally the manipulation of abstract representations of the actual objects and phenomena, In this way, as the curriculum "goes" upwards, more complex concepts and methods can be introduced. The key features of the spiral curriculum are:

- the student revisits a topic or theme several times throughout her/his school years;
- the complexity of the topic and theme increases with each visit;
- new learning is related to previous learning and is put in context the old one.

This changing emphasis can allow for progression that is critical for informatics including: increasing difficulty of problems, enabling students to become more comprehensive in their problem-solving process as they progress, move from block-based programming environments to text-based. An additional argument in favor of the spiral curriculum was provided by Winch (Winch, 2013) who identified the need to introduce early in the curriculum all three main types of knowledge: concepts, propositions and know-how, because these types of knowledge are interdependent.

In discussing the informatics core curriculum for early school education, due to space constraints, we will limit our attention to only two Unified aims and their Attainment targets. Similarly, we will limit the lists of student achievements and concepts learned to those items that appear in the examples in Sect. 5. The three remaining Unified aims refer to: III. Achievements in using computers, digital devices, and computer networks; IV. Achievements in developing social competencies; V. Achievements in observing law and safety principles. It should be noted that no single Attainment target can be considered in isolation. The examples in Sect. 5 illustrate how the achievement of one target can be accompanied by the achievement of several other targets from many different Unified aims.

---

[1] The complete set of Unified Aims in published in (Webb et al., 2017).

Informatics Core Curriculum for Grades 1–3, Limited to Two Unified Aims:

I. Achievements in understanding, analyzing, and solving problems. The student:
   1) arranges in a logical order: pictures, texts, commands (instructions) consisting of, among others: for daily activities;
   2) Creates a command or sequence of commands for a specific action plan leading to achieving a goal;
   3) Solves tasks and puzzles leading to the discovery of algorithms.
II. Achievements in programming and problem-solving by using computers and other digital devices. The student:
   1) Programs visually: simple situations or stories based on own ideas and ideas developed together with other students, single commands, and sequences of commands controlling an object on a computer screen or other digital device;
   2) Creates simple drawings, text documents, combining text with graphics, e.g., invitations, diplomas, leaflets, announcements; enlarges, reduces, copies, pastes, and deletes graphic and text elements – while improving skills in writing, reading, arithmetic, and presenting ideas;
   3) Saves the results of work in the indicated place.

In the next two subsections, we first list some achievements that students of grades 1–3 are expected to develop, and then the concepts whose meaning they should become familiar with. The items on these lists are not intended to be used to assess students, although they may be useful for this purpose in conjunction with various assessment methods. These student achievements and the concepts they learn are primarily intended to help teachers in designing appropriate classroom activities.

These lists were created on the basis of the informatics curriculum for grades 1–3 and constitute methodological material for teachers in grades 1–3. Both lists are also very useful for teachers in grades 4–6 to know what students in grades 1–3 are coming up with. The complete lists are also used by teachers taking part in personal development courses for preparing lesson plans for their future classroom activities.

Students' Achievements in Grades 1–3, Limited to Two Unified Aims:
Algorithmics (creativity, logical and computational thinking): considers problem situations in everyday activities; solves simple puzzles leading to the discovery of algorithms; breaks down a problem into simpler parts: represents data in the form of illustrations, symbols, numbers; explains what an algorithm is and how simple algorithms work; creates algorithms; arranges activities/objects in a linear order; searches for an item in a collection; creates algorithms: linear, with repetition and conditions; creates algorithms for execution without a computer (unplugged).

Programming (solving problems with a computer): creates programs from ready-made blocks; builds own programs for various situations, algorithms, robots; logically concludes about the operation of a program and its effects; launches and tests own programs; avoids errors in programs and corrects errors; uses in programs: sequences, loops, conditions, variables, events.

Applications: uses computer applications to create and process graphics, text and numerical information; searches, collects, analyses, evaluates, processes and presents data and information; uses acquired skills to support learning other subjects; uses technology responsibly and safely.

Concepts Learned in Grades 1–3, Limited to Two Unified Aims:
Algorithmics: problem; problem decomposition; sequence of elements; algorithm; linear algorithm; algorithm with repetitions and conditions; algorithm for searching an element, for ordering elements; execution of an algorithm outside the computer;

Programming: instruction; picture-text commands; program, code; linear program; program with repetitions, conditions, events, variables; program testing; debugging; executing a program outside computer; program for a robot;

Applications: applications for drawing, writing, calculating and presenting; web applications; use of informatics and technology in other subjects; examples of the use of technology at school; technology around us;

3 Informatics Learning with Computational Thinking and a Computer in the Background

In this Section, we briefly present two methods used to develop students' informatics knowledge, skills and competences. In the presented approach, both of these methods occur in the background, not only for students, what is obvious in the case of the youngest students, but also for teachers planning classes. The teacher's main goal is to plan students' activities in such a way that they contribute to the shaping and development of their achievements and build their understanding of emerging concepts. Regarding the two methods, students use the ways of reasoning that constitute computational thinking when solving various puzzles, tasks and problems, and their activities take place in an environment in which they can freely choose and use various artifacts. Below we shortly comment on these two methods based on (Sysło, 2023).

Computational Thinking
Computational thinking (CT) is not a characterization of informatics (computer science), it is a collection of mental tools and practices originated in computing but addressed to areas far beyond informatics. It is a problem solving approach addressed to all students to use in various school subjects. Although coming from informatics, CT is not only the study of informatics, though computers play an essential role in the design of problems' solutions.

Seymour Papert used the concept of CT for the first time in his groundbreaking book *Mindstorms* in 1980 (Papert, 1980), but it was the paper of Jeannette Wing (Wing, 2006) that contributed to the enormous popularity of this concept. As she wrote: *Computational thinking is a fundamental skill for everyone, not just for computer scientists. To reading, writing, and arithmetic, we should add computational thinking to every child's analytical ability*. And in 2008 she appreciated the role of early school education (Wing, 2008): *if we wanted to ensure a common and solid basis of understanding and applying computational thinking for all, then this learning should best be done in the early years of childhood*.

CT has a longer history, as Peter Denning pointed out: *Computational thinking has a long history within computer science, known in the 1950s and 1960s as "algorithmic thinking"* (Denning, 2009). Denning's opinion is confirmed by our 1997 informatics core curriculum, in which we defined the problem-solving process as the sequence of algorithmic thinking steps. Moreover, each step in algorithmic thinking can be associated with selected mental tools of CT, which form another definition of CT (Sysło, 2023). Thus, CT as algorithmic thinking in the problem solving process has a long tradition in our informatics education. However, in our approach we avoid to use the terms like "CT education", "teaching CT", "CT classes" and similar, as used by many authors. CT is an approach and a collection of mental tools used by students in the process of problem solving. Therefore, the following definition of CT fits our approach the best (Wing, 2014): *Computational thinking is the thought processes involved in formulating a problem and expressing its solution(s) in such a way that a computer – human or machine – can effectively carry out.*

In conclusion, we propose not to directly teach CT, but allow students to discover, develop, and use mental tools of CT in solving problems from various areas, in particular for integrating different subjects areas in early school education. Similarly, as we suggest not to "teach Scratch" but to "teach programming using Scratch".

Informatics with a Computer in the Background

Informatics (Computer Science) unplugged was originally defined as: *a collection of activities and ideas to engage a variety of audiences with great ideas from computer science, without having to learn programming or even use a digital device* (Bell, Vahrenhold, 2018). Almost every informatics concept can be explained to students without using a computer. Our experience and research show that unplugged classes can indeed stimulate students' interest in understanding and learning informatics and can have a positive impact on the development of students' use of CT.

The unplugged approach was used in schools in Poland in the mid-1980' before it was established in the late 1990' (Sysło, 2023). There were only few computers in schools and students spent a lot of time designing and writing their solutions and programs on paper before the programs could be run on a computer. Also teachers were using traditional tools. It was time of unplugged introduction to informatics and preparation for programming. However, we have never, in the past and in the last years, referred to activities as unplugged or plugged-in, these phases of teaching and learning have been naturally intertwined and integrated. Today it is difficult to maintain the 'unplugged' approach in its original meaning when all schools are well equipped with digital equipment and all students carry technology in their pockets. In a blending of unplugged and plugged-in approach, unplugged may play a role of introduction to using CT tools. Combining both types of activities may help students to better comprehend concepts and constructions such as variables, loops, conditionals, events.

Understanding the unplugged approach as an introduction to informatics without using a computer, mainly not to program it, we have extended the range of unplugged approach to teaching and learning in environments with **a computer in the background** (Sysło, 2023), in which digital technologies are in the background of learning activities, closer or further, more or less integrated, but not as the technology used in teaching and learning, although in the process of problem solving computationally. We distinguish 4 types of environments in which a computer can have its place in the background, in some sense: (1) classical unplugged, eventually with some computer puzzles; (2) Bebras tasks; (3) educational robotics; (4) algorithmics and programming unplugged. In Sect. 4, we shortly characterize some environments from these 4 groups that may accompany informatics classes in early school education in the background, and in Sect. 5, we illustrate their use in developing selected informatics concepts and achievements of students in grades 1–3. The resources described in Sects. 4 and 5 are used in our in-service courses for early school education teachers.

From pedagogical point of view, our approach supported by computers and with computers in the background contributes to constructionist learning, learning by doing and making meaningful decisions and objects in the real world and computational models of real-world situations. Our learning environments for grades 1–3 are extensions of classical unplugged ones by encouraging students to purposely and properly choose and use computers and digital technologies when solving various problems.

4 Learning Environments with Technology in the Background

We shortly characterize here popular learning environments used in early school education, and in the next chapter we illustrate our integrated approach with selected examples of students' activities in these environments while developing skills and achievements in the field of informatics.

Informatics for Kids (I4K) – Digitalized Classical Unplugged

By classical unplugged activities we mean the activities used to engage young students with basic ideas, concepts and methods from computing and with problem solving, but without using any digital device.

We created a package of simple applications that can be used in the implementation of the informatics core curriculum for grades 1–3. Hence its name "Informatics for Kids" – **I4K** (pl. *Informatyka dla Smyka*). The 25 apps can also be integrated with other educations in grades 1–3: mathematics, science, languages, arts, etc. Some apps contain Bebras tasks or code.org puzzles. The instructions for students in the package are read by the lector, as not all students in grades 1–3 are fluent readers. Access to this package is free and available after registering on platform dzwonek.pl.

The use of these applications can be manifold, as we illustrate in Sect. 5. Some of them imitate students' activities on the playground, but their computer implementations are much more diverse, multiple and enable interaction and repeated execution. On the other hand, ideas from these applications can be transferred to children's activities on the playground with appropriate materials (cards, templates, etc.). Classes using I4S can take various forms. A group of students can start unplugged activities on the playground then some students can leave the group to practice solving selected puzzles on a computer or tablet with I4K. However, it will probably be easier to organize unplugged classes first and then move the whole class to the computer lab. A student registered for this package may also use it at home with siblings or parents.

Bebras Tasks

Bebras's tasks are illustrated stories describing "real" problem situations, used in the International Bebras Challenge: https://www.bebras.org/, https://www.bobr.edu.pl/. These tasks are related to informatics concepts, topics and methods, usually indirectly, hidden in stories. For students, tasks are an opportunity to discover informatics concepts and algorithms and use some mental tools that make up CT (Dagienė et al. 2019). To solve such a task, the student must: choose one of four possible multiple-choice items or create a solution in interaction with the computer – write an answer (a string of characters) in an open window or create a solution by manipulating the graphical elements of the task formulation. A computer is only a medium for presenting the tasks and is used to create and save task solutions – it does not help the student solve the task in any way (Beaver's tasks can also be transferred from the screen to paper and solved outside the computer.). After a challenge, we publish augmented versions of all tasks with an additional section containing: a correct solution and its development, and comments that are extended version of the original task section "It's informatics". The comments are addressed to both, students and to teachers.

For the sets of tasks that we prepare for our students we prefer interactive (open) tasks for which we can be sure that the answers are obtained by students in the process of solving the tasks, i.e. using, most often unconsciously, certain mental tools of CT and inventing an algorithm. In competitions in 2020–2023, there were 8–12 out of 15 such open tasks for students in grades 1–3.

We convince our teachers that Beaver's tasks should not appear only during the competition, but can constitute educational resources throughout the year. For this purpose, we create a repository of all tasks tagged with informatics concepts, algorithms, and mental tools of CT (see (Datzko, 2021) for a classification of Bebras tasks), so that the teacher can select tasks appropriate to the topic of the lesson. We also use these tasks during the in-service courses for teachers of early school education when introducing new informatics concepts and methods. Furthermore, we suggest that teachers use some of Bebras's collections of tasks to measure students' achievements, especially when they "graduate" from integrated early childhood education, which is very important for students' successful spiral development as preparation for the next stages of education (Román-González et al., 2019).

Educational Robotics

Robots are very useful at many stages of integrated informatics education in grades 1–3. First, a student may imitate the robot's movements on the playground or in another environment at the commands of another student. Then physical robots, such as Dash&Dot can be used as a continuation of the kinesthetic activities of students, when for example a robot is supposed to imitate the movements of children or vice versa, on the floor or on the screen. Manipulating physical robots promotes children' constructionist learning through the development of mental representations of the objects. Robotics also encourages students to think creatively and apply some mental tools in the process of building solutions (Grover, 2011), (Chevalier et al., 2020). In Sect. 6, we show how specific robots can be used to introduce students to programming.

The Hour of Code; code.org
The informatics core curriculum for early school education refers to robots in: "The student: [...] sequences of commands controlling an object on a computer screen or other digital device;" (II, 1)). An excellent environment for this type of activities are puzzles in the Hour of Code initiative (https://code.org), which is very popular in Poland – in 2018 there were more than 650 M students registered to code.org from our schools. Such a popularity of this initiative is due to many thoughtful solutions such as: (1) the heroes of the puzzles are characters known to students from their favorite comics and games; the students can interact with them in code.org; (2) puzzles are in sets of increasing difficulty; (3) the solutions of puzzles consist in arranging a program in a block-based language to pre-prepared scenarios; (4) the students can run, debug and improve solutions many times. Although there is no direct connection of the code.org activities with CT concepts, solving such puzzles arranged in courses which correspond to particular algorithmic and programming constructions, students apply abstraction and pattern matching, then decomposition and finally algorithms in solving puzzles. Moreover, using event blocks students can program interaction what is a quite advanced informatics topic. During in-service courses for teachers in early school education we suggest to use puzzles from code.org as first step in spiral approach of learning programming, see Sect. 6.2.

5 Implementation Examples

We present some proposals for implementing the informatics core curriculum in early school education. As we described in Sect. 4, students' informatics-related activities may take place in a computer lab or in a classroom converted into a playground, a free place on the floor surrounded by desks with PC's and tablets. The final choice belongs to the teacher and also to the students and should be determined only by the students' assumed achievements.

How to use a Mouse (grade 1); at PC's with I4K or code.org
Kids usually are very skillful in using touch screens in tablets and smartphones but many of them have a problem to use a mouse for **selecting an item** and especially to **drag and drop** an object on the screen. They can practice these mouse operations arranging traditional puzzles, painting some pictures or arranging arrows in an algorithm to reach a certain location. They can do it in several application of I4K or in code.org, where one can find puzzles for students who cannot read.

Robotics (grade 1); on the Floor

In the photo on the left, the students control Dash robots that deliver Christmas presents and on the right they program Genibot using note/sound cards to play a melody they have learned to play on the xylophone. The students develop **practical algorithms**.

Bebras Tasks (grades 1–3), at PC's with the Bebras Challenge, on the Floor.

In the task on the left, the student is asked to click the tower that will be in the tenth position after arranging the towers from the lowest to the highest. In the task on the right, the student is asked to click the coins that will make the sum 13. The first task is concerned with **ordering**, and the second one is concerned with **the binary system**.

Collecting, sorting (grades 1–2), at PC's with I4K, on the Floor, with Robots.

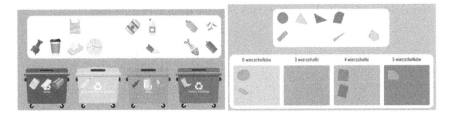

Garbage collection is a practical application of the **bucket sort**. It can be applied to many object types, for instance geometric figures which kids learn in math lessons. Garbage collection can have a real version when kids sort on the floor real garbage using Dash robots playing the role of bulldozers.

Sudoku (grades 1–3), at PC's with I4K, on Desks, on the Floor.

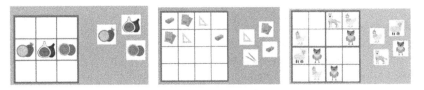

Sudoku is a fantastic puzzle that aims to introduce students to using mental tools of computational thinking without boring them with information about what computational thinking is or even without fully realizing that they are thinking computationally. The simplest Sudoku is a Latin square – the fruits have to be different in each row and in each column. Sudoku with school supplies is just one bigger. Then, when trying to solve Sudoku with animals, the student tries to find a place where he can place the missing animal (he uses decomposition) and the sequence of his decisions creates an algorithm.

When solving subsequent Sudoku puzzles, the student applies the same principle to different objects, so he thinks abstractly, and when moving to larger sizes, he generalizes. Students can solve unplugged Sudoku with various objects on the floor, with real fruit and school supplies.

Math puzzles (grades 1–3), at PC's with I4K, on Desks, on the Floor.

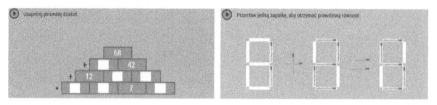

At the early school of education students still like math and we should rather give them interesting math challenges instead of tedious and boring calculations. We offer in I4K pyramids of math operations and puzzles with matches. Note that solving a pyramid kids have to find, first – a starting window, and then – a sequence (**algorithm**) of operations to fill in the empty windows. Puzzles with matches can be played on the floor with real matches.

Graphics, Art (grades 1–3), at PC's with I4K, on Desks, on the Floor.

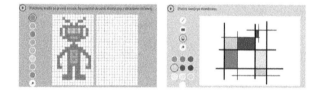

Copying the images on a square grid can be an illustration of the **representation of images** on the screen in the **raster graphics**. The tasks are to copy the image or to make its mirror reflection. In the application on the right, students can create their own Mondrians and then the class or school can organize an art exhibition of their creativity.

6 Spiral Implementation of Two Topics

We continue here with two fundamental topics: sequencing and programming focusing on their spiral development in grades 1–3, as well as the spiral continuation in later stages of education. Sequencing (alias ordering, sorting) and programming are the two most important informatics topics throughout all stages of informatics education in schools, starting from early school education. It is therefore important how these two topics are implemented at the earliest stage and, at the same time, how they are spirally developed at this and subsequent stages. These two topics are not independent. Piaget already drew attention to students' ability to sequencing from an early age (Piaget, 1969). This skill is extremely important when programming, which is a sequence of commands used to create a series of actions to instruct a computer. To create a program, students should think sequentially in terms of decision what must be *next, before,* and *until* (Pea, Kurland, 1984).

Implementing Informatics Core Curriculum in Early School Education in Poland   55

6.1 Sequencing

The informatics core curriculum for early school education refers to sequencing in several places: "The student: arranges in a logical order: pictures, texts, commands (instructions) consisting of, among others: for daily activities" (I, 1); "Creates a command or sequence of commands for a specific action plan" (I, 2); "Programs [...] sequences of commands" (II, 1). Sequencing or arranging things in a linear order is one of the basic skills students should acquire in early school education. The figures below show two of many tasks from I4K in which students are to arrange the activities in a linear order. For some students, it is a problem to decide if the order of activities on the right picture is linear. All such tasks from I4K can be transferred to the floor as unplugged activities.

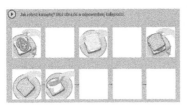 

It is clear that when sequencing objects or activities, students also use other mental tools of computational thinking, such as **pattern recognition** (comparing pictures), **logical thinking** (relations between pictures), **algorithmic thinking** (building a sequence), and **debugging** (verifying and correcting solution).

Students' subsequent spiral activities related to sequencing in grades 1–3 concern creating a sequence of commands to be executed by a robot or on a computer in the form of a program. At subsequent stages of school education (from grade 4), students learn ordering algorithms and program them. Sequencing also appears in many other subjects, such as science (organizing data) or history (ordering the dates of events).

6.2 Programming

The informatics core curriculum for early school education refers to programming in its section II, which is about: "Achievements in programming and problem-solving by using computers and other digital devices." Then it states: "The student: Programs visually: simple situations or stories based on her/his own ideas and ideas developed together with other students, single commands, and sequences of commands controlling an object on a computer screen or other digital device".

Classes with robots can play a role of introduction to programming when students turn on robots and control their moves to achieve certain goals with the help of programs made in a language characteristic for given types of robots. In such classes students have opportunity to learn that robots can understand they own language to communicate with them: graphical collection of interactive instructions (Dash&Dot), colors (Ozobot, in the picture above), cards (Genibot, in the picture above). In these first steps of programming, students learn that programming does not have to be about "writing a program" and that programming a digital device can be as simple as using the robot's own language.

According to the curriculum, students in grades 1–3 begin their adventure with programming in a block-based programming environment. It may be a robot programming environment (e.g. Dash&Dot), The Hour of Code and code.org initiative or Scratch. In the upper grades of primary school, students begin programming in a text-based language such as Python or C++. In such a situation, a natural question arises: What is a possible spiral transition between these programming environments? The figure below illustrates a smooth transition from two block-based environments (The Hour of Code and Scratch) to the text-based environment (Python). However, only the first two environments are suitable for early school education. The smoothness and ease of this transition is based on the observation that although the first two environments use blocks, the blocks actually contain command texts from which it is easy to build a text-based program.

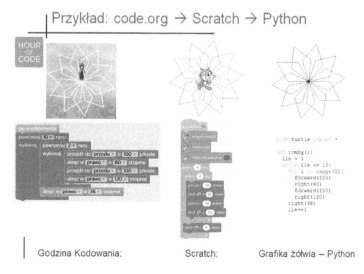

Acknowledgments. The author thanks the reviewers for their valuable suggestions that improved the presentation.

References

1. Bell, T., Vahrenhold, J.: CS unplugged – how is it used, and does it work? In: Böckenhauer, H.J., Komm, D., Unger, W. (eds.) Adventures Between Lower Bounds and Higher Altitudes. LNCS, vol. 11011, pp. 497–521. Springer, Cham (2018). https://doi.org/10.1007/978-3-319-98355-4_29

2. Bers, M.U.: Coding as a Playground: Programming and Computational Thinking in the Early Childhood Classroom. Routledge (2018)
3. Bruner, J.S.: The Process of Education. Harvard University Press, Cambridge (1960)
4. Chevalier, M., Giang, C., Piatti, A., Mondada, F.: Fostering computational thinking through educational robotics: a model for creative computational problem-solving. Int. J. STEM Educ. **7**(41) (2020)
5. Chiazzese, G., Arrigo, M., Chifari, A., Lonati, V., Tosto, C.: Exploring the effect of a robotics laboratory on computational thinking skills in primary school children using the Bebras tasks. In: TEEM 18, pp. 25–30 (2018)
6. Dagienė, V., Futschek, G., Stupuriene, G.: Creativity in solving short tasks for learning computational thinking. Construct. Found. **14**(3), 382–415 (2019)
7. Datzko, C.: A multi-dimensional approach to categorize Bebras tasks. In: Barendsen, E., Chytas, C. (eds.) ISSEP 2021, LNCS, vol. 13057, pp. 83–94 (2021). https://doi.org/10.1007/978-3-030-90228-5_7
8. Denning, P.J.: Beyond computational thinking. Commun. ACM **52**(6), 28–30 (2009)
9. Grover, S.: Robotics and engineering for middle and high school students to develop computational thinking. In: Annual Meeting of the American Educational Research Association, New Orleans (2011)
10. Papert, S.: Teaching Children Thinking. In: World Conference on Computer Education. IFIPS, Amsterdam (1970)
11. Papert, S.: Mindstorms. Children Computers, and Powerful Ideas. Basic Books, New York (1980)
12. Pea, R.D., Kurland, D.M.: On the cognitive effects of learning computer programming. New Ideas Psychol. **2**(2), 137–168 (1984)
13. Piaget, J.: The Child's Conception of Time (1927, Original, Fr.). Routledge (1969)
14. Román-González, M., Moreno-León, J., Robles, G.: Combining assessment tools for a comprehensive evaluation of computational thinking interventions. In: Kong, S.C., Abelson, H. (eds.) Computational Thinking Education. Springer, Singapore (2019). https://doi.org/10.1007/978-981-13-6528-7_6
15. Sysło, M.M., Kwiatkowska, A.B.: Introducing a new computer science curriculum for all school levels in Poland. In: Brodnik, A., Vahrenhold, J. (eds.) ISSEP 2015. LNCS, vol. 9378, pp. 141–154 (2015). https://doi.org/10.1007/978-3-319-25396-1_13
16. Sysło, M.M.: Computer Science Education with a Computer in the Background. In: ISSEP 2023 Local Proceedings, pp. 89–101 (2023)
17. Wing, J.M.: Computational thinking. Comm. ACM **49**(3), 33–35 (2006)
18. Wing, J.M.: Computational thinking and thinking about computing. Philos. Trans. R. Soc. Math. Phys. Eng. Sci. **366**(1881), 3717–3725 (2008)
19. Wing, J.M.: Computational Thinking Benefits Society (2014). http://socialissues.cs.toronto.edu/index.html%3Fp=279.html
20. Webb, M.E., et al.: Computer science in K-12 school curricula of the 21st century: why, what and when? Educ. Inf. Technol. **22**, 445–468 (2015)
21. Webb, M., et al.: Computer Science in the School Curriculum: Issues and Challenges. In: WCCE 2017, IFIP AICT 515, pp. 421–431 (2017)
22. Winch, C.: Curriculum design and epistemic ascent. J. Philos. Educ. **47**, 128–146 (2013)

Problem Solving, Algorithms and Programming

Mastering Control Structures in Secondary Education: Student Observations and Descriptions of Program Logic

Corinna Mößlacher[2(✉)][iD], Katharina Brugger[3], Tatjana Angermann[1], and Andreas Bollin[1]

[1] Department of Informatics Didactics at University of Klagenfurt, Klagenfurt, Austria
{tatjana.angermann,andreas.bollin}@aau.at
[2] University College of Teacher Education Carinthia, Klagenfurt, Austria
corinna.moesslacher@ph-kaernten.ac.at
[3] Carinthia Education Directorate, Klagenfurt, Austria
katharina.brugger@aau.at

Abstract. The acquisition of control structures in programming poses a significant challenge for K12 students, often requiring more time than typically allocated in standard lecture schedules. This study uses three distinct experiment groups to investigate the efficacy of different instructional approaches to learning control structures. One group (our baseline) consisted of K12 students with prior programming experience. Another group included novices who received a conventional introduction to control structures. Finally, a third group, also comprised of novices, engaged in an intensive unit employing the "human robot" method, which heavily emphasized control structures. Our findings indicate that even for students with prior experience, mastery of control structures demands extended practice and instructional time. Notably, the "human robot" method significantly enhanced the understanding of control structures among novices, suggesting that more dedicated time and innovative teaching strategies are crucial for effectively teaching these fundamental concepts. Consequently, we recommend that computer science lessons allocate additional time and employ active learning techniques to ensure students develop a robust grasp of control structures.

Keywords: K12 · problem solving · control structures · programming education

1 Introduction

Mastering control structures is fundamental to learning to program, forming the backbone of logical thinking and algorithm development. Control structures, such as loops and conditionals, are essential for creating efficient and effective programs [4]. However, educators often face the challenge of conveying these concepts within the limited time in standard lecture schedules. Traditional teaching methods may not provide the depth of understanding required for K12 students to apply these concepts effectively in more complex programming scenarios. Additionally, students new to programming frequently adopt a trial-and-error/tinkering approach [6,15], particularly when using block-based programming languages, which can impede their conceptual understanding and long-term retention of control structures.

In response to these challenges, educational strategies have evolved to include block-based programming [12] and unplugged activities [1,2]. Block-based programming enables students to focus on the semantics and logic of programming without the burden of syntax. Unplugged activities, on the other hand, leverage everyday algorithms, such as planning daily routines or understanding game instructions, to illustrate control structures in a tangible, relatable manner. Despite these innovative approaches, the problem persists: many students struggle to develop a robust understanding of control structures, as evidenced by their performance in subsequent programming tasks.

Given students' persistent difficulties in mastering control structures, our research seeks to identify the most effective instructional intervention for teaching these concepts. Specifically, for the work described in this paper, we aim to determine whether the '"human-robot" method (where students take over the role of a robot and get programmed to solve problems by their classmates) and observations during hands-on activities with programmed robots better fosters the learning of control structures.

For this, our study examines the effectiveness of these two instructional strategies through an experimental design involving three distinct groups of students. Group one (G01) includes lower secondary class students with little prior programming experience using Scratch[1]. After a short introduction to the so-called "human robot" (that only included tasks with sequential instruction and no control structures to introduce the concept of an algorithm), they were given the task of observing robots called Bit:Bots[2]. Group two (G02) consists of novices introduced to programming through the "human robot" method, including tasks emphasizing control statements and loops. In contrast, group three (G03), with the most programming experience using BBC micro: bits[3], had no introduction before analyzing the Bit:Bots.

The paper is structured as follows: We present related work, describe our study with focus on the setting and the different cohorts as well as the observed tasks in the workshop. Then, we present the results of the collected data from the students' worksheets - specifically the differences in the cohorts. In the conclusion, we describe possible impacts on our workshops and introductory programming lessons.

---

[1] https://scratch.mit.edu/ (accessed 7 June 2024).
[2] https://4tronix.co.uk/blog/?p=1490 (accessed 7 June 2024).
[3] https://microbit.org/ (accessed 7 June 2024).

2 Related Work

Block-based programming environments, such as Scratch and Blockly, have been widely adopted due to their intuitive interfaces, enabling beginners to create programs by snapping together blocks representing different commands. This method has lowered the entry barrier for learning to program and fostered creativity and experimentation [12,13]. Grover and Pea [4] discussed the effectiveness of these environments in developing computational thinking skills among K-12 students, emphasizing the importance of focusing on logic and problem-solving rather than syntax. Studies by Maloney et al. [7] further highlight the benefits of Scratch in making programming accessible to a broader audience, noting its role in engaging students in meaningful computational tasks.

Despite the advantages of block-based environments, students often develop misconceptions about programming concepts and program flow. Pea [11], Sorva [14], Mühling [9], and Du Boulay [3] identified several common misconceptions that learners hold, such as misunderstanding the sequential nature of program execution and the behavior of control structures. Mühling also investigated misconceptions in novice programmers, highlighting the need for targeted interventions to address these misunderstandings. These misconceptions can persist and impede progress in more advanced programming tasks.

Our research aims to fill the gap in understanding the most effective instructional interventions for teaching control structures in programming. While the above-mentioned studies have explored the benefits of block-based environments and identified common misconceptions, there is limited empirical evidence comparing different hands-on and unplugged approaches specifically focused on control structures. By examining the efficacy of the "human robot" method against observations during hands-on activities, our study provides insights into how these different strategies impact the understanding and application of control structures among novice programmers. This comparative analysis contributes to the existing body of knowledge by offering practical recommendations for educators to enhance programming education.

3 Study

As described in the introduction, three cohorts of students, with a total n of 73 students, participated in our study. Four workshops were conducted. The setting differed, but all groups had to do the Bit:Bot activity and complete a worksheet. This section describes the setting and tasks in the workshop, the common core part of the study, the background and information of the three study groups, and the data collection and evaluation process.

3.1 Setting and Tasks

Each group participated in a workshop that introduced Bit:Bot programming.

Before starting programming themselves, all classes participating in the workshop were divided into six groups. Each group received a Bit:Bot robot with an existing program. Their task was to try out the program, describing their behavior in as much detail as possible. No further input was given except for a small description of the robots' sensors and buttons.

Each of the six robots was programmed differently and marked with colored stickers. They also differed in the difficulty of the program. After describing one robot, the students were able to switch robots. The participants were given about thirty minutes for this task. Each group managed to work with two to three Bit:Bots in the allotted time. Table 1 briefly describes each program and its control structures. The tasks came from our repository of Bit:Bot programs that we have used in our workshops for the past 3–4 years.

Table 1. Overview of the available stations (by color code), their Bit:Bot program, possible observable control flows, and their complexity.

Color	Task	Control Flow	Difficulty
Blue	The robot is controlled by pressing a button, pauses between commands, and can move and turn	conditional, sequential	Easy
Multi	The robot waits for a button press, turns until a sensor is activated, stops/moves, displays random numbers, stops at number '6'	conditional, sequential	Difficult
Yellow	The robot randomly changes color and direction, with pauses in between	sequential	Medium
Green	Has adjustable counter: robot moves forward and turns 90° when A+B are pressed	conditinal, sequential, loops/repetition	Medium
Pink	The robot moves forward, turning left at obstacles	conditional, sequential	Medium
Turquoise	The robot uses a compass, can be rotated manually, and aligns to the north	conditional, sequential	Difficult

3.2 Cohorts and Workshop

This study focuses on the introduction phase of these workshops.

All cohorts were lower secondary class students from three different schools. This leads to different prior knowledge regarding programming experiences. However, they did not know the "human robot" or Bit:Bots and can be classified as follows (for a summary, Table 2 provides an overview of all cohorts):

Cohort G01 started with a twenty-minute introduction to algorithms and sequences of instructions using the "human robot". The groups were divided and challenged to lay instructions sequences to a specific place on the map. No loops or conditionals were used for G01. After this introduction, G01 received the prepared Bit:Bots for the analysis.

Table 2. Quick overview of the background of the three different cohorts.

Cohort One (G01)	
School Context:	Two public, lower secondary school classes
Quantity:	35 students in total
Age:	Between 12 and 14 years
Prior Knowledge:	Little to no knowledge about block-based coding with Scratch
Cohort Two (G02)	
School Context:	One private, lower secondary school class
Quantity:	12 students in total
Age:	Between 13 and 14 years
Prior Knowledge:	No knowledge about programming
Cohort Three (G03)	
School Context:	One public, lower secondary school class
Quantity:	21 students in total
Age:	Between 13 and 14 years
Prior Knowledge:	Prior knowledge about block-based programming with micro:bits - event control, conditionals and loops

Cohort G02 received a more detailed introduction, lasting about thirty minutes, to algorithms and sequences of instructions using the "human robot". The groups were challenged to lay instruction sequences to a specific place on the map AND to use loops and conditionals. A usage for loops was required to let the robot walk a square. The conditional method was used to examine boxes on the map and to react differently depending on the content of the boxes. After this introduction, G02 received the prepared Bit:Bots for the analysis.

Cohort G03 directly received the prepared Bit:Bots for the analysis without an introduction to the "human robot" since they had the most prior programming knowledge compared to G01 and G02.

Every cohort analyzed existing programs by observing the behavior of the Bit:Bots. However, each group received different input regarding algorithms and unplugged programming beforehand. This leads to the next workshop module because we used the "human robot" for this.

The "human robot" is an unplugged activity for teaching programming and control structures. The material was developed by the computer science lab (Informatik-Werkstatt) at the Department of Informatics Didactics at University of Klagenfurt.[4]

In the workshop part of the "human robot," the participants are divided into three different roles. First, the 'programmer' team. This team places predefined instruction cards on a table in consultation. These cards show the commands "one step forward/backward" and "one turn to the left/right." These sequences of instructions later guide a robot through a maze to a predefined destination. The second team, the 'interpreter' team, reads these instructions. Third, the

---

[4] https://www.rfdz-informatik.at/informatik-werkstatt/.

'robot' executes them. The representation of the "human robot" can be seen as a notional machine [5].

Munasinghe et al. [10] have shown that using unplugged activities similar to the "human robot" as an introduction can facilitate the development of programming skills in students. However, their presented example similar to the "human robot" - the Kidbots by CSUnplugged[5] - does not include control structures such as conditionals and loops. The "human robot", as in our case, does so. Figure 1 shows an example of a conditional. It should be noted that the conditional, as well as the loop, does not include terms ("if...else" or "for...") used in block-based or text-based coding in our workshops. We have chosen a visual representation so as not to provide any wording that will later be included in the worksheet.

Fig. 1. An example of a conditional that is used in the "human robot" A possible written form of this instruction would be: "Do you see the ball?" (Note: in the box you just opened). "If yes: take the ball, if no: close the box".

3.3 Data Collection and Classification

To collect the needed data, we printed worksheets with instructions for analyzing the Bit:Bot robots. Although the groups were divided into teams analyzing one robot, the worksheets had to be completed individually and independently of each other. Figure 2 shows the analysis phase of one team in practice.

The task was to describe in one's own words what the robot was performing. The students only received information that the robot could drive, with buttons and a distance sensor at the front. If one team finished the analysis,

---

[5] https://www.csunplugged.org/en/topics/kidbots/.

Fig. 2. Three students executing the analysis phase with the multi-colored Bit:Bot

they needed to swap their robots with another. Each team analyzed at least two robots during the phase, which took around thirty minutes. After the workshop, the handwritten description was transcribed in a tabular form by someone not involved in conducting the workshop units.

Every group was recorded in a separate table. Each row is seen as an item and depicts a description of one robot, referenced by its color. Further information about every item is the corresponding child's and their team's index. No personal information was collected at all during the study.

After collecting the data, a classification was carried out. G01 had 99 usable descriptions, G02 had 25 usable descriptions, and G03 had 55 usable descriptions. Of these 179, 24 were selected randomly; a classification was created and applied to 20 other descriptions to test for their suitability. The classification was further improved on this basis. In parallel, ChatGPT4o was used to perform qualitative content analysis, according to Mayring [8]. The proposed classes were analyzed and merged into a common classification. Two researchers completed the classification independently, merged the data in a joint session, and contradictory assessments (about 10 % of the descriptions) were documented or resolved.

Several factors were collected in the study (we were looking at the observation type, the complexity of the description, the technical accuracy, the detection of control structure types, and the area of application), but in this paper, we only look at the factor describing the control structures. They were classified as follows:

Sequential Control: Recognition of responses that describe the sequential processing of commands or actions without branches or loops. Distinction between **direct** (*'first this – then that'*) or **indirect** (enumeration that shows the chronological sequence)

Conditional Control: Answers that show an understanding of conditional statements (*if-then logic, selection decisions based on conditions*). Differentiation between **direct** (*'if-then'*) or **indirect** (when it is implied what happens then; examples: *'X: right, Y: left'* or *'at X it drives ...'*)

Loops/Repetitions: Responses that describe the recognition of repeatedly performed actions, including infinite loops and conditional loops. Distinction

between **direct** (*'more often'*, *'repeatedly'*) or **indirect** (when it is implied that something happens repeatedly)
Not Recognized: No control structures have been recognized.

4 Results

We evaluated the results in the context of recognizing conditional statements and loops. Figure 3 shows the detection of conditional statement for G01 whereas Fig. 4 respectively Fig. 5 shows the results for G02 and G03.

4.1 Conditional Control and Loops

When comparing the cohorts concerning conditional control statements, significant variations in performance were evident.

In group G01, students failed to recognize any control structures in five out of six tasks despite some of these tasks being categorized as difficult.

In contrast, group G02, which underwent the detailed "human robot" preliminary exercise, markedly improved. All students in G02 recognized conditional statements in four tasks, and in two of these tasks, they directly described the target statements.

Group G02 consistently outperformed G01 in every task. The proportion of students failing to recognize statements was lower in G02 across five tasks correctly. The exception was the Turquoise task, where the proportion was slightly higher; however, all recognized statements in this group were direct rather than indirect.

Group G03, which had the most prior programming experience, identified all statements in three tasks. While the proportion of unrecognized statements was relatively low in the remaining tasks, the proportion of direct statements was surprisingly low, sometimes even lower than in G01. This result is unexpected, considering their prior exposure to block-based programming should have facilitated easier formulation of these statements.

Regarding loop recognition, group G02 again excelled, with all students successfully describing loops. In contrast, the other groups had significantly more students who provided no direct or indirect description of a loop (Fig. 6).

4.2 Validity

In the context of our study, several threats to validity must be considered:

Firstly, the cohorts were drawn from different types of schools. Groups G01 and G03 were from public middle schools, whereas G02 was from a private middle school that follows Waldorf education principles. Despite these differences, the educational standards for this age group in the region should ensure comparable writing skills across these cohorts. Therefore, we consider any potential bias due to the school type insignificant.

Control Structures in Secondary Education 69

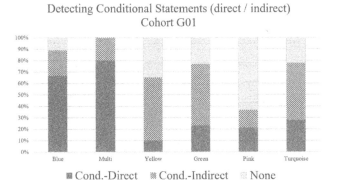

Fig. 3. Relative amount of direct and indirect mentions of control structures of G01 (n = 99 descriptions)

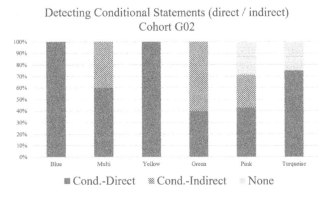

Fig. 4. Relative amount of direct and indirect mentions of control structures of G02 (n = 25 descriptions)

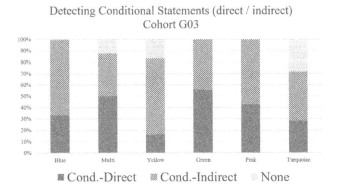

Fig. 5. Relative amount of direct and indirect mentions of control structures of G03 (n = 55 descriptions)

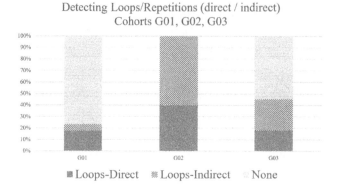

Fig. 6. Relative amount of direct and indirect mentions of loops or repetitions for station "green" for all 3 cohorts (n = 98 descriptions). (Color figure online)

A more significant concern is the small sample size of cohort G02 compared to the other groups. We could not conduct an additional workshop with another class from the same school to achieve a sample size comparable to G01. Although the small sample size limits the interpretability of G02's results, observable trends allow us to draw preliminary conclusions. In addition, not all students in every cohort analyzed all programs. They were randomly selected to analyze two to three robots each.

Thirdly, we must acknowledge the issue of inter-rater reliability in evaluating qualitative descriptions. Two independent raters assessed each item and compared their evaluations to mitigate this. Discrepancies were minimal, and consensus was reached through discussion. Additionally, a classification run with ChatGPT4 showed no significant deviations, further supporting the reliability of our evaluations.

Finally, the relatively weak results from group G03 may be attributable to the timing of their programming instruction, which did not occur immediately before the survey. This gap may have affected their recall and articulation of programming concepts. Despite expecting that engagement with block-based programming languages would foster a durable understanding, this was not evident in our cohort.

5 Conclusion

Our study aimed to explore the efficacy of different instructional approaches in helping secondary school students recognize and describe control structures in programming. Despite our expectations, the findings indicate significant challenges and variations in students' understanding across cohorts.

The results show that traditional methods and prior experience with block-based programming may not be sufficient to ensure a robust grasp of control structures. Specifically, students in groups G01 and G03, despite their varying backgrounds, exhibited difficulty identifying and articulating control structures accurately. In contrast, group G02, which engaged in the detailed "human robot" preliminary exercise, demonstrated a better understanding, though this was not uniformly strong across all tasks.

These observations underscore the necessity for more innovative and intensive instructional strategies. The "human robot" method appears promising, yet it requires further refinement and consistent application to be fully effective. Additionally, our study highlights the importance of timing and reinforcement in programming education, as gaps between instruction and assessment can negatively impact student performance.

In conclusion, while our research provides valuable insights into the teaching and learning of control structures in programming, it also reveals substantial areas for improvement. Future work should focus on developing and testing more comprehensive educational interventions, ensuring regular reinforcement, and addressing the diverse needs of students. By doing so, we can better equip students with the fundamental programming skills necessary for their academic and professional futures.

References

1. Bell, T.: Cs unplugged or coding classes? Commun. ACM **64**(5), 25–27 (2021). https://doi.org/10.1145/3457195
2. Bell, T., Witten, I., Fellows, M.: Computer Science Unplugged - an enrichment and extension programme for primary-aged children. iN: Computer Science Unplugged (csunplugged.org) (2002)
3. Boulay, B.D.: Some difficulties of learning to program. J. Educ. Comput. Res. **2**(1), 57–73 (1986). https://doi.org/10.2190/3LFX-9RRF-67T8-UVK9
4. Grover, S., Pea, R.: Computational thinking in k-12 a review of the state of the field. Educ. Research. **42**, 38–43 (2013). https://doi.org/10.3102/0013189X12463051
5. Kohn, T., Komm, D.: Teaching programming and algorithmic complexity with tangible machines. In: Pozdniakov, S.N., Dagienė, V. (eds.) ISSEP 2018. LNCS, vol. 11169, pp. 68–83. Springer, Cham (2018). https://doi.org/10.1007/978-3-030-02750-6_6
6. Lewis, C.M.: How programming environment shapes perception, learning and goals: logo vs. scratch. In: Proceedings of the 41st ACM Technical Symposium on Computer Science Education, SIGCSE 2010, pp. 346–350. Association for Computing Machinery, New York (2010). https://doi.org/10.1145/1734263.1734383
7. Maloney, J., Resnick, M., Rusk, N., Silverman, B., Eastmond, E.: The scratch programming language and environment. ACM Trans. Comput. Educ. (TOCE) **10**(4) (2010). https://doi.org/10.1145/1868358.1868363
8. Mayring, P.: Qualitative content analysis - theoretical foundation, basic procedures and software solution. Klagenfurt. SSOAR. Open Access Repository (2014)
9. Mühling, A., Ruf, A., Hubwieser, P.: Design and first results of a psychometric test for measuring basic programming abilities. In: Proceedings of the Workshop in Primary and Secondary Computing Education, WiPSCE 2015, pp. 2–10. Association for Computing Machinery, New York (2015). https://doi.org/10.1145/2818314.2818320

10. Munasinghe, B., Bell, T., Robins, A.: Unplugged activities as a catalyst when teaching introductory programming. J. Pedagogical Res. **7**(2), 56–71 (2023)
11. Pea, R.D.: Language-independent conceptual "bugs" in novice programming. J. Educ. Comput. Res. **2**(1), 25–36 (1986). https://telearn.hal.science/hal-00190538
12. Resnick, M., et al.: Scratch: programming for all. Commun. ACM **52**(11), 60–67 (2009). https://doi.org/10.1145/1592761.1592779
13. Seraj, M., Katterfeldt, E.S., Bub, K., Autexier, S., Drechsler, R.: Scratch and google blockly: how girls' programming skills and attitudes are influenced. In: Proceedings of the 19th Koli Calling International Conference on Computing Education Research. Koli Calling 2019. Association for Computing Machinery, New York (2019). https://doi.org/10.1145/3364510.3364515
14. Sorva, J.: Visual program simulation in introductory programming education. Doctoral dissertation. Ph.D. thesis, Department of Computer Science and Engineering, Aalto University (2012)
15. Woo, K., Falloon, G.: Problem solved, but how? an exploratory study into students' problem solving processes in creative coding tasks. Thinking Skills Creat. **46**, 101193 (2022). https://doi.org/10.1016/j.tsc.2022.101193. https://www.sciencedirect.com/science/article/pii/S1871187122001948

From Guesswork to Game Plan: Exploring Problem-Solving-Strategies in a Machine Learning Game

Clemens Witt[1](✉)[iD], Thiemo Leonhardt[2][iD], Erik Marx[1,3][iD], and Nadine Bergner[2][iD]

[1] TUD Dresden University of Technology, Dresden, Germany
{clemens.witt,erik.marx}@tu-dresden.de
[2] RWTH Aachen University, Aachen, Germany
{leonhardt,bergner}@informatik.rwth-aachen.de
[3] Center for Scalable Data Analytics and Artificial Intelligence (ScaDS.AI) Dresden/Leipzig, Dresden, Germany

Abstract. Problem-solving strategies have been investigated in various informatics education contexts. However, no substantial research has yet been conducted on the problem-solving behavior of students in the field of Machine Learning (ML). This study aims to bridge this gap by analyzing the self-directed problem-solving processes employed by students in grades 8 to 10 ($n = 93$) when developing decision trees as classification models. A digital multi-touch puzzle game and a custom-developed toolchain were utilized to visually capture and subsequently analyze students' gameplay behaviors using quantitative content analysis techniques. The results of this study indicate that learners within the examined age group predominantly employ exploratory problem-solving strategies in the self-directed construction of decision trees. In contrast, structured approaches are employed much less frequently and demonstrate lower persistence, yet they are significantly more correlated with successful game completion. These findings underscore the necessity of developing learning environments that promote the application and facilitate the persistence of structured problem-solving strategies, enabling learners to engage with the functioning and development of decision trees in a systematic and purposeful manner.

Keywords: Problem-Solving Strategies · Machine Learning · ML · Decision Trees · K-12 Education · Artificial Intelligence · AI

1 Introduction

The conveyance of central concepts in the fields of Artificial Intelligence (AI) and Machine Learning (ML) presents a unique challenge in informatics education due to their complexity and abstract nature. In recent years, a wide range of publications have aimed to define and classify key competency development areas and learning objectives in AI and ML [10,14,18]. In order to comprehend how learners resolve informatic problems, there have been numerous years of investigation in the field of programming education. This research has identified effective problem-solving strategies that adhere to commendable computational approaches, such as *Divide and Conquer*, but also non-informatic approaches that are unlikely to result in success. However, similar research does not yet exist in the field of ML. As a result, the strategies learners employ to solve problems in ML remain unclear. To initiate research on problem-solving strategies within the field of ML, we selected the study of decision trees as the primary focus of our investigation. Unlike more complex ML models such as neural networks or transformers, decision trees offer a direct visualization of the features that lead to specific decisions [11]. They organize data into increasingly homogeneous groups through repeated splitting based on decision rules in a tree structure, allowing for the prediction or classification of new data [1,16]. Their structural similarity to human decision-making processes [12,13] also allows individuals without specialized knowledge to intuitively understand and effectively use them [16,20]. It is therefore not surprising that decision trees are already being used to a significant extent in several ML teaching concepts [5,14,17,18]. The existing unplugged activities (e.g., [8,9]) and computer-based learning applications (e.g., [2,19]) in this field are designed to facilitate learners' active exploration and experimentation with decision trees [14].

Building on prior investigations of problem-solving strategies in the context of informatics education, this study aims to address the research gap of problem-solving strategies in the field of ML education, guided by the following research questions:

1. What problem-solving strategies do students employ when independently solving a task for developing classification models in the form of decision trees?
2. What correlations exist between the problem-solving strategies used and the achievement of the learning objective?
3. What patterns emerge in the usage behavior of problem-solving strategies, especially with regard to persistence and switching behavior?

2 Theoretical Background

The study of learners' problem-solving behavior has long been a prominent area of research in informatics education, particularly in the context of programming education. One of the earliest studies investigating learners' programming behavior was conducted by Perkins et al. in 1986 [15]. This study observed students in grades 4 to 6 as they worked on introductory programming tasks and identified three essential problem-solving strategies: *Stoppers*, *Movers*, and *Tinkerers*.

Stoppers are learners who cease their efforts at challenging points in the problem-solving process. Perkins et al. propose that this behavior is a consequence of a lack of self-efficacy, or the belief in one's ability to solve complex problems independently.

Movers are learners who are continuously engaged in the process of trying out ideas, constantly modifying and testing their approaches without pausing long enough to appear stuck. Hosseini et al. further differentiate the Movers pattern by introducing the substrategies *Builders, Reducers,* and *Massagers* [6]. **Builders** work incrementally, continuously adding new features to improve the correctness of their solution. This approach aligns with the Hill-Climbing strategy described by Kiesmüller [7]. **Reducers** initially focus on developing a functional solution and then enhance its efficiency by removing unnecessary components. In contrast, **Massagers** try to optimize existing concepts through minimal, continuous modifications, without implementing substantial structural changes.

Tinkerers are learners who attempt to solve problems through experimentation, making predominantly small changes. In contrast to Movers, they are distinguished by a greater willingness to experiment and a high tolerance for frustration. They are confident in their ability to solve the given problems and are not hesitant to alter aspects of their approaches. The effective application of the Tinkering approach necessitates the capacity to comprehend the functionality and consequences of implemented solutions in order to avoid chaotic and unstructured experimentation.

Hosseini et al. extend the original taxonomy of Perkins et al. by introducing a new category, *Strugglers*, which bridges the gap between the patterns of Stoppers and Tinkerers. **Strugglers** are learners who exhibit a high degree of experimentation and persistence, yet lack a systematic approach [6]. Gamper et al. [4] identify two behavioral patterns that can be subsumed under the *Struggler* pattern. They classify learners as **Watchers** when they repeatedly submit flawed solutions without making significant changes. This behavior is likely motivated by the hope of randomly or luckily identifying the problems in their solutions based on the feedback received. Learners are classified as **Restarters** when they abandon an existing problem-solving approach and begin anew from scratch. This pattern was also previously described by Perkins et al. [15].

In addition to the described behaviours and problem-solving strategies, Kiesmüller identifies the structuring of problem spaces into subproblems as a crucial goal in developing competence in learning to program [7]. Kiesmüller describes two central strategies for structuring problem spaces: The initial structuring of a problem space may follow the divide and conquer principle, where all subproblems are identified before developing a solution approach. This is referred to as a **Top-Down Strategy**. Conversely, the **Bottom-Up Strategy** is applied when subproblems are identified and addressed successively. This strategy is characterized by an iterative approach, where step-by-step solutions for individual subproblems are developed and eventually integrated into a comprehensive solution.

In particular, in comparison to Perkins et al., Kiesmüller [7] presents the role of trial-and-error and exploratory approaches as significantly more ambivalent. The **Thoughtless Trial-and-Error** strategy involves searching for suitable solutions primarily through random experimentation. In contrast, the **Thought-**

ful **Trial-and-Error** strategy is analogous to a generate-and-test-like approach. In this strategy, potential solution fragments are selected and evaluated in a systematic manner. Although this methodology is not yet fully systematic, as the problem's mechanics are not yet fully understood, it is more targeted and reflective than random experimentation.

Fig. 1. Playing area (left) and feedback display (right) of the learning game "Match the Monkeys"

3 Methodology

ML learning games such as *Artbot*[1] provide learners with the opportunity to engage with the topic of decision trees. In order to analyze the various problem-solving strategies, we opted to develop a custom learning game that focuses on the structural development of decision trees. The learning game "Match the Monkeys" (see Fig. 1) transforms the unplugged activity "Good-Monkey-Bad-Monkey-Game", originally developed by Lindner et al. [9], into an interactive, browser-based application. In the game, the objective for the learners is to distinguish between biting and non-biting monkeys based on their visual characteristics. To accomplish this, they construct a decision tree in the form of a multi-touch puzzle game. The learners are provided with continuous visual feedback on the accuracy of their classification model in relation to the data: correctly identified monkeys are highlighted in green, while misclassified monkeys are highlighted in red. A notable distinction between the unplugged activity and the digital learning game is the provision of a predefined set of filter elements. The absence of the necessity to formulate own distinction rules simplifies the gameplay and allows for a stronger focus on the structure and methodology of creating decision trees.

The development of decision trees in the learning game "Match the Monkeys" can be considered comparable to the learning tasks in the context of programming education, since both require the structured decomposition of a complex problem into smaller sub-problems. In working with the provided data, learners are required to develop a system to distinguish between biting and non-biting

[1] https://art-bot.net/.

monkeys. The construction of a decision tree with high classification accuracy can be viewed as analogous to the successful execution of a decision tree learning algorithm. In contrast to traditional programming learning tasks, the assignment in the game "Match the Monkeys" is distinguished primarily by the formalisation of the problem-solving process. Rather than creating an algorithm in the form of program code and subsequently executing it on a computer system, learners develop algorithmic solutions implicitly and interpret them progressively by linking the elements of the decision tree themselves.

3.1 Data Acquisition

The recording of gameplay sessions for the learning game "Match the Monkeys" was conducted during three introductory workshops on the topic of ML in March 2024. A total of 93 students participated in the workshops, comprising 44 students from tenth grade and 49 students from two eighth-grade classes who had not previously studied the topic of ML. The gameplay session served as an introduction to the workshop section on models in the field of ML. Each student independently played the learning game using two tablets. To record the students' game play, the game was equipped with a routine that periodically took screenshots of the game screen at a rate of two frames per second. This frequent capture ensured that even the most subtle game actions were documented. The screenshots were continuously sent to a database along with the current Unix timestamp and the randomly assigned session ID, creating a comprehensive screencast of each game session. In total, 166,000 screenshots were collected, which is equivalent to approximately 23 h of gameplay footage.

3.2 Category System and Coding Process

The analysis of problem-solving strategies in the recorded game sessions was conducted using the method of quantitative content analysis [3], with five coders involved.[2] In preparation for the coding training, we used the problem-solving strategies described in Sect. 2 to develop an initial category system.

The described problem-solving strategies were adopted in their most differentiated form. The modifications made to the category descriptions were limited to the necessary adjustments to the context of the learning game. The *Watchers* strategy described by Gamper et al. [4] was extended beyond its original definition to include the possibility of exploratory testing of existing decision trees. In the game "Match the Monkeys", this behavior specifically encompasses the experimental addition and removal of labels in the form of leaves. The *Reducers* strategy proposed by Hosseini et al. [6] was omitted because, to achieve the game's goal, creating an optimal tree is already necessary from the beginning due to the limited playing area. Furthermore, the *Massagers* strategy described by Hosseini et al. was integrated with the *Thoughtless Trial & Error* strategy

---

[2] The annotated sessions, along with the full category system and code examples, are available at the following link: https://doi.org/10.17605/osf.io/snuvq.

Table 1. Adapted category system used in the coding process

Category	Definition
Stopping	The construction of the decision tree is interrupted for the majority of the current observation interval or is aborted before the end of the game time
Watching	During the game, identical incorrect decision trees are constructed multiple times or are attempted to be verified using leaves in an exploratory manner
Restarting	A decision tree built during the game is completely removed
Trial & Error Tinkering	The assembly of filter and output elements, or the trial of different filter combinations, is conducted without any discernible system
Thoughtful Tinkering	The assembly of filter and output elements, or the trial of different filter combinations, is conducted in an exploratory manner, with a discernible system
Building	A gradual combination of filter elements is employed to achieve the correct classification of individual monkeys or groups of monkeys
Bottom-Up Structuring	The distinguishing characteristics between biting and non-biting monkeys are gradually identified, and the appropriate filter elements are selected and assembled accordingly. Work on a subsequent node does not proceed until the current node has been completed with the correct leaf
Top-Down Structuring	The monkeys are classified into multiple subgroups based on combinations of characteristic features before filter elements are selected and combined

proposed by Kiesmüller [7] to form the *Trial & Error Tinkering* strategy. A comprehensive overview of the adapted problem-solving strategies can be found in Table 1.

To ensure efficient review and coding of the video material, a web-based evaluation tool was developed. This application allowed for the review of recorded game sessions and the annotation of game sequences with the described problem-solving strategies. To facilitate the coding process, a coding assistant was provided that enabled coding of predetermined time segments. For the coding training, five game sessions were randomly selected and individually coded by each coder based on the initial category system. The coding assistant was primarily used with an interval duration of 30 s. Any inaccuracies in the definitions of the individual categories and any coding difficulties that were encountered were shared and subsequently discussed collectively, along with the corresponding discrepancies in the session codings. The results of this discussion were used not only to adjust specific formulations of the category system, but also to develop a coding aid in the form of a flow chart, as illustrated in Fig. 2. This approach permitted the annotation of game sessions in the subsequent second phase of the coding training to be conducted in a more criterion-guided and consistent manner. In the second phase, five additional sessions were selected at random and individually coded. To identify individual coding errors, a secondary review was conducted by the research lead. During this review, all assigned codes were examined for their alignment with the coding aid and category definitions. Subsequently, the original coder was encouraged to review and, if necessary, revise the identified errors.

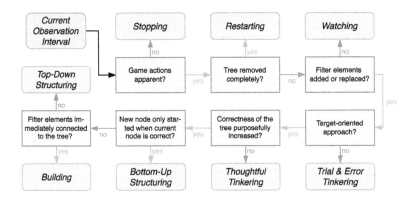

Fig. 2. Coding aid derived from the adapted problem-solving strategy definitions

The intercoder reliability attained through the coding training was determined using Krippendorff's Alpha. In the second training phase, a reliability of $\alpha = 0.75$ was achieved after review among all coders. This indicates good consistency in the codings and confirms the effectiveness of the coding training and the optimization measures applied to the category system. The training concluded with a discussion of minor discrepancies among the coders and the collective formulation of additional best practices for coding. The remaining game sessions were then randomly assigned to the coders. During the individual processing of the sessions, the coders were instructed to report any irregularities and doubtful cases in a shared chat. These passages were then reviewed and contextually categorized by the other coders.

4 Results

Of the 93 recorded game sessions, a total of 92 sessions could be included in the analysis. Only one session had to be excluded due to a suspected loss of connection between the game and the feedback tablet. Within the included sessions, a total of 29 students achieved the game objective. The average game duration was 14 min and 54 s, with a significant difference ($p = 0.007$) between successful (13:04) and unsuccessful (15:45) sessions.

Thoughtful Tinkering was the most common problem-solving strategy observed in the sessions, accounting for 30.64% of the time, followed by Trial &

Error Tinkering at 24.71%. In their initial attempts at problem-solving, 48.31% of learners employed the Thoughtful Tinkering strategy, while 34.83% initially opted for a Trial & Error Tinkering approach. The Watching pattern of reviewing developed decision trees was detected in 17.33% of the observed 30-second intervals. Compared to these exploratory approaches, the group of more structured strategies, including Building, Bottom-Up Structuring, and Top-Down Structuring, was observed much less frequently, with a total share of 5.02%. The complete restructuring of solution approaches in the sense of the Restarting pattern occurred in 7.13% of the observed intervals. During 15.19% of the total playing time no relevant game actions were detected (Stopping).

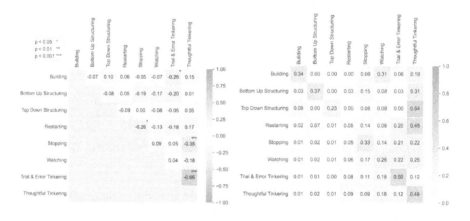

Fig. 3. Strategy Correlation Matrix (left) and Strategy Transition Matrix (right)(The matrix describes the strategy transition tendencies of the learners, from row to column, between two observation intervals in the examined game sequences.)

Regarding the usage rates of the individual strategies, several opposing trends were observed in the game sessions. As shown in Fig. 3 (left), the strategy pattern Trial & Error Tinkering was observed less frequently among learners who used the strategy patterns Building or Thoughtful Tinkering. Furthermore, learners who utilized the Thoughtful Tinkering or Restarting strategies exhibited a reduced tendency to interrupt their solution development.

In terms of game success, only weak correlations were found between the use of individual strategies and game outcomes. The Building ($\rho = 0.37, p < 0.001$) and Bottom-Up Structuring ($\rho = 0.35, p < 0.001$) strategies were positively related to game success, while the Watching ($\rho = -0.24, p < 0.05$) strategy showed a negative correlation. The strongest overall positive correlation with game success was observed for the group of strategies consisting of Building, Bottom-Up Structuring, and Top-Down Structuring ($\rho = 0.59, p < 0.001$). These strategies were used for an average of 2.71% of the game time in unsuccessful sessions, while their share in successful sessions was 13.71%. In contrast, a moderate negative relationship with game success was found for the combination of the more exploratory strategies, comprising Thoughtful Tinkering, Trial & Error Tinkering, and Watching ($\rho = -0.41, p < 0.001$).

As illustrated in the main diagonal of the strategy transition matrix in Fig. 3 (right), all strategies, with the exception of Restarting and Top-Down Structuring, are most likely to be continued in the next observation interval. After the application of the Restarting strategy, 45% of the learners continue with the Thoughtful Tinkering strategy, while 20% switch to a Trial & Error Tinkering approach. The Top-Down Structuring strategy has only a 25% probability of being continued in the next interval. In contrast, there is a 54% probability of switching to the Thoughtful Tinkering strategy. The transition probabilities for the Watching strategy also show a broader distribution. While there is a 26% probability of continuing in the next interval, there are similar probabilities of transitioning to Thoughtful Tinkering (25%) and Trial & Error Tinkering (22%).

5 Discussion

The findings presented in the preceding section offer valuable insights into the problem-solving behavior of students in grades 8 to 10 when developing decision trees as classification models independently. The following section discusses the implications of these findings and provides recommendations for designing learning environments focused on the conveyance of decision trees based on these insights.

Regarding the problem-solving strategies employed in the examined game sessions, it can be stated that Thoughtful Tinkering and Trial & Error Tinkering were the most frequently observed behaviors, collectively accounting for over 55% of the total game time. Over 83% of learners selected one of these two approaches as their initial strategy. This observation suggests that learners adopt an exploratory and experimental approach to independently tackle the given problem and to become familiar with the game environment. As illustrated in the strategy transition matrix (see Fig. 3, right), the two Tinkering strategies are not only relevant in the context of the initial strategy choice; with rates approximately 50% each, they have the highest probability of being employed over multiple observation intervals among the strategies examined. Moreover, following the restart of a previously developed solution fragment, there is a 65% probability that the next solution approach will be based on one of these two strategies. The transition tendencies also indicate a close connection between the Watching strategy and the two Tinkering strategies. This group of exploratory problem-solving strategies accounted for more than 72% of the total game time in the examined sessions. This stands in striking contrast to the group of structured problem-solving strategies, comprising Building, Bottom-Up Structuring, and Top-Down Structuring, which made up only about 5% of the total game time. It is therefore essential to emphasize that these two strategy groups exhibit an inverse relationship with regard to the achievement of the game objective. Only in one session in the entire set of games examined the game objective was achieved exclusively via exploratory problem-solving strategies.

With regard to achieving the learning objective, this observation suggests that the group of structured problem-solving strategies can often be identified as a necessary prerequisite for the successful completion of the game. It is, therefore, of significant importance to support learners' to think structurally about the given problem. However, an examination of the strategy transition matrix reveals that these structured strategies have significantly lower persistence compared to the two Tinkering strategies. When applying the Building or Bottom-Up Structuring strategies, the probability of transitioning to the group of exploratory strategies in the next interval is approximately equivalent to the chance of staying in the respective strategy. In the case of the Top-Down Structuring strategy, this probability is more than twice as high. Therefore, it is insufficient to merely encourage learners to break down complex problems into manageable sub-problems using structured strategies; the sustained application of these strategies is an equally significant issue. In order to facilitate students' consistent and systematic development of solution approaches independently, it is essential to provide ongoing support for their problem-solving processes.

The analysis of strategy transitions in the "Match the Monkeys" learning game indicates that feedback on classification accuracy was insufficient for most learners to maintain a systematic problem-solving behavior. This aligns with Kiesmüller's observation that error messages in programming environments often lack actionable feedback due to technical wording and disregard for individual problem-solving behavior [7]. Consequently, it appears advisable to develop feedback systems that evaluate solution quality and consider individual problem-solving behavior in order to generate adaptive feedback for ML learning games.

In addition to the aforementioned results, it is imperative to consider the following limitations of the study. The sample of 93 students from grades 8 to 10 examined represents a specific demographic group and does not reflect the full range of educational backgrounds and age groups for whom the learning about decision trees is relevant. In order to make more precise statements about the strategy transition tendencies within the group of structured problem-solving strategies, it would also be necessary to examine a much larger sample, given that they constitute a relatively small proportion of the total game time. The game "Match the Monkeys" represents an artificially created learning environment the design of which may influence the strategy choices of learners. Consequently, it is not possible to rule out the possibility that traditional, more established learning environments may require the application of additional substrategies that have little relevance in the game. With regard to the analysis of problem-solving strategies in the learning game itself, it is also possible that the selected observation interval of 30 s did not adequately capture subtle nuances in the students' problem-solving behavior. Despite the adjustments made during the coding training, it is still conceivable that the definitions of the problem-solving strategies were interpreted slightly differently among the coders. Finally, it should be noted that the decision trees considered in this study have significantly lower complexity than more modern ML models, such as neural networks or transformers. Consequently, the presented results cannot be directly applied to the process of developing ML models in general without further research.

6 Conclusion and Outlook

This study employed quantitative content analysis to examine the problem-solving strategies of students in grades 8 to 10 in constructing decision trees within a digital learning game. The findings indicate that learners predominantly employed exploratory problem-solving strategies. While structured strategies were used less frequently, they were more closely associated with successful completion of the learning objective. These results highlight the importance of creating learning environments that not only encourage structured problem-solving approaches but also support their persistent application, ensuring students systematically engage with the construction of decision trees. To corroborate and expand these results, engaging students directly in the evaluation process by collectively reviewing recorded game sessions could elucidate their problem-solving rationale more effectively. These insights can inform the development of adaptive ML learning applications on the topic of decision trees that integrate individual problem-solving behaviors into feedback and support mechanisms.

References

1. Breiman, L.: Classification and Regression Trees. Routledge, New York (1984)
2. Elia, M., Gajek, C., Schiendorfer, A., Reif, W.: An interactive web application for decision tree learning. In: European Conference on Machine Learning and Principles and Practice of Knowledge Discovery in Databases, pp. 11–16. PMLR (2021)
3. Früh, W.: Inhaltsanalyse: Theorie und Praxis. No. Nr. 2501 in UTB Medien- und Kommunikationswissenschaft, Psychologie, Soziologie, UVK Verlagsgesellschaft mbH, Konstanz, 9. edn. (2017)
4. Gamper, P., Heinemann, B., Ehlenz, M., Schroeder, U.: Identifying problem solving strategies of programming novices in a serious game. In: 2021 International Conference on Advanced Learning Technologies (ICALT), pp. 91–93 (2021). https://doi.org/10.1109/ICALT52272.2021.00035
5. Heinemann, B., et al.: Drafting a Data Science Curriculum for Secondary Schools. In: Proceedings of the 18th Koli Calling International Conference on Computing Education Research, pp. 1–5. ACM, Koli (2018). https://doi.org/10.1145/3279720.3279737
6. Hosseini, R., Vihavainen, A., Brusilovsky, P.: Exploring problem solving paths in a Java programming course. In: Psychology of Programming Interest Group Conference, PPIG 2014, pp. 65–76. University of Pittsburgh (2014)
7. Kiesmüller, U.: Diagnosing learners' problem-solving strategies using learning environments with algorithmic problems in secondary education. ACM Trans. Comput. Educ. **9**(3), 1–26 (2009). https://doi.org/10.1145/1594399.1594402
8. Lindner, A., Berges, M., Rösch, M., Franke, F.: Implementing a portable learning lab on artificial intelligence: it's AI in a Box! In: Pellet, J.P., Parriaux, G. (eds.) Informatics in Schools. Beyond Bits and Bytes: Nurturing Informatics Intelligence in Education, pp. 26–39. Springer, Cham (2023). https://doi.org/10.1007/978-3-031-44900-0_3

9. Lindner, A., Seegerer, S., Romeike, R.: Unplugged activities in the context of AI. In: Pozdniakov, S.N., Dagienė, V. (eds.) ISSEP 2019. LNCS, vol. 11913, pp. 123–135. Springer, Cham (2019). https://doi.org/10.1007/978-3-030-33759-9_10
10. Long, D., Magerko, B.: What is AI literacy? competencies and design considerations. In: Proceedings of the 2020 CHI Conference on Human Factors in Computing Systems, pp. 1–16. ACM, Honolulu (2020). https://doi.org/10.1145/3313831.3376727
11. Lundberg, S.M., et al.: From local explanations to global understanding with explainable AI for trees. Nat. Mach. Intell. **2**(1), 56–67 (2020). https://doi.org/10.1038/s42256-019-0138-9
12. Mariescu-Istodor, R., Jormanainen, I.: Machine learning for high school students. In: Proceedings of the 19th Koli Calling International Conference on Computing Education Research, Koli Calling 2019, pp. 1–9. Association for Computing Machinery, New York (2019). https://doi.org/10.1145/3364510.3364520
13. Martignon, L., Vitouch, O., Takezawa, M., Forster, M.R.: Naive and yet enlightened: from natural frequencies to fast and frugal decision trees. In: Thinking: Psychological Perspectives on Reasoning, Judgment and Decision Making, chap. 10, pp. 189–211. John Wiley & Sons, Ltd. (2003). https://doi.org/10.1002/047001332X.ch10
14. Michaeli, T., Seegerer, S., Kerber, L., Romeike, R.: Data, trees, and forests - decision tree learning in K-12 education. In: Proceedings of the Third Teaching Machine Learning and Artificial Intelligence Workshop, pp. 37–41. PMLR (2023)
15. Perkins, D.N., Hancock, C., Hobbs, R., Martin, F., Simmons, R.: Conditions of learning in novice programmers. J. Educ. Comput. Res. **2**(1), 37–55 (1986). https://doi.org/10.2190/GUJT-JCBJ-Q6QU-Q9PL
16. Podgorelec, V., Šprogar, M., Pohorec, S.: Evolutionary design of decision trees. WIREs Data Min. Knowl. Disc. **3**(2), 63–82 (2013). https://doi.org/10.1002/widm.1079
17. Podworny, S., Fleischer, Y., Hüsing, S.: Grade 6 students' perception and use of data-based decision trees. In: Peters, S.A., Zapata-Cardona, L., Bonafini, F., Fan, A. (eds.) Bridging the Gap: Empowering and Educating Today's Learners in Statistics. Proceedings of the Eleventh International Conference on Teaching Statistics, pp. 1–6. International Association for Statistical Education, Rosario (2022). https://doi.org/10.52041/iase.icots11.T2H3
18. Touretzky, D.S., Gardner-McCune, C.: Artificial intelligence thinking in K–12. In: Kong, S.C., Abelson, H. (eds.) Computational Thinking Education in K–12, pp. 153–180. The MIT Press (2022). https://doi.org/10.7551/mitpress/13375.003.0013
19. Voulgari, I., Zammit, M., Stouraitis, E., Liapis, A., Yannakakis, G.: Learn to machine learn: designing a game based approach for teaching machine learning to primary and secondary education students. In: Interaction Design and Children, pp. 593–598. ACM, Athens (2021). https://doi.org/10.1145/3459990.3465176
20. Zieffler, A., Justice, N., delMas, R., Huberty, M.D.: The use of algorithmic models to develop secondary teachers' understanding of the statistical modeling process. J. Stat. Data Sci. Educ. **29**(1), 131–147 (2021). https://doi.org/10.1080/26939169.2021.1900759

A Learning Environment to Promote the Computational Thinker: A Bebras Perspective Evaluation

Oliver Kastner-Hauler[1](✉), Karin Tengler[1], Barbara Sabitzer[2], and Zsolt Lavicza[2]

[1] Department of Media Education, University of Education Lower Austria, 2500 Baden, Austria
{oliver.kastner,k.tengler}@ph-noe.ac.at
[2] Department of STEM Education, Johannes Kepler University Linz, 4040 Linz, Austria
{barbara.sabitzer,zsolt.lavicza}@jku.at

Abstract. Digital education curricula underwent substantial changes worldwide in the last decade, emphasizing computational thinking and problem-solving skills, as introduced in Austria in 2018 for students aged 10–14. This study evaluates the effectiveness of a novel learning environment in promoting these skills and facilitating the implementation of new curricula. The research utilized the BBC micro:bit device for physical computing and block-based programming, alongside an open educational resource textbook. A quasi-experimental pre- and post-test design, based on tasks from the Bebras International Challenge, assessed four units of learning activities conducted over 5–8 weeks. Results demonstrate the potential of the learning environment materials to foster confidence in computational thinking among teachers and students, suggesting a successful promotion of the Computational Thinker in middle schools through practical everyday classroom application aligned with new digital education curricula.

Keywords: computational thinking · bebras tasks assessment · microbit · physical computing · block-based programming · digital education

1 Introduction

Developing computational thinking (CT) skills in young learners is crucial in today's digital world [12]. CT enables students to become digital creators [45] and adapt to emerging careers [52]. Initiatives such as the *Bebras International Challenge* [5] and the *Hour of Code* [17] promote CT, which is essential for developing problem-solving skills across disciplines. Educators are employing STEAM teaching [16], recognizing the congruence between CT and problem-solving [27], as implemented in frameworks such as PISA 2022 [36].

New curricula for middle schools (10–14 years) have been introduced internationally in recent years to develop Computational Thinkers. In 2018, Austria implemented Basic Digital Education (BDE), which includes CT, as a compulsory exercise. By 2022, BDE became a mandatory subject. To support teachers in the field, an Open Educational Resource (OER) textbook was created, focusing on coding and CT with the micro:bit [3]. This was later expanded with flipped classroom tasks [24] and adaptations for upper primary grades (8–10 years) [25].

To address the gap in teaching materials for CT, the authors designed a learning environment (LE) combining the micro:bit, OER textbook adaptions, and Bebras tasks for assessment [44]. This freely available resource supports CT adoption in classrooms, especially for less technically trained teachers. The LE empowers teachers to design and adapt CT lessons confidently, aiming to help students apply CT to everyday tasks – extending beyond Austria.

This research promotes computational thinking (CT) in lower secondary grades for students aged 10–14 using physical computing with micro:bit [20] and block-based coding via Makecode [34]. The designed learning environment demystifies CT [46] and translates its facets for classroom use. The haptic component of the physical computing device enhances learners' self-efficacy in applying CT algorithms practically. Self-directed learning paths guide users through examples in the learning environment (LE). Results indicate the LE effectively promotes playful acquisition of CT and problem-solving skills in lower secondary grades.

2 Background and Related Work

2.1 Computational Thinking (CT)

The integration of CT in education has gained momentum, accelerated by the COVID pandemic. Wing [55] laid the foundation for this trend, building on Papert's earlier work with LOGO [40]. Resnick, Papert's student and collaborator at MIT Media Lab, continued this path with Scratch [43], that is very popular in education. Both LOGO and Scratch embody Papert's constructionist theory [15], emphasizing learning-by-doing and knowledge construction through hands-on experience. CT is now viewed as a universal thinking skill across the curriculum rather than just a sole computing skill [28].

Shute et al. [46] and others identify common core CT facets: decomposition, abstraction, algorithms, and debugging. Iteration and generalization were subsequently added [14]. Palts and Pedaste [39] provide a comparative overview of frameworks. We synthesize these findings into five CT facets: (1) decomposition, (2) abstraction, (3) algorithms, (4) generalization, and (5) evaluation - incorporating debugging in (5), iteration in (3), and pattern recognition in (4). This operational definition supports classroom teacher preparation and fosters transdisciplinary STEM/STEAM education with CT [42].

2.2 Physical Computing

Physical Computing emerged with sensor- and actuator-equipped devices [18]. The micro:bit, with its built-in sensors and interfaces, facilitates communication and data handling. After coding on the computer, algorithms are visualized on the device, promoting hands-on CT learning [41]. External sensors and actuators can extend capabilities using toolkits or self-built circuitry [3,26]. This approach emphasizes haptic tinkering and playful coding within a STEM/STEAM context [19].

2.3 Block-Based Programming

The increasing importance of computing at school necessitates fundamental programming or coding skills [51]. Visual block-based programming environments (VBBPEs) like Scratch and Makecode offer accessible entry points [8,47]. Unlike text-based programming, VBBPEs eliminate language barriers and facilitate experimentation [53]. Color-coded blocks support intuitive code construction without prior vocabulary knowledge. Makecode's multilingual support [10] further reduces language bias. Furthermore, VBBPEs foster problem-solving and CT development in young learners [48].

2.4 Bebras Tasks and Problem-Solving

The Bebras International Challenge aims to promote CS and CT interests among school students of all ages [5]. By emphasizing higher-order thinking skills [9], Bebras' posed problems address problem-solving and knowledge construction [49]. Various CS/CT concepts, such as algorithms and data flow [37], are explored without requiring prior knowledge or experience.

While not originally designed as assessment tools, Bebras tasks can evaluate CT knowledge gained through interventions [44]. Researchers have linked Bebras tasks to problem-solving skills and CT domains assessment [54]. We adapted Bebras tasks for pre- and post-test questionnaires to assess the LE for CT with our intervention. Details about task selection are provided in the "Materials and Methods" section.

3 Materials and Methods

This paper investigates the initial design of a newly created LE for physical computing with the micro:bit. We employ a quasi-experimental pre-post assessment using Bebras tasks [30] to examine its impact on CT and problem-solving. The LE will be refined through educational design research (EDR) to derive design principles [32]. Follow-up research will explore broader implications. Our research question for this paper is:

RQ: Does the design of the physical computing learning environment with the micro:bit device scaffold and support the acquisition of both computational thinking and problem-solving skills?

3.1 The Study

3.1.1 Research Design

Since 2019, our project has introduced the micro:bit and CT to primary and secondary schools. Previous EDR cycles investigated CT task difficulty [23], flipped OER textbook adaptation [24], and combined effects of physical computing and block-based programming [25]. This paper focuses on a sub-study for lower secondary students (ages 10–14) using the micro:bit and assessing CT through Bebras tasks. Teachers received in-service training on the OER textbook wiki and the CT assessment questionnaire and formed a supervised online community for support. We analyzed the impact of the LE on students' CT skills during problem-solving [4].

3.1.2 Participants

Participants were recruited through their teachers in a quasi-experimental design. Students in grades 5–8 (aged 10–14) were exposed to a new CT including curriculum. Our sample consisted of n = 240 students (f = 119, m = 121) from a larger project carried out during pandemic circumstances all over Austria. We focused on teachers who had participated in initial onboard training and with whom we had direct personal contact. Students were divided into two age groups (10–12 and 12–14) based on the Bebras Challenge. Each group included an experimental and control group.

We followed the research guidelines of the Austrian Agency for Research Integrity [35] and ethical standards of the authors' affiliated universities. Informed consent was obtained from students' next of kin collected from their teachers. Data confidentiality and participant anonymity were ensured through unique pseudonymous codes, allowing for individual-level pre-post matching while complying with legal and ethical research requirements.

3.1.3 Instruments

Students completed pre- and post-tests using online Bebras tasks, selected by an expert panel of university teachers familiar with CS/CT and block-based coding. Each age group (Benjamins and Cadets) answered 10 Bebras tasks, categorized into three difficulty levels (easy, medium, hard). Difficulty and point allocation increased correspondingly, with incorrect answers resulting in point deductions. Pre- and post-tests each contained five tasks (two easy, two medium, one hard) packaged separately for each age group. A 14-point positive bias was applied to avoid negative scores, resulting in a 0–56 point range. This design ensured different question sets for pre- and post-tests, preventing memorization effects on the measurement instrument.

The expert panel selected 20 questions from an initial pool of 40 for the final assessment, implementing them via LimeSurvey [29] or on paper – used versions can be retrieved [22]. Each question offered four single-choice answers and a fifth option to omit. The panel reviewed and recalibrated difficulty levels across age groups, adjusting 6 out of 24 questions, which resulted in only one question being lowered in difficulty [50]. They created two packages of 5 questions each for pre- and post-tests for both age groups, ensuring an even distribution of difficulty levels. In cases of uncertainty, more difficult questions were assigned to the post-test to ensure statistical integrity. This process addressed inconsistencies in original difficulty classifications and optimized the assessment for online implementation and cross-age group comparability.

We analyzed valid pre- and post-test responses from students with no prior coding or Bebras experience. The assessments included two questions to filter this pre-condition for statistical examination. A paired t-test assessed improvements in problem-solving and CT abilities. SPSS 28 was used to analyze Bebras tasks' scores and to generate descriptive statistics.

3.2 Materials

3.2.1 BBC micro:bit and Makecode

This project utilized the BBC micro:bit hardware [33] and Makecode visual block-based programming environment (VBBPE) [34]. The micro:bit's onboard sensors and actuators make it cost-effective for classroom STEM/STEAM activities [21]. In Austria, a nationwide initiative distributed micro:bits to selected teachers and students to introduce programming and foster CT, like similar efforts in other countries [1].

3.2.2 Learning Environment

Four learning units for playful CT experimentation were created following the 5E instructional model for inquiry-based learning (IBL) [7] to show immediate success and further motivate the students. The basis for each of the units is furnished by the OER textbook wiki and is extended by additional materials and pedagogical tips and tricks from in-service teacher training.

The micro:bit intervention started in Unit 1 (Appendix - Table 2) with hardware familiarization and basic programming using Makecode. Students were then introduced to the OER textbook wiki, a digital resource designed to support problem-solving through guided inquiry. The subsequent phase involved physical computing activities, beginning with simple shape representations on the micro:bit's 5x5 LED matrix display and progressing to button-triggered interactions. A foundational "flashing heart" tutorial prepared students for the first OER example, "On the trail of chance." This example, and subsequent OER content, employed a step-by-step approach with visual code blocks and clear instructions, facilitating independent learning for more advanced students while providing ample support for those requiring additional guidance. Unit 2 (Appendix - Table 2) builds upon the first unit, increasing complexity. It introduces the accelerometer, external circuitry, and sound generation. The second OER example, supported by the wiki, follows these foundations.

Units 3 and 4 expand upon previous units, offering a medium-level OER task in Unit 3 and a flexible choice for Unit 4. Upon completion, students will have completed four OER examples: one easy, two medium, and one of any difficulty.

4 Results

Prior to and immediately following the four-unit LE intervention, pre- and post-test assessments were administered to each class. To ensure comparability, both assessments were designed to be completed within a single 50-minute lesson. Consistent with previous research, the post-test was slightly shorter than the pre-test [25,56]. To establish a reliable dataset, outliers with completion times below 10 minutes were excluded. Data normality was confirmed through Q-Q plots (see Appendix - Fig. 1), indicating the suitability of parametric statistical tests. A rigorous four-eye approach was employed during data processing. The subsequent sections detail the findings from this analysis.

The maximum score for each assessment was 56 points and was achieved nineteen times in the post-test for the whole student group n = 240. The Benjamins 5/6 scored five times maximum and the Cadets 7/8 twelve times with the maximum score in the experimental groups. The control group for Cadets was the only control group to score two times with maximum value at the post-test. No one student scored with the maximum value on the pre-test. The first impact of the intervention in a favorable direction is shown in Table 1 by a higher mean value of correct answers, naturally more expressed in the experimental groups. Furthermore, the Benjamins control group denoted a higher mean for pre-test than post-test, to be discussed later on.

Table 1. Bebras Tasks Pre-/ Post-Test Scores for Benjamins Grades 5/6 and Cadets Grades 7/8.

Grade	Bebras Tasks	Group *	N	Mean	Median	SD	Variance
5/6 Benjamins	pre	E	57	26.67	28.0	11.760	138.298
		C	16	32.69	33.5	9.527	90.763
	post	E	57	28.23	35.0	16.935	286.786
		C	16	24.75	22.5	10.003	100.067
7/8 Cadets	pre	E	144	24.07	22.5	12.688	160.974
		C	23	21.22	19.0	12.310	151.542
	post	E	144	32.24	32.0	13.303	176.979
		C	23	25.00	24.0	15.115	228.455

* Group: E = Experimental Group, C = Control Group.

The results of a paired samples t-test showed that, on average, the Cadets' experimental group was able to raise the score statistically significant from pre-test (M = 24.07, SD = 12.688) to post-test (M = 32.24, SD = 13.303), t(143) = 5.496, p < .001, d = .458. The Benjamins' experimental group was able to achieve a statistically non-significant raise from pre-test (M = 26.67, SD = 11.760) to post-test (M = 28.23, SD = 16.935), t(56) = −.643, p = .523, d = −.085. The control group for Cadets showed a statistically non-significant raise from pre-test (M = 21.22, SD = 12.31) to post-test (M = 25, SD = 15.115), t(22) = −.888, p = .384, d = −.185. And the control group for Benjamins showed statistical significance with an opposite effect from pre-test (M = 32.69, SD = 9.527) to lower post-test (M = 24.75, SD = 10.003), t(15) = 2.234, p = .041, d = .558.

For a better illustration of the similarities and differences between the experimental and control groups in their respective age groups see Appendix - Fig. 2. As can be obtained from Table 1, the experimental group for Cadets improved quite strongly from pre-test M = 24.07 to post-test M = 32.24 but with a wider spread. The control group for Cadets scored overall lower from pre-test M = 21.22 to post-test M = 25.00. The experimental group for Benjamins improved slightly from pre-test M = 26.67 to post-test M = 28.23. The control group for Benjamins produced a lower post-test M = 24.75 than for the pre-test M = 32.69. Additionally, the used data set shows that no student from the Benjamins Control group scored zero in both pre- and post-test. The next section will explore plausible rationales for the observed phenomena.

The intervention's impact is quantified with a value of Cohen's d = 0.458 for the larger Cadets group n = 144 and statistically significant with p < .001. Reaching closely a Cohen's d ≥ 0.5 it is still classified as a medium effect size, but within the upper range of value. This suggests that the designed learning environment, as a result of the intervention, has led to an improvement in problem-solving and computational thinking skills, particularly measurable for Cadets in grades 7/8.

5 Discussion

This study aimed to evaluate newly designed instructional materials for CT and problem-solving with the micro:bit based on an OER textbook [3] and its wiki. The LE was distributed through in-service teacher training before the intervention. Two assessments with five Bebras tasks each were conducted pre- and post-intervention across experimental and control groups. Over 5–8 weeks, students explored block-based coding with Makecode and the micro:bit. The study focused on Bebras tasks to assess CT and problem-solving development. The findings and limitations will be discussed in the following.

Data from the study (n = 240) showed a positive effect of the intervention for the older Cadets group (n = 167), with a medium effect size. However, no statistical evidence of an intervention effect was found for the younger Benjamins group (n = 73), although the experimental group showed an increased mean score from pre- to post-test, while the control group decreased. This may be due to the uneven age distribution, with only 7 of 73 Benjamins in grade 6. Some teachers failed to follow procedures, leading to data irregularities, such as outliers and suspiciously high scores, which were excluded. In addition, some teachers omitted their code for deletion, which affected the dataset as their self-testing data was included. Notably, no student in the Benjamins control group scored zero after outliers were removed, potentially due to pre-set defaults in the assessment web form that included many out-of-scope self-testers (Appendix - Fig. 2).

In investigating the issues, we identified that arbitrary interpretations of the LE implementation, particularly regarding lesson numbers and tasks, led to the observed problems. This misinterpretation undermined the basis for comparability. To address this, we recommend stricter supervision during in-service teacher training, ensuring clear communication of the project's key implementation details. If personal presence during teacher onboarding isn't feasible, a detailed video message should be provided. Additionally, in-service training should emphasize the mutual benefits of the project, encouraging educators to actively engage with data collection. Future efforts should focus on preventing misinterpretations and ensuring data comparability.

The use of Bebras tasks for pre- and post-test assessments with a control group is widely accepted in the CT research community [44]. Bebras tasks fall into two categories: multiple choice and interactive. Due to resource constraints, we focused solely on multiple-choice tasks, which may be a limitation. Considering Bebras tasks as problem-solving tools, it would be valuable to examine the effects of CS unplugged activities included in these tasks [6]. A future research cycle is planned to explore this through a "Bebras-unplugged" trial group.

6 Conclusion and Outlook

This study is part of a multi-cycle educational design research [31] aimed at developing instructional materials and best practices for integrating CT into classrooms. The main goal is to enhance CT and problem-solving skills while increasing awareness and confidence in applying CT in daily life. This paper focuses on a sub-study involving a newly designed learning environment for lower secondary students (10–14 years). Four units, adapted from an OER textbook, emphasized physical computing and inquiry-based learning (see Appendix - Table 2. Bebras tasks were used for pre- and post-intervention assessments. Future work will explore design principles and further CT assessments to inform the development of instructional materials.

With this study, we can conclude that the promotion to become Computational Thinkers for students aged 10–14 can be effectively achieved by combining block-based coding, physical computing, and Bebras tasks. The intervention had a significant impact on older students (12–14 years, n = 167), while younger students (10–12 years, n = 73) showed practical improvement without statistical significance. Further exploration is needed, as a one-tool-fits-all approach is not yet feasible at this stage of research. However, our research contributes to the development of better instructional materials for classroom use, with promising potential to extend CT in schools through targeted assessment tools and iterative design and evaluation of curricula.

The resources evaluated here can be used to teach and study CT in the context of physical computing in school grades 5–8. Our approach, combining Makecode, micro:bit, inquiry-based learning, and Bebras tasks, provides a promising strategy to promote CT skills and Basic Digital Education in a fun and engaging manner in middle schools. Results indicate a positive impact on CT classroom adoption. Scaffolding materials support both teachers and students in developing and applying CT and problem-solving skills.

Acknowledgements

Funding. No funding was used for this research.

Data Availability. The article includes the original contributions presented in the study, further inquiries can be directed to the corresponding author.

Disclosure Statement. No potential conflict of interest was reported by the authors.

Ethics. The research involving human participants was reviewed and approved by all the universities of the authors. Written informed consent to participate in this study was obtained from the participants' legal guardian/next of kin.

Artificial Intelligence (AI). AI-tools assisted in language refinement and clarity enhancement under human supervision. DeepL [11] improved translations and style, while ChatGPT [38], Claude [2], and Gemini [13] aided in text refinement and shortening. All original ideas, analysis, interpretations, and conclusions remain the sole responsibility of the authors.

Appendix

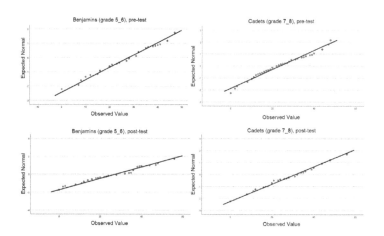

Fig. 1. Sample Distribution Alignment Q-Q Plots: Benjamins and Cadets Groups

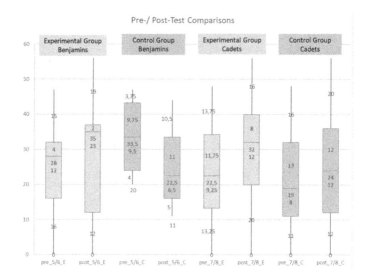

Fig. 2. Assessment Score Boxplot: Experimental (_E) and Control (_C) Groups for Pre-/Post-Test with Bebras Tasks

Table 2. First units* of the Learning Environment – micro:bit example tasks with difficulty levels easy and medium:

Content	Unit 1	Unit 2
Objectives	- Getting to know the micro:bit - First steps with the Makecode VBBPE - Connecting USB/power and transferring programs to the micro:bit - How to use Makecode tutorials - Getting to know the OER textbook wiki - How to use wiki "spoiler" links - Complete an easy example	- Advanced steps with the Makecode VBBPE - How to use Makecode tutorials and videos - How to connect external circuitry - Complete a medium example
Activities	- Tutorial "flashing heart" - OER textbook wiki introduction - Hands-on micro:bit: computer connection with USB cable (wiki) - Drag and drop .hex program file onto micro:bit (USB) - Easy OER example at choice - e.g. "On the trail of chance - heads or tails" - Open-ended coding - extensions of example tasks	- Makecode video "accelerometer" - Tutorial "hack your headphones" - Play sounds on micro:bit and computer - Trigger sound event by shaking the device - Medium OER example at choice - e.g. "Audio alert - Where is my pen eraser?" - Open-ended coding - extensions of example tasks
Physical Computing	- Giving shape to algorithms - Transfer self-drawn stick figures to device - Animate screen - Interact with device using buttons and sensors - Physically play "heads or tails"	- Giving sound and shape to algorithms - Display "angry" screen for attempted theft - Interact with buttons, sensors, and actuators (audio buzzer) - Connect external buzzer (micro:bit v1 only)
CT	- Decomposition: how to randomize - Abstraction: representing heads and tails with 5 × 5 matrix stick figures - Generalization: transfer from tutorials and OER - Algorithms: variables, flow control, conditions, event trigger (buttons & sensors) - Evaluation: debug and create final functioning code	- Decomposition: theft attempt - Abstraction: representing sound and shape for theft attempt - Generalization: transfer from tutorials, videos, and OER materials - Algorithms: variables, flow control, conditions, event trigger (buttons & sensors) - Evaluation: debug and create final functioning code

* Units 3 and 4 not displayed follow the same schema outlined here and instructed during teacher training. Unit 3 must contain a medium-level OER example task, unit 4 can be of any difficulty level to assure equal conditions for assessment.

References

1. Abonyi-Tóth, A., Pluhár, Z.: Wandering Micro:bits in the public education of Hungary. In: Pozdniakov, S.N., Dagienė, V. (eds.) ISSEP 2019. LNCS, vol. 11913, pp. 189–199. Springer, Cham (2019). https://doi.org/10.1007/978-3-030-33759-9_15
2. Anthropic: Claude (2024). https://www.anthropic.com. Large Language Model
3. Bachinger, A., Teufel, M. (eds.): Digitale Bildung in der Sekundarstufe - Computational Thinking mit BBC micro:bit V1 + V2. Austro.Tec, Grieskirchen, 2nd edn (2022)
4. Basu, S., Rutstein, D.W., Xu, Y., Wang, H., Shear, L.: A principled approach to designing computational thinking concepts and practices assessments for upper elementary grades. Comput. Sci. Educ. **31**(2), 169–198 (2021). https://doi.org/10.1080/08993408.2020.1866939
5. Bebras.org: What is Bebras? (2023). https://www.bebras.org/about.html
6. Bell, T., Vahrenhold, J.: CS unplugged—how is it used, and does it work? In: Böckenhauer, H.-J., Komm, D., Unger, W. (eds.) Adventures Between Lower Bounds and Higher Altitudes. LNCS, vol. 11011, pp. 497–521. Springer, Cham (2018). https://doi.org/10.1007/978-3-319-98355-4_29
7. Bybee, R.W.: Using the BSCS 5E instructional model to introduce STEM disciplines. Sci. Child. **56**(6), 8–12 (2019)
8. Cárdenas-Cobo, J., Puris, A., Novoa-Hernández, P., Parra-Jiménez, Á., Moreno-León, J., Benavides, D.: Using scratch to improve learning programming in college students: a positive experience from a non-WEIRD country. Electronics **10**(10), 1180 (2021). https://doi.org/10.3390/electronics10101180
9. Dagiene, V., Mannila, L., Poranen, T., Rolandsson, L., Stupuriene, G.: Reasoning on children's cognitive skills in an informatics contest: findings and discoveries from Finland, Lithuania, and Sweden. In: Gülbahar, Y., Karataş, E. (eds.) ISSEP 2014. LNCS, vol. 8730, pp. 66–77. Springer, Cham (2014). https://doi.org/10.1007/978-3-319-09958-3_7
10. Dasgupta, S., Hill, B.M.: Learning to code in localized programming languages. In: Proceedings of the Fourth ACM Conference on Learning @ Scale, Cambridge, MA, pp. 33–39. ACM (2017). https://doi.org/10.1145/3051457.3051464
11. DeepL GmbH: Translator & Write (2023). https://www.deepl.com. online machine translation service, AI-powered writing assistant
12. Döbeli Honegger, B.: Mehr als 0 und 1: Schule in einer digitalisierten Welt. hep verlag, Bern (2016). https://mehrals0und1.ch/
13. Google: Gemini (2023). https://gemini.google.com. Large Language Model
14. Grover, S., Pea, R.: Computational thinking in K-12: a review of the state of the field. Educ. Res. **42**, 38–43 (2013). https://doi.org/10.3102/0013189X12463051
15. Harel, I.E., Papert, S.E.: Constructionism. Ablex Publishing, New York (1991)
16. Houghton, T., et al.: STEAMTEACH Austria: towards a STEAM professional development program. Int. J. Res. Educ. Sci. **8**(3), 502–512 (2022). https://doi.org/10.46328/ijres.2747
17. Hourofcode.com, Partovi, H.: Hour of Code: Anybody can Learn Coding (2022). https://hourofcode.com/
18. Igoe, T.: Making Things Talk: Practical Methods for Connecting Physical Objects, 3rd edn. O'Reilly Media, Inc., San Francisco (2017)

19. Juškevičienė, A., Stupurienė, G., Jevsikova, T.: Computational thinking development through physical computing activities in STEAM education. Comput. Appl. Eng. Educ. **29**(1), 175–190 (2021). https://doi.org/10.1002/cae.22365
20. Kalelioglu, F., Sentance, S.: Teaching with physical computing in school: the case of the micro:bit. Educ. Inf. Technol. **25**(4), 2577–2603 (2020). https://doi.org/10.1007/s10639-019-10080-8
21. Kalogiannakis, M., Tzgkaraki, E., Papadakis, S.: A systematic review of the use of BBC Micro:bit in primary school. In: 12th Edition of the International Conference New Perspectives in Science Education, p. 486. Pixel e Filodiritto Editore, Bologna (2021). https://doi.org/10.26352/F318_2384-9509
22. Kastner-Hauler, O.: Bebras tasks based pre-/post-test for students computational thinking with the BBC micro:bit. (German) (2024). https://pub.ph-noe.ac.at/id/eprint/25/
23. Kastner-Hauler, O., Sabitzer, B., Tengler, K.: BBC MICRO:BIT experiments - spicing up computational thinking skills. In: INTED2020 Proceedings, Valencia, pp. 5077–5083 (2020). https://doi.org/10.21125/inted.2020.1385
24. Kastner-Hauler, O., Tengler, K., Demarle-Meusel, H., Sabitzer, B.: Adapting an OER textbook for the inverted classroom model - how to flip the classroom with BBC micro:bit example tasks. In: 2021 FIE Conference, Lincoln, NE, USA, pp. 1–8. IEEE (2021). https://doi.org/10.1109/FIE49875.2021.9637170
25. Kastner-Hauler, O., Tengler, K., Sabitzer, B., Lavicza, Z.: Combined effects of block-based programming and physical computing on primary students' computational thinking skills. Front. Psychol. **13**, 875382 (2022). https://doi.org/10.3389/fpsyg.2022.875382
26. Katterfeldt, E.S., Cukurova, M., Spikol, D., Cuartielles, D.: Physical computing with plug-and-play toolkits: key recommendations for collaborative learning implementations. Int. J. Child-Comput. Interact. **17**, 72–82 (2018). https://doi.org/10.1016/j.ijcci.2018.03.002
27. Labusch, A., Eickelmann, B., Vennemann, M.: Computational thinking processes and their congruence with problem-solving and information processing. In: Kong, S.-C., Abelson, H. (eds.) Computational Thinking Education, pp. 65–78. Springer, Singapore (2019). https://doi.org/10.1007/978-981-13-6528-7_5
28. Li, Y., et al.: Computational thinking is more about thinking than computing. J. STEM Educ. Res. **3**, 1–18 (2020). https://doi.org/10.1007/s41979-020-00030-2
29. LimeSurvey.org: LimeSurvey - Turn questions into answers (2022). https://limesurvey.org/
30. Lockwood, J., Mooney, A.: Developing a computational thinking test using Bebras problems. In: 2018 EC-TEL Conference, p. 12 (2018). https://ceur-ws.org/Vol-2190/TACKLE_2018_paper_1.pdf
31. McKenney, S., Reeves, T.C.: Conducting Educational Design Research, 2nd edn. Routledge, Milton Park (2018). https://doi.org/10.4324/9781315105642
32. McKenney, S., Reeves, T.C.: Educational design research: portraying, conducting, and enhancing productive scholarship. Med. Educ. **55**, 82–92 (2021). https://doi.org/10.1111/medu.14280
33. Microbit Educational Foundation: Let's code with the micro:bit (2015). https://microbit.org/code/
34. Microsoft: Microsoft MakeCode for micro:bit (2021). https://makecode.microbit.org/
35. OeAWI: Guidelines for Good Scientific Practice. Austrian Agency for Research Integrity (2019). https://oeawi.at/wp-content/uploads/2018/09/OeAWI_Brosch%C3%BCre_Web_2019.pdf

36. OECD: PISA 2022 Assessment and Analytical Framework. PISA, OECD Publishing, Paris (2023). https://www.oecd-ilibrary.org/education/pisa-2022-assessment-and-analytical-framework_dfe0bf9c-en
37. Oliveira, A.L.S., Andrade, W.L., Guerrero, D.D.S., Melo, M.R.A.: How do bebras tasks explore algorithmic thinking skill in a computational thinking contest? In: 2021 FIE Conference, pp. 1–7 (2021). https://doi.org/10.1109/FIE49875.2021.9637151
38. OpenAI: Chatgpt-4 (2023). https://openai.com/gpt-4. Large Language Model
39. Palts, T., Pedaste, M.: A model for developing computational thinking skills. Inform. Educ. **19**, 113–128 (2020). https://doi.org/10.15388/infedu.2020.06
40. Papert, S.: Mindstorms; Children, Computers and Powerful Ideas. Basic Books, New York (1980)
41. Przybylla, M., Romeike, R.: Physical computing and its scope - towards a constructionist computer science curriculum with physical computing. Inform. Educ. **13**(2), 225–240 (2014). https://doi.org/10.15388/infedu.2014.14
42. Psycharis, S., Kalovrektis, K., Sakellaridi, E., Korres, K., Mastorodimos, D.: Unfolding the curriculum: physical computing, computational thinking and computational experiment in STEM's transdisciplinary approach. Eur. J. Eng. Res. Sci. 19–24 (2018). https://doi.org/10.24018/ejeng.2018.0.CIE.639
43. Resnick, M., et al.: Scratch: programming for all. Commun. ACM **52**(11), 60–67 (2009). https://doi.org/10.1145/1592761.1592779
44. Román-González, M., Moreno-León, J., Robles, G.: Combining assessment tools for a comprehensive evaluation of computational thinking interventions. In: Kong, S.-C., Abelson, H. (eds.) Computational Thinking Education, pp. 79–98. Springer, Singapore (2019). https://doi.org/10.1007/978-981-13-6528-7_6
45. Scott, J., Bundy, A.: Creating a new generation of computational thinkers. Commun. ACM **58**(12), 37–40 (2015). https://doi.org/10.1145/2791290
46. Shute, V.J., Sun, C., Asbell-Clarke, J.: Demystifying computational thinking. Educ. Res. Rev. **22**, 142–158 (2017). https://doi.org/10.1016/j.edurev.2017.09.003
47. Sukirman, Pramudita, D.A., Afiyanto, A., Utaminingsih: Block-based visual programming as a tool for learning the concepts of programming for novices. Int. J. Inf. Educ. Technol. **12**(5), 365–371 (2022). https://doi.org/10.18178/ijiet.2022.12.5.1628
48. Tsarava, K., et al.: A cognitive definition of computational thinking in primary education. Comput. Educ. **179**, 104425 (2022). https://doi.org/10.1016/j.compedu.2021.104425
49. Vaníček, J., Simandl, V.: Microworlds for programming bebras tasks in czechia. In: ITiCSE 2023 Proceedings, p. 653. ACM (2023). https://doi.org/10.1145/3587103.3594223
50. van der Vegt, W.: How hard will this task be? Developments in analyzing and predicting question difficulty in the Bebras challenge. In: Olympiads in Informatics, vol. 12, pp. 119–132 (2018). https://doi.org/10.15388/ioi.2018.10
51. Waite, J., Sentance, S.: Teaching programming in schools: a review of approaches and strategies. Raspberry Pi Foundation (2021). https://www.raspberrypi.org/app/uploads/2021/11/Teaching-programming-in-schools-pedagogy-review-Raspberry-Pi-Foundation.pdf
52. WE Forum: The Future of Jobs Report 2023. World Economic Forum (2023). https://www.weforum.org/reports/the-future-of-jobs-report-2023/
53. Weintrop, D., Wilensky, U.: Comparing block-based and text-based programming in high school computer science classrooms. ACM Trans. Comput. Educ. **18**, 1–25 (2017). https://doi.org/10.1145/3089799

54. Wiebe, E., London, J., Aksit, O., Mott, B.W., Boyer, K.E., Lester, J.C.: Development of a lean computational thinking abilities assessment for middle grades students. In: SIGSCE 2019 Proceedings, Minneapolis, MN, USA, pp. 456–461. ACM (2019). https://doi.org/10.1145/3287324.3287390
55. Wing, J.M.: Computational thinking. Commun. ACM **49**(3), 33–35 (2006). https://doi.org/10.1145/1118178.1118215
56. Zapata-Cáceres, M., Martín-Barroso, E., Román-González, M.: BCTt: beginners computational thinking test. In: Understanding computing education, vol. 1, pp. 46–56. Proceedings of the Raspberry Pi Foundation Research Seminars (2021). http://rpf.io/seminar-proceedings-vol-1-zapata-caceres-et-al

Programming Tasks in the Bebras Challenge: Are They a Good Idea in Terms of the Contestants' Workload?

Václav Šimandl[✉] [iD], Václav Dobiáš [iD], and Jiří Vaníček [iD]

University of South Bohemia, České Budějovice, Czech Republic
`{simandl,dobias,vanicek}@pf.jcu.cz`

Abstract. In the Czech version of the Bebras Challenge, programming tasks in which a programming code is built from blocks are used alongside traditional contest tasks. This paper deals with the comparison of these programming tasks with other informatics tasks in terms of the workload of their solvers. Programming tasks can strongly attract the contestants' attention. The aim of the paper is to find out to what extent pupils pay attention to programming tasks at the expense of other tasks and how this differs for successful and unsuccessful contestants. We prepared national round tests in which there were typically two programming tasks and ten other tasks in each age category. We conducted quantitative research with a total of 184,949 respondents from the 2023 contest.

We discovered that pupils spend more time on programming tasks than on the other tasks. When designing tests that include programming tasks, it is necessary to take this into account, and thus either limit the number of tasks, increase the test time, or include less challenging tasks. Our research on programming tasks revealed that, for most age categories, successful pupils ran different versions of their solution fewer times than unsuccessful ones. We also discovered that successful solvers spent more time on the task than unsuccessful solvers. The youngest pupils were the outliers in these findings.

Our paper contributes to the understanding of the extent to which it is a good idea to include programming tasks in informatics contests like the Bebras Challenge.

Keywords: Computational thinking · Algorithmization · Block programming · Bebras Challenge · Workload of pupils · Time consumption

1 Introduction

1.1 Programming and Computational Thinking

Programming has strong relationships to computational thinking [1–3]. Tikva and Tambouris identified a total of 101 studies addressing this topic [2]. Åkerfeldt et al. claims that the number of publications related to this area is growing exponentially [3].

Programming can be seen as a playground for the development of computational thinking [4, 5]. According to Lye and Koh, programming exposes students to computational thinking, which involves problem-solving using computer science concepts like abstraction and decomposition [6].

Environments designed to learn programming play an important role in teaching and learning computational thinking through programming [2]. Such environments have undergone a gradual evolution, from Papert's Logo to currently used block-based environments such as Scratch, Makecode, and Blockly.

Programming tasks involving the building of code from blocks seem to be increasingly accepted as legitimate tasks for developing pupils' computational thinking [7–9]. In recent years, block programming environments have become a common learning tool in countries where informatics education reforms have taken place.

1.2 Block Programming in Bebras Tasks

One of the main goals of the Bebras Challenge is the development of computational thinking [10]. Bebras improves computational thinking in areas of simpler computational concepts and brings a smaller improvement in the more complex ones [11]. As claimed by Boom et al., Bebras can be used directly to measure computational thinking [12].

If both Bebras and block programming aim to develop computational thinking, then it is possible to use their synergy and to include such tasks in the Bebras Challenge concept. The answer in the form of constructing programming code from blocks could be added to the traditional ways of answering a programming task (multiple choice, drag and drop, clicking on an object).

Such a project of creating a module with block programming tasks for the Bebras Challenge has been implemented in the Czech Republic in the past 3 years. This project was reported at this ISSEP conference in 2022 [13]. Since 2021, the Czech version of the Bebras Challenge uses such tasks in all age categories (which are intended for pupils aged 8 to 19). About 16–25% of all tasks in the contest are programming tasks.

The created module allows the data of the contestants to be collected, e.g. their success rate, the time at which they ran their program, and the number of these executions. This allowed us to determine how difficult these tasks are and thus to discover another criterion for assessing difficulty of a programming task [14]. This paper provides answers to some of the other questions, e.g. how burdensome programming tasks are to the contestants compared to other, traditional Bebras tasks.

The Czech version of the Bebras Challenge supports the use of block programming tasks. We prepared a software module which allows such tasks to be created, included in the test, and automatically evaluated. The created module allows pupils to build a program from the offered set of blocks, to observe the situation that described the programming problem, and to get feedback to debug the program. Four templates of so-called microworlds were created for different types of situations. In these microworlds, the program controls a sprite that performs the required actions. Each of the microworlds contains:

- A stage, i.e. the area on which the programmed action takes place
- The area for building the program

- A menu of usable commands, which may differ for different tasks in the same microworld
- A panel providing feedback on the completion of the task

The individual microworlds differ in the type of programmed action and the set of basic commands:

- Karel the Robot – movement of the sprite in a square grid with placing and collecting objects and detecting obstacles
- Movie – creating an animation by positioning and adjusting the size and rotation parameters of the sprite depending on time
- Turtle – drawing graphics from lines as a trace of the sprite's movement
- Printouts – simulating printouts of calculation results

The first two microworlds (Karel the Robot, Movie) were introduced in detail in [13], now we will introduce the remaining two.

The Microworld Turtle. This microworld is based on Seymour Papert's Logo language microworld [15]. The controlled sprite moves in the direction of its rotation on the drawing board, according to commands, and rotates by a given angle. As it moves, it can leave a trail behind it, creating segments that form patterns. The pupils' task is to create a program to draw the shape that is pre-drawn on the board (see Fig. 1). The sprite does not detect any obstacles. From the program structures, it uses only a loop with a fixed number of repetitions.

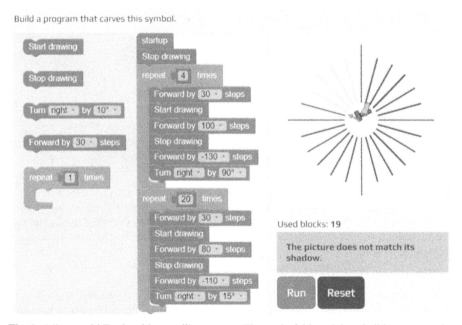

Fig. 1. Microworld Turtle with a pupil's program. The goal of this task is to build a program that carves a symbol in stone. The arrow shows the direction of movement of the hammer. In this task, pupils are not constrained by the length of the program.

This microworld has been the basis of legacy programming environments since the 1980s [16, 17]. Therefore, it is well-known and there are a large number of tried-and-tested tasks that can be used in the contest. Another advantage is the usability for younger pupils as it contains a small set of basic language commands and programming structures.

The Microworld Printouts. Unlike the others, this microworld has no visible sprite that is controlled by the program. The object being programmed is a virtual printer that prints the results of calculations with variables and expressions. In this microworld, the only command that has a visible result is the print command. This prints the current numeric value of a variable. The built program thus prints a column of numbers (see Fig. 2). The task for pupils is to create a program that prints a prescribed set of numbers given by their enumeration (e.g. 1, 3, 5, 7, 9) or description (e.g. all single-digit odd numbers). At any moment during the execution of the program, pupils see the contents of all the variables used.

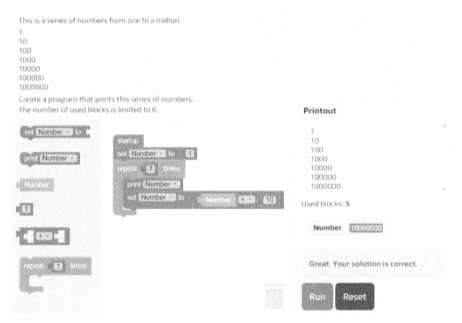

Fig. 2. Microworld Printouts. The set of numbers printed on the right shows the result after running the built program. To correctly solve this particular task, pupils have to reveal that each number in the printout is ten times larger than the previous one. They then need to program this printout. In doing so, they are limited to using only one variable, called Number, and a total of six blocks in the program.

This microworld is more complex due to the absence of a controlled sprite and is intended for upper-secondary school pupils. Besides finding the relationship between the numbers printed, another challenge may be the limited maximum number of blocks allowed in the program or the number of variables used. This forces pupils to use repetition, conditions, and arithmetic calculations to solve the task.

The Tasks Each of the microworlds allows a number of tasks of a similar type to be created. Programming tasks created in this way may have different purposes:

- To familiarize students with the microworld environment
- To teach a new concept or its application in a new context
- To test programming skills in a real contest task

In each microworld, we created tasks so that they were comparable in complexity to the other Bebras tasks. To provide similar complexity, we used the Bebras Challenge archive which contains a number of programming tasks. However, these tasks do not provide feedback on the program being created or are of a different type, e.g. the program is given and the task is to determine the final state, to choose the best algorithm, to find an error or optimal input.

2 Motivation and Aim of the Research

In the contest, traditional Bebras tasks are mixed with new programming tasks of building a program from blocks. In our previous research [13], we found out that such programming tasks are usable in the contest and that in principle they are not more difficult than other tasks. However, it is unclear how much effort contestants must spend to solve them. This is important because the Bebras Challenge requires all contest tasks to be completed in a similar amount of time. Tasks with significantly different solving time would complicate the creation of national tests and the selection of tasks for them.

Programming tasks can strongly attract the contestants' attention by their increased interactivity. The aim of this paper is to find out to what extent pupils pay attention to the programming tasks at the expense of the other tasks. Based on this aim, we posed the main research question:

RQ1: How time-consuming are programming tasks compared to other tasks?

In previous research [4], we found it useful to compare the results of successful and unsuccessful contestants, i.e. those who did and did not solve a particular task. The unsuccessful ones may be motivated differently, may spend more time on the solution or, on the contrary, may give up the solution more quickly.

If we focus on programming tasks, we can use another indicator besides time - the number of iterations of the program being created. In the light of this, we posed two additional research questions:

RQ2: What is the number of executions of programming tasks for successful and unsuccessful solvers?
RQ3: What is the time spent on programming tasks in case of correct and incorrect answers?

The insights grounded in the findings of the study might be valuable for educators. The suggestions could be beneficial to future iterations of the Bebras Challenge and similar educational initiatives. They might offer practical recommendations for designing tests that include programming tasks. We believe that the research will contribute to understanding the balance between programming and traditional tasks in informatics contests.

3 Methodology

To fulfill the aims of the research, we used data obtained from the Czech version of the Bebras Challenge. In order to answer the research questions, we conducted quantitative research.

We used data from the year 2023. The contest was held in five age categories, from Grade 3 to Grade 13, i.e. from 8 to 19 years of age. In all categories, pupils solved 12 contest tasks, some of which were programming tasks (see Table 1). Contestants had a time limit of 30 min to solve the tasks in the youngest category, and 40 min in the other categories.

Table 1. Number of programming tasks by contest categories.

Grade	3–4	5–6	7–8	9–10	11–13
Programming tasks	1	2	2	2	2

3.1 Data Collection

We used the data recorded by the contest software during the contest. We did not work with personal data of the pupils; all data were anonymized before starting the analysis. We collected summary data about:

- Each contestant (start time, finish time, suspension by the teacher)
- Each answer (task and contestant identifiers, time stamp, answer correctness)

In programming tasks, we took data from each execution of the program as the answer. To ensure data integrity, we excluded contestants who were suspended by their teachers for cheating, not completing the test or competing for a very short time. In total, we included 184,949 contestants.

3.2 Data Processing and Analysis

To answer **RQ1**, we used information about which tasks each contestant answered and when he/she did so. We were interested in each contestant's answering a task (even if he/she changed the answer later). Based on this, we determined the order of the answers sent by the contestant. We determined the time spent on solving a task as the interval between answering the previous task and answering this task. If a contestant answered a task repeatedly, we added up the partial solution times for that task. We examined the average time to solve the programming tasks and the other tasks by grade. We investigated in which cases this difference was statistically significant. We formulated the (null) hypothesis that the average time to solve the programming and other tasks is the same. We tested this hypothesis using the Two-Sample Wilcoxon test.

To answer **RQ2** and **RQ3**, we focused on programming tasks. We used information about how many times during the process of solving the task the contestant ran his/her program, when he/she did so, and whether he/she solved the task successfully. In **RQ2**, we collected the average number of program executions for successful and unsuccessful task solvers by grade. We formulated the (null) hypothesis that the average number of executions is the same for successful and unsuccessful solvers. We tested this hypothesis using the Two-Sample Wilcoxon test. Moreover, for the successful task solvers we were concerned with the average number of executions after solving the task.

In the case of **RQ3**, we followed a similar procedure, but we examined the average time to solve the task. We formulated the (null) hypothesis that the average time in which the task is solved is the same for successful and unsuccessful solvers. In all cases of statistical testing, we chose a significance level of $\alpha = 0.01$.

4 Results

4.1 RQ1: How Time-Consuming are Programming Tasks Compared to Other Tasks?

In this research question, we were interested in the extent to which programming tasks consumed contestants' time that could be spent solving other tasks.

Table 2. Average time spent on one task by task type and grade (times are in seconds)

Grade	3	4	5	6	7	8	9	10	11	12	13
Programming tasks	255	237	367	339	340	319	329	318	304	310	301
Other tasks	110	102	113	110	147	148	135	153	189	184	185

We found that, in all grades, contestants spent much more time on one programming task than on one task of any other kind (see Table 2). This difference reached a maximum in Grade 5 and Grade 6. Among these pupils, the time spent on the programming task was more than three times longer than on the other tasks. It was only in high school pupils that it fell below twice as long. Based on statistical testing, we found that the differences in all grades were statistically significant (in all cases, the p-value was 2.2 e-16).

4.2 RQ2: What is the Number of Executions of Programming Tasks for Successful and Unsuccessful Solvers?

A common way of solving programming tasks is to iterate the program and receive feedback on errors. Therefore, we focused on tracking the number of program iterations. In this way, we were interested in whether we would detect a different approach to solving in the successful and unsuccessful contestants. Since the build of a new variant is always followed by the execution of the program to check its correctness, we could determine this by the number of times the program was run while solving the task.

We found that in the two youngest grades, successful solvers ran the program more times compared to contestants who were unsuccessful in solving it (see Table 3). In other words, they left the task earlier when they were unsuccessful in finding the solution. This finding could be interpreted in such a way that the younger pupils are less resistant to giving up. Thus, for younger pupils, it can be argued that more persistent pupils are also more successful.

Table 3. Average number of program executions and time spent on programming tasks for successful and unsuccessful solvers by grade. The columns called "Unsuccessful difference" present data on the difference between unsuccessful and successful solvers. If a number in these columns is negative, it means that unsuccessful solvers ran the program fewer times respectively were faster than successful ones. All differences are statistically significant at the $\alpha = 0.01$ level.

Grade	Number of program executions		Time (in seconds) spent on one task	
	Successful	Unsuccessful difference	Successful	Unsuccessful difference
3	10.13	−3.55	268	−38
4	9.53	−1.39	224	13
5	8.02	1.74	338	43
6	7.56	2.69	307	60
7	8.82	1.99	331	−19
8	8.39	2.18	310	−20
9	10.64	1.81	380	−85
10	7.55	2.93	335	−41
11	13.14	2.36	351	−60
12	12.76	1.78	361	−70
13	11.52	0.97	328	−42

The opposite phenomenon was observed for older pupils (from Grade 5 onwards). The successful ones ran the program fewer times than the unsuccessful ones. This can be explained so that the unsuccessful pupils were stubbornly trying to find a solution. They got too fixated on the task, which they did not solve in the end. This may have impaired their overall test performance.

We were also interested in whether pupils would run the program once more after successfully solving the task. This assumption was confirmed – a number of pupils ran the program again after the first successful execution, when the whole animation played correctly. Some of them did so more than once. This finding shows the strong motivational potential of this type of task. This was found to be more frequent among the youngest pupils, roughly twice as frequent as among the older pupils.

4.3 RQ3: What is the Time Spent on Programming Tasks in the Case of Correct and Incorrect Answers?

In the previous RQ2, we dealt with the comparison between successful and unsuccessful solutions in terms of the number of program variants created. Following this, we were interested in this comparison in terms of time spent. We discovered that for younger pupils (from Grade 4 to Grade 6), unsuccessful solvers spent more time solving than successful solvers (see Table 3). This could indicate a low level of metacognitive skills in younger pupils. For the other pupils, those who were unsuccessful spent less time solving than the successful ones.

In the case of the youngest pupils (Grade 3), this can be explained by them quickly becoming tired and therefore losing interest in solving the task. The average time for solving a task is almost 4 min; long enough for such young children to lose concentration.

For older pupils (from Grade 7 onwards) there may be more reasons. In addition to the above, their self-regulation and awareness of the limited time available to solve the whole set of tasks may be the reason. These pupils may have chosen not to continue solving the task because further effort would have been too time-consuming. This finding is positive because the unsuccessful pupils did not waste too much time solving the programming task at the expense of many other tasks.

As stated in Sect. 4.2, we already knew that some pupils like to run the correct program again. We were interested in the amount of time spent in this way because it is unproductive in terms of the test result. This time ranges from 6 s among the oldest pupils to 15 s among the youngest. On average, it did not exceed half a minute for the whole test, i.e. about one percent of the total time. This is probably "execution for fun", which may contribute to the contestant's motivation to solve the rest of the test.

5 Discussion and Conclusion

The results showed that, on average, pupils spent more time on programming tasks (with building a program from blocks) than on other short informatics (Bebras) tasks during the test. But this is not caused by higher complexity of programming tasks, because it is comparable between these two types of tasks. When creating tests involving programming tasks, the longer time should be taken into account. It is suitable to limit the number of tasks, increase the test time or include less demanding tasks. In our research, we cannot report that solving these tasks limited the pupils or was at the expense of the overall test result, because in most cases the pupils did not use up the entire test time.

We discovered that for most grades, successful pupils ran different versions of their solution fewer times than unsuccessful ones. We also revealed that successful solvers spent more time on the task than unsuccessful ones. The youngest pupils were the outliers in this finding.

The level of metacognition is an important part of the ability to solve problems. Li et. al. Point out the importance of metacognition in the acquisition of computational thinking [19]. The level of metacognition, for example, affects the way we learn to use unfamiliar software [20]. In the results of our paper, the gradual development of metacognitive skills depending on the age of pupils is evident. Younger pupils spend an unnecessarily long time on tasks that they are eventually unable to solve. If they do solve the task, they spend additional time re-running it. All these activities are counterproductive in terms of getting the best result in the contest. We consider these to be manifestations of the insufficient level of metacognitive skills in younger pupils.

Comparing data in Table 3 leads us to the question of why unsuccessful solvers spend less time on the task than successful ones but have more executions. Successful solvers seem to spend more time thinking about the solution, while unsuccessful ones seem to more often choose the trial-and-error method. This is consistent with the differences in problem solving between novices and experts [21, 22].

Many of the pupils who successfully solved the programming task re-ran the correct program, some of them repeatedly. It is possible that, in this moment, the motivation to solve such a programming task outweighed the motivation to perform well on the whole test; the contestants wanted to enjoy their "victory" over the task. It is possible that programming tasks within Bebras tasks have a similar motivational power in general.

The following factors contribute to the fact that programming tasks are more time consuming compared to other tasks:

- The attractiveness of the task (something is happening in the scene, often it is an animation)
- The time required to build the program
- The possibility of debugging the solution in response to the feedback provided

Further research may focus on the extent to which these factors influence the time spent on programming tasks. It could investigate non-programming tasks that have immediate feedback and the possibility of resubmitting a solution. Examples of such tasks are https://1url.cz/v1RGE or https://1url.cz/U1RGp. These could be compared with programming tasks in terms of attractiveness and workload for contestants. Based on this, it would be possible to determine whether the programming tasks are unique within the contest, or whether they have some parameters in common with other Bebras tasks.

A limitation of the research is the use of data collected while solving tasks in different microworlds. It is possible that some microworlds are more attractive to pupils than others, for example due to greater interactivity.

A limitation of the research may be that the contestants' workload was only measured in a quantitative way using one indicator - time spent on the task. The number of iterations could not be used to compare programming tasks with other tasks that do not provide feedback.

Another limitation could be that data collection was completed online. The researchers were not present in the classroom. If a teacher was not thorough and did not follow rules of the contest, it may have led to negative occurrences such as cheating or not providing the expected time to solve the test. It is also not certain whether the pupils were working or thinking throughout the entire duration of the contest.

The technical limit of the research is the uncertainty as to whether the pupils really attended the grade they had declared to be.

The course followed by the described project leads to strengthening the position of programming in school informatics as a suitable environment for pupil development. Unlike other topics in school informatics, some teachers – beginners without a relevant computer science background – may be afraid of teaching programming because they are not skilled in programming. Many teachers who fall into this category use Bebras tasks in their teaching. Programming tasks develop computational thinking and produce problems similar to other Bebras tasks. Including them in the Bebras Challenge can help these teachers to overcome the mental block that leads to the elimination of programming from the curriculum. These teachers may then accept programming tasks as relevant to their teaching and thus change their view of programming. Moreover, programming Bebras tasks are positively evaluated by both pupils and teachers [23]. Despite the time-management problems described above, including such tasks in the contest seems to be a good idea.

References

1. Tang, X., Yin, Y., Lin, Q., Hadad, R., Zhai, X.: Assessing computational thinking: a systematic review of empirical studies. Comput. Educ. **148** (2020). https://doi.org/10.1016/j.compedu.2019.103798
2. Tikva, C., Tambouris, E.: Mapping computational thinking through programming in K-12 education: a conceptual model based on a systematic literature review. Comput. Educ. **162** (2021). https://doi.org/10.1016/j.compedu.2020.104083
3. Åkerfeldt, A., Kjällander, S., Petersen, P.: A research review of computational thinking and programming in education. Technol. Pedagogy Educ. **33**(3), 375–390 (2024). https://doi.org/10.1080/1475939X.2024.2316087
4. Vaníček, J., Dobiáš, V., Šimandl, V.: Understanding loops: What are the misconceptions of lower-secondary pupils? Inf. Educ. **22**(3), 525–554 (2023). https://doi.org/10.15388/infedu.2023.20
5. Bers, M.U., González-González, C., Armas-Torres, M.B.: Coding as a playground: promoting positive learning experiences in childhood classrooms. Comput. Educ. **138**, 130–145 (2019). https://doi.org/10.1016/j.compedu.2019.04.013
6. Lye, S.Y., Koh, J.H.L.: Review on teaching and learning of computational thinking through programming: what is next for K-12? Comput. Hum. Behav. **41**, 51–61 (2014). https://doi.org/10.1016/j.chb.2014.09.012
7. Li, W., Liu, C.Y., Tseng, J.C.R.: Development of a metacognitive regulation-based collaborative programming system and its effects on students' learning achievements, computational thinking tendency and group metacognition. Br. J. Educ. Technol. **55**(1), 318–339 (2023). https://doi.org/10.1111/bjet.13358
8. Wu, B., Hu, Y., Ruis, A.R., Wang, M.: Analysing computational thinking in collaborative programming: a quantitative ethnography approach. J. Comput. Assist. Learn. **35**(3), 421–434 (2019). https://doi.org/10.1111/jcal.12348
9. Wong, G.K.W., Cheung, H.Y.: Exploring children's perceptions of developing twenty-first century skills through computational thinking and programming. Interact. Learn. Environ. **28**(4), 438–450 (2018). https://doi.org/10.1080/10494820.2018.1534245
10. Bebras Challenge. https://www.bebras.org/
11. Zapata-Cáceres, M., Marcelino, P., El-Hamamsy, L., Martín-Barroso, E.: A Bebras computational thinking (ABC-thinking) program for primary school: evaluation using the competent computational thinking test. Educ. Inf. Technol. (2024). https://doi.org/10.1007/s10639-023-12441-w
12. Boom, K.D., Bower, M., Siemon, J., Arguel, A.: Relationships between computational thinking and the quality of computer programs. Educ. Inf. Technol. **27**, 8289–8310 (2022). https://doi.org/10.1007/s10639-022-10921-z

13. Vaníček, J., Šimandl, V., Dobiáš, V: Bebras tasks based on assembling programming code. In: Bollin, A., Futschek, G. (eds.) Informatics in Schools. A Step beyond Digital Education. ISSEP 2022. LNCS, vol. 13488, pp. 113–124. Springer, Cham (2022). https://doi.org/10.1007/978-3-031-15851-3_10
14. Dobiáš, V., Šimandl, V., Vaníček, J.: Number of program builds: another criterium for assessing difficulty of a programming task? Inf. Educ. **23**(3), 525–540 (2024). https://doi.org/10.15388/infedu.2024.23
15. Papert, S.: Mindstorms: Children, Computers, and Powerful Ideas. Basic Books, New York (1980)
16. Blaho, A., Kalaš, I.: Imagine Logo: učebnice programování pro děti (Imagine Logo: The textbook of programming for kids). Computer Press, Brno (2006)
17. Harms, K.: Atari Logo looking good. Antic. **2**(6) (1983). https://www.atarimagazines.com/v2n6/logo.php
18. Hour of Code: Code with Anna and Elsa. https://studio.code.org/s/frozen/
19. Li, W., Liu, C.Y., Tseng, J.C.R.: A effects of the interaction between metacognition teaching and students' learning achievement on students' computational thinking, critical thinking, and metacognition in collaborative programming learning. Educ. Inf. Technol. **28**, 12919–12943 (2023). https://doi.org/10.1007/s10639-023-11671-2
20. Dobiáš, V., Šimandl, V.: Self-regulated learning in the context of digital literacy. Int. J. Lit. **31**(1), 83–104 (2024). https://doi.org/10.18848/2327-0136/CGP/v31i01/83-104
21. Plháková, A.: Učebnice obecné psychologie (Textbook of General Psychology). Academia, Praha (2004)
22. Nolen-Hoeksema, S., Fredrickson, B.L., Loftus, G.R., Wagenaar, W.A.: Atkinson & Hilgard's Introduction to Psychology, 15th edn. Wadsworth Pub Co., Belmont (2009)
23. Vaníček, J., Šimandl, V., Dobiáš, V.: Situational algorithmic tasks with the assembling of program code as a tool for developing computational thinking. J. Technol. Inf. Educ. **14**(2), 101–119 (2022). https://doi.org/10.5507/jtie.2022.014

Teaching Task Specification Efficiently in Introductory Programming Courses in Higher Education

Győző Horváth[✉]

Eötvös Loránd University, Pázmány Péter sétány 1/c., 1117 Budapest, Hungary
gyozo.horvath@inf.elte.hu

Abstract. In introductory programming courses in higher education, systematic problem-solving consists of three interdependent steps: 1) the specification of the task, 2) the algorithm of the solving program, and 3) the implementation of the algorithm. During the specification phase, numerous decisions are made that help to describe subsequent steps, making specification a crucial stage in the design process, mainly when we use stricter analogous programming approaches, like derivation. However, the formal language used for the specification requires a considerable level of abstraction, so in practice this part of the task solution is often incomplete or incorrect from students. In this article, we aim to explore the challenges associated with the specification step in introductory programming courses in higher education. Additionally, we introduce a tool designed to alleviate these issues and elevate the specification process to the same level of experience as writing algorithms and code during problem solving.

Keywords: formal specification · analogous programming · teaching programming · higher education

1 The Role and Form of the Specification

In higher education, several approaches are used to teach programming in introductory courses. At the Faculty of Informatics of Eötvös Loránd University, students traditionally first learn about algorithms in the framework of the procedural paradigm, upon which the object-oriented paradigm is built later. During programming education, we try to give the students the tools they can use to create *correct* algorithms and programs to solve problems with computers [1–3]. There are several methods to determine whether an algorithm solves a problem correctly or not. Informal tools can be used, such as textual formulation of our expectations, or input-output testing known from the black-box testing method, but the common feature of these approaches is that they cannot *fully* guarantee the correctness of the operation of the algorithm. The latter can only be guaranteed by formal tools and mathematical models.

At the Faculty of Informatics, ELTE, it was Ákos Fóthi [4] who developed a *formal description of programming* based on the work of Dijkstra [5] and Hoare [6], and used the set theory of the relational model and the tools of first-order logic to prove that given algorithmic structures indeed solve the specific task. The formal description focuses on the state space of the task, and the control structures perform transitions in this state space. Thus, when describing a task, we need to specify the state space of the data or variables, we need to formulate statements for the initial state in the language of first-order logic, and we need to specify the final state that is considered acceptable for a given initial state. Finally, the solving algorithm can be derived from the task description given in this way.

In this method, the core part of task solutions is the task description, called the *specification*. This is a concise, precise, and formal description of the task, in order to check or even ensure the correctness of the solving program (depending on which direction we look at the problem). The specification and algorithm are therefore very closely related. The algorithm can be derived from the specification, or vice versa, the correctness of the algorithm is ensured by the specification. The elements of the specification are [4, 7–10]:

- the description of *the structure of the state space*, distinguished in some descriptions by
  - the description of the structure of the *input data*, and separately
  - the description of the structure of the *output data*;
- the logical condition of restrictions on input data, the so-called *precondition*;
- an identically true logical condition describing the relationship between properly connected input-output data, the so-called *post-condition*.

In introductory programming courses, however, we cannot expect students coming freshly from high school to prove the correctness of the algorithms they create using formal toolkits that rely on deep mathematical concepts. Instead, we aim to ensure the creation of *correct algorithms* by identifying general task types, creating general specifications for them, and deriving their algorithms with formal methods. This results in proven correct specification-algorithm pairs for given task types, known as *programming patterns*. We then construct the solution of a specific task by drawing analogies to the general solution. This method is called *analogous programming* [7, 11].

There are several ways of using analogous programming. In the computer science courses of ELTE, we follow a more formal, rigid type of analogous programming, which is called *derivation*. This approach considers the formal description of the specific task, *the specification*, as the starting point, and aligns this specification with the specification of a general programming pattern. This is done with the aim that, just as the general algorithm can be derived from the specification of the general programming pattern, the algorithm of the specific task can similarly be derived from the specification of the specific task through similar steps. Therefore, it is enough to identify the differences between the specific and the general tasks and make the appropriate renamings.

As an example, let us consider the maximum selection programming pattern. The general task is the following: Given an interval $[m..n]$ of integers and a function $f : [m..n] \rightarrow \mathcal{H}$. A complete ordering relation is defined on the elements of the set $\mathcal{H}$. Let's determine where the function f takes the largest value on the non-empty interval $[e..u]$, and specify what this maximum value is! Fig. 1 shows the general specification of this programming pattern. The input specifies the $[m..n]$ interval, the output contains the max and ind results. The precondition ensures that the interval is non-empty, and the postcondition gives the relation between the input and output elements.

Input: $m \in \mathbb{Z}, n \in \mathbb{Z}$
Output: $ind \in \mathbb{N}, max \in \mathcal{H}$
Precondition: $n \geq m$
Postcondition: $ind \in [m..n] \land max = f(ind) \land \forall i \in [m..n] : max \geq f(i)$

Fig. 1. The general specification of the maximum selection pattern.

The algorithm for this specification can be seen in Fig. 2 in a Nassi-Schneiderman diagram. The correctness of this algorithm can be proven with formal methods, but in introductory courses we just provide the correct specification-algorithm pair for the students without any complex proof.

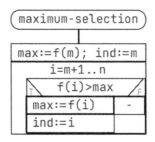

Fig. 2. The general algorithm of the maximum selection pattern.

When students are given a specific task, they must first recognize the programming pattern to be used, and then define the task according to that specification. Once the specification for the specific task is created, its postcondition is compared to the postcondition of the specification for the general task and the differences are summarized in a table (derivation table). These differences are applied to the algorithm of the general task and thus the solution of the current task is obtained. Figure 3 shows the specification, the derivation table and the algorithm for a task, where the largest number is needed to be specified from an array of numbers. Since the algorithm of the general task was derived from its specification, and it is therefore correct, the algorithm of the current task will also be correct, since we corresponded to the general specification at the model level. We can see, therefore, that in this approach the specification plays a very important role during solving a task and creating its algorithm.

Input: $n \in \mathbb{N}, x \in \mathbb{Z}^n$
Output: $ind \in \mathbb{N}, largest \in \mathcal{Z}$
Precondition: $n \geq 1$
Postcondition: $ind \in [1..n] \land largest = x[ind] \land \forall i \in [1..n] : largest \geq x[i]$

$m \rightarrow 1$
$max \rightarrow largest$
$f(i) \rightarrow x[i]$

```
  largest-number
┌─────────────────────┐
│ largest:=x[1]; ind:=1│
├─────────────────────┤
│      i=1+1..n       │
├─────────────────────┤
│    x[i]>largest     │
├──────────────┬──────┤
│ largest:=x[i]│      │
│    ind:=i    │  -   │
└──────────────┴──────┘
```

Fig. 3. The specification, the derivation table and the algorithm of the task derived from the maximum selection pattern.

2   Experiences, Problems, and Goals in Teaching Specification

The introductory programming course takes a practical view of the specification and considers it one of the steps of systematic problem solving. In this process, students first determine 1) what the task is (*specification*), 2) design the steps of the solving program (*algorithm*), 3) implement this using a chosen programming language (*coding*), 4) check if the solution works correctly and efficiently solves the task (*testing*), and if not, then 5) *find* and 6) *fix* the error, 7) finally, they create a *documentation* of the operation and structure of the program. While every step in problem-solving is necessary, our programming education places special emphasis on the first three steps: specification, algorithm, and coding. During these steps, students progress from defining the task to breaking down the solution into steps, and eventually reaching the working code. Each of these three steps has its own descriptive language: the specification uses formal mathematical tools, the algorithm requires a new abstract language or notation system (such as a structogram in our case), and coding requires understanding the tools and principles of the chosen programming language. As a result, this expects students to learn and apply three abstract languages during problem-solving.

Among these steps, the specification proves to be particularly difficult for students to understand, learn, and apply. The nature of breaking down a complex problem into simple steps is close to our everyday thinking and algorithm description languages contain relatively few elements, making it easy to learn. Using a programming language is either already known to them, or if it initially seems intimidating, later becomes appealing as it involves the tangible process of creation. In contrast, the high level of abstraction required by the formalism of the specification uses many notations that are often unfamiliar to students, making this descriptive language inherently foreign to them. This is a particularly painful point for our students because we solve tasks in the introductory programming course using the derivation technique, which crucially involves understanding and creating specifications. This makes the role of the specification in systematic problem solving essential, highlighting the gap between the knowledge expected from students and their actual lack of understanding even more contrasting.

The problem primarily lies in the applied formalism. Routine use of the language and notation of first-order logic cannot be expected from newly arriving students. In fact, often even the instructors are not precisely aware of the exact set of rules they are working with. The use of basic logical operations (and, or, not) and quantifiers is still consistent, but in certain cases, such as determining the uniqueness of elements in a sequence, ad-hoc notations are applied.

Based on the teaching experiences of recent years, it can be said that most students do not understand the purpose of the specification. They do not see that a post-condition of a specification is a "contract" where correctly related input and output data give an identically true logical value. Another problem is that even for simple tasks, but especially in cases where complex problems require the application of multiple programming patterns, student solutions are full of errors. Some of these are syntactic errors, where the descriptive formula mentioned above is violated, such as missing commas, incorrectly defined sequences or structures, and unclear parentheses in logical expressions. Instructors often "graciously" correct these deficiencies, understanding the student's intent, but it is evident that the student is not yet fluent in this language. A more significant issue is that the written specifications can also be semantically incorrect, which the student does not realize due to the lack of feedback during the creation process, thus missing the feedback-reinforcement phase so crucial in the learning process. From an instructor's perspective, interpreting and evaluating these specifications needs a lot of effort from them. The contradictory of this situation can be described as expecting students to use tools intended for formal correctness proof while they do not even know how to model data at a basic level.

It is therefore legitimate for students to have the opportunity to practice writing specifications, given its integral role in problem solving. This article's starting point was this demand and the recognition that currently no tools are available for this purpose. The question it aims to address is how we can help students write correct specifications in a way that is also practicable. In this article, I propose ways to make specification teaching more effective and provide opportunities for students to practice it.

3 Design Considerations for a Practicable Specification

Practical Benefits. In addition to its hidden potential for proving correctness, the specification, that appears as the first step in systematic problem solving, has the following important and *practical benefits* during problem processing:

- Modelling: Structuring the data of the task into abstract structures, data representation.
- Preparing an algorithm: In most cases, specifying the relationship between the data in the state space also provides ideas on how to solve the problem (executable specification).
- Testing: As preparations for the previous two points, it is advisable to provide specific input-output data, which can be used later to test the completed implementation.

Correctness by Compliance. In the following, a tool supporting the above practical aspects of problem solving will be defined. Additionally, the primary goal is to enable students to write *syntactically* and *semantically* correct specifications while understanding what the specification is about. It is important during this process that *the formal language of the specification* should correspond to the formalism found in the literature for the introductory programming course. The use of a notation system is essential, one that can be relatively easily matched and transformed into a format that allows for formal correctness proof. As long as this connection is maintained, the analogue programming model can be utilized.

Practicability. Following this, we need to consider how to make specification *practicable* for students. The purpose of practice is to make students apply their acquired knowledge to an unfamiliar task. They learn from this by receiving feedback on their solution, preferably as soon as possible. Fortunately, a large number of tasks can be found in various online collections. When a task is assigned, the student can submit their solution to the instructor, who evaluates it and provides feedback. This method has several drawbacks: on one hand, the student receives feedback on their task very slowly, and on the other hand, the burden of evaluation and feedback falls on the instructor. Another solution could be to create a collection of tasks where solutions are also available to read. In this case, the instructor is not involved in the evaluation process; it is the responsibility of the student.

Automation. It would be much better if the practice and evaluation of specifications could be done in an *automated system*. The first question in this context is in what form the specification should be given to this system. There are several options:

- Hand-drawn sketches: Traditionally, specifications are "paper-based" due to the many specialized notations used in them: various logical characters, subscripts and superscripts, large sums, elements positioned above or below. However, automatically analyzing a hand-drawn sketch would be too complicated.
- Equation editors: Fortunately, equation editors in word processors allow these formulas to be written. However, editing such equations can be either too cumbersome or require learning another specialized language.
- LaTeX, AsciiMath: These are simple text formats where expressions can be specified in a code-like, "flat" manner, but they still require learning a new language.

Syntax. Among the above options, the last two provide the opportunity for automatic evaluation since they have fixed formats, and from them only the latter can be easily entered in the machine due to its code-like form, but it requires learning a new language. Consequently, it seems that each option has its own drawbacks. Based on these, it seems like a good solution to create a *custom Domain-Specific Language* (DSL) tailored for task specifications, which practically resembles the "hand-drawn" solutions, but with each element presented in a flat, code-like manner. This way, there is the freedom to align it as closely as possible with the requirements and needs, while maintaining the connection to the formal background and intent of the specification. Specifications written in this language can be syntactically checked, and immediate feedback can be provided to the student.

Semantics. Free text input is important because the same task can have many different solutions. It is essential to design the specification tool to support freedom to any thoughts and creative processes. However, this poses a significant burden on *semantic checking*. How do we know if the solution to a given task is the right one? The interesting thing about this question is that it contains a logical pitfall: in principle, the specification tells us when the task is correct, but what we want to know is when the specification is correct for a given task. Formal and informal methods are available to check the correctness of the specification:

- Official specification: We can create an official solution for the task. However, comparing it to another one can be rejected immediately. The challenge lies in proving the equivalence of two different specifications, which would require symbolic execution using formal methods.
- Automated theorem proving systems: As a formal solution, we could employ automated theorem proving systems capable of understanding first-order logic. However, these are highly complex systems, and translating specifications into their own language would be a considerable task.
- Black box testing: An informal method where we decide the correctness of a specification based on whether the post-condition holds true for input-output pairs we find correct. If the post-condition holds for all of them, then there is a

certain likelihood that it is correct. This method is commonly used for testing codes, and its application is valid here as well. Its theoretical background is provided by the substitution rule of first-order logic: if a statement is true in general, then it will give true when specific values are substituted.

Supported Features. It is crucial that the language created in this way *supports the elements used in introductory courses*. Here are some examples, without claiming completeness:

- Specifying data, sets, sequences (arrays), direct products (records), potentially nested declarations.
- Mathematical operators: $=, \neq, <, >, +, -, *, /, div, mod$, parentheses for grouping.
- Basic mathematical functions.
- Existential and universal quantifiers.
- Expansion of the state space.
- Use of programming patterns (task types) in abbreviated form.
- Definition and invocation of functions, including recursive functions.

Visualization. Finally, it is important that the tool enables understanding of the "operation" of the specification by *visualising the evaluation in steps*. We consider the specification to be a contract between the client and the programmer, which describes in the formal language of mathematics what we expect from the task, or in other words, when a task is considered correct. Practically, we can achieve this by substituting input and output data from the program into the post-condition and checking whether the logical expression evaluates to true. The evaluation phases after substitution could be presented step by step.

4 Introducing the Specification Tool

A special tool was developed in the form of a client-side web application that meets the above criteria (see Fig. 4) [12]. The main area of the tool is the editor located on the left side. This is where one can write the defined specification language. Some of the main functions of the language can be seen in the example of Listing 1.

Listing 1. An example specification to decide whether the heights of consecutive students increase montonically (the task).

Listing 1. An example specification to decide whether the heights of consecutive students increase montonically (the task).

```
In:    n ∈ N, students ∈ Student[1..n],
       Student = Name x Height, Name = S, Height = N
Out:   mon ∈ L
Pre:   n >= 1 and ∀i ∈ [1..n-1]:(students[i].name <= students[i+1].name)
Post:  n = 1 -> mon = true and
       n > 1 -> mon = EVERY(i=1..n-1, students[i].height <= students[i+1].height)
```

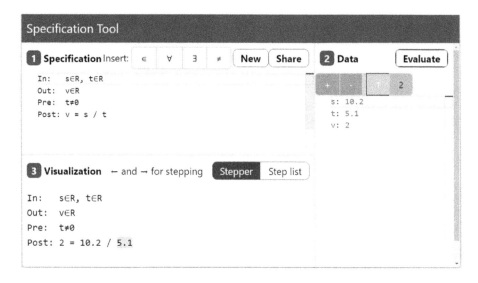

Fig. 4. The user interface of the specification tool during solving a task.

This language is specified in the PEG (Parsing Expression Grammars) format [13]. During the traversal of the source code, an abstract syntax tree is built, which is later traversed during evaluation with the current data. During traversal, the data found in the input, output, and auxiliary data is created typewise and becomes accessible for the logical expression evaluated in the input and output. We can define two complex types: array and record. The program recursively traverses and builds the type tree from them. If an error is encountered during traversal, it can be seen under the editor.

To determine semantic correctness, test data is needed. These can be provided in YAML[1] format on the right-hand side. From the type tree built during traversal, we construct a JSON[2] schema, so the right-hand editor can provide error messages corresponding to the expectations of our specification if the provided data is not in the correct structure. The correctness of the specification is automatically checked with the provided data. If semantic errors occur, such as comparing a number with a string, we also receive error messages. Even if the substitution is successful, we may still receive an error message if the precondition or post-condition evaluation is not true. This way, we can provide and verify invalid tests as well. If both syntax and semantic checks are successful, the background of the test number turns green.

At this point, we can check the evaluation of the post-condition by clicking the "Evaluate" button. The specification appears at the bottom left, indicating

---

[1] YAML is a human-friendly data serialization language (YAML Ain't Markup Language, https://yaml.org/).
[2] JSON is data description language built on top of the object and array literals of JavaScript language (JavaScript Object Notation, https://www.json.org/).

the current evaluation step in yellow. We can step through the evaluation using the left-right arrow keys. At the end of the evaluation, the post-condition should show either true or false.

The written specification can be shared. By clicking the "Share" button, the tool generates a compressed textual representation from the contents of the editing fields, which is embedded in the URL and also copied to the clipboard. This makes it very easy to share and review prepared or completed solutions.

5   Methodological Analysis and Expectations

Using the specification tool prepared in this way, we can assign various types of tasks that can focus on different aspects of problem solving and specification. These types of tasks can be used both in class and as homework assignments.

Empty task the most common type of task, where the task is issued textually, and the student must provide the correct solution. In this case, the student creates the specification, adds test data, and makes corrections in the specification until the tests turn green. It is recommended to start with the tests in this case. The test data help to form an understanding of the structure of the data, making it easier to describe the input, output, and even the precondition. It's worth preparing multiple tests so that we can quickly verify the correctness of the specification.

Test-driven problem solving a classic type of task for a textbook. In addition to the textual description, we also prepare the test data we consider correct, while leaving the specification blank. We save this state in a link and assign it as a task to the students, asking them to write a specification that satisfies the tests. Moreover, this procedure serves as a good example of test-driven development.

Testing a rarer type of task where a solution is given, and the student must write tests for it. It improves reading specifications, especially data modelling.

Data representation students should prepare input and output descriptions for the data structures given in the tests. Preconditions and post-conditions are not necessary. This is currently a theoretical possibility because the syntactic checker expects them to be correctly provided, but it could be a very important skill to practice.

My specification tool offers significant methodological advantages, and the following benefits are expected:

Interaction. Perhaps the most important advantage of the tool is that students can interact with the specification. The qualitative difference compared to the paper version cannot be emphasized enough. In both cases, the person solving the task develops a mental model of the solution before formally writing it down. On paper, there is no feedback if someone is unsure whether a comma, colon, or parentheses are needed, or in what order to provide the data. I.e. there is no feedback on the mental model during the creation process. In the specification tool, however, immediate feedback is provided in the form of error messages, indicated by red underlines, signalling that something is wrong and needs correction. It means that Immediate feedback is given on the conceptual model, speeding up the learning process. But more importantly, all of this happens at semantic level as well. With showing the syntax errors, only a syntactic model is confirmed, whereas indicating the correctness of the specification, immediate feedback is given on the semantic model of the solution. This allows for the specification to be shaped, developed, and refactored in any way.

Creativity. It comes from the above that the tool allows the free expression of thoughts. It provides the safety net that immediate feedback is given even when something is done well or poorly.

Support for the Teaching Process. Through links, tasks can be easily prepared, distributed, and submitted. Working with a standard and widely supported web toolset, links can be embedded in documentation, learning management systems, emails, and messages. The correctness is immediately indicated by the green-red state of the tests. Supporting both in-class and out-of-class activities becomes easier, and teacher evaluation becomes faster.

More Effective Task Solving. As a long-term goal, it can be expected that students will be able to better concentrate on the mental model of the task, allowing them to progress faster. By creating a set of tasks, they can practice more, which can also help improve their effectiveness.

6 Summary

Among the systematic steps of problem solving, specification stands out from the others in such a way that it poses the greatest challenge for students freshly coming from high school in introductory programming courses at the higher education level. The main reason for this is the strong formalism and a mode of thinking that differs from the usual algorithmic approach. Since these cannot be abandoned, I have created a tool to help students practice writing specifications more easily. For this purpose a web application was developed that is accessible and usable by everyone, using a fully precise and formal language defined by me for specifying tasks, consistent with the literature. The correctness of the specifications is verified using a black-box approach by providing test data. The tool provides immediate feedback on both syntactic and semantic correctness. Additionally, it includes a visualization tool that breaks down the evaluation of the post-condition into steps, showing how the specification works. The tool already demonstrates numerous methodological advantages, but further measurements are planned to validate this. Possible future developments include:

- possibility to specify the text of tasks,
- creating an online problem set,
- supporting various dialects of the specification languages.

References

1. Gegg-Harrison, T.S., Bunce, G.R., Ganetzky, R.D., Olson, C.M., Wilson, J.D.: Studying program correctness by constructing contracts. In: ITiCSE 2003: Proceedings of the 8th Annual Conference on Innovation and Technology in Computer Science Education (2003)
2. Todorova, M., Armyanov, P.: runtime verification of computer programs and its application in programming education. GSTF J. Math. Stat. Oper. Res. (2012)
3. Huisman, M., Monti, R.E.: Teaching design by contract using snap! arXiv:2107.05679v1 (2021)
4. Fóthi, Á.: Bevezetés a programozáshoz, ELTE Eötvös Kiadó (2005) (Introduction to programming, in Hungarian)
5. Dijkstra, E.W.: A Discipline of Programming. Prentice Hall, Upper Saddle River (1976)
6. Hoare, C.A.R.: Proof of correctness of data representations. Acta Informatica $\mathbf{1}(4)$, 271–281 (1972)
7. Gregorics, T., Sike S.: Generic algorithm patterns. In: Proceedings of Formal Methods in Computer Science Education (2008)
8. Szlávi, P., Zsakó, L., Törley, G.: Programming theorems have the same origin. Central-Eur. J. New Technol. Res. Educ. Pract. $\mathbf{1}(1)$, 1–12 (2019)
9. Szlávi, P., Zsakó, L.: Módszeres programozás: Programozási bevezető. μlógia 18, 8th, revised edition (2004). (Systematic programming: Introduction to programming, in Hungarian)
10. Szlávi, P., Zsakó, L.: Módszeres programozás: Programozási tételek. μlógia 19, 6th, revised edition (2004). (Systematic programming: Programming patterns, in Hungarian)
11. Gregorics, T.: Abstract levels of programming theorems. Acta Universitatis Sapientiae Informatica $\mathbf{4}(2)$, 247–259 (2012)
12. The Specification Tool. https://progalap.elte.hu/specifikacio/. Accessed 31 May 2024
13. Bryan, F.: Parsing expression grammars: a recognition-based syntactic foundation. ACM SIGPLAN Not. $\mathbf{39}(1)$ (2004)

Teacher's Perspective

A Glimpse Into Primary and Secondary Teachers' Knowledge to Teach Informatics

Gabriel Parriaux[1](✉), Jean-Philippe Pellet[1], and Vassilis Komis[2]

[1] University of Teacher Education, Lausanne, Switzerland
{gabriel.parriaux,jean-philippe.pellet}@hepl.ch
[2] University of Patras, Patras, Greece
komis@upatras.gr

Abstract. In this article, we present a regional overview of teachers' knowledge to teach informatics. It was obtained through a self-reported quantitative evaluation instrument of informatics teachers' knowledge addressing the seven domains of the Technological Pedagogical Content Knowledge (TPACK) model. Sixty-four teachers of French-speaking Switzerland participated from various educational levels, including primary, secondary, and higher education. While primary teachers had mostly informatics education during their teacher education, upper-secondary teachers all had informatics as a major or secondary topic in the university.

Using dimensionality reduction techniques (Principal Component Analysis and Factor Analysis), we extract the latent features from the knowledge expressed according to the seven domains of TPACK. Subsequently, executing an agglomerative hierarchical clustering, we group the teachers in clusters and explore the relations between those clusters and their professional profile. As a result, we can say that upper-secondary teachers express higher knowledge both on the didactical and foundational aspects of informatics teaching. Primary and lower-secondary teachers express low self-efficacy in domains related to the contents of informatics and higher self-efficacy in domains related to technology. This process facilitated the identification of adjustments that could be integrated into teacher education programs to address these needs.

Keywords: teachers' knowledge to teach informatics · TPACK · primary and secondary teachers · dimensionality reduction · clustering

1 Introduction and Context

Many countries, especially western countries, experience a movement towards the introduction of informatics[1] content into school teaching. Several examples can be mentioned like UK [3], Germany [4] or New Zealand [2] among others.

---

[1] In this article, we consider "informatics" and "computer science" as synonyms and do not treat wider aspects of digital education.

This introduction can take different forms, sometimes as a dedicated subject, sometimes as a content integrated into other disciplines, and happen at different school degrees, from primary to lower and upper secondary.

In this context, there is the need to provide teachers with the necessary knowledge and competencies to teach this new content, as it has been shown for other disciplines like sciences that teachers' knowledge has a strong influence on student learning [9].

In Switzerland, primary teachers are generalists who teach nearly all disciplines, unlike upper-secondary teachers who are specialists teaching only one discipline, sometimes two, but rarely more. Lower-secondary teachers are in the middle and are usually specialist teachers, but often for more disciplines at the same time. We acknowledge that it might be quite different from one country to the other.

In terms of education, we formulate the hypothesis that primary teachers have a low disciplinary education, as they have to share their time during pre-service education between a lot of disciplines, and that upper-secondary teachers have a much deeper disciplinary education, as they often possess a Master's (or even a PhD) degree in their discipline. Lower-secondary teachers being, again, somewhere in the middle in terms of disciplinary education.

But the knowledge and competencies required to teach a discipline are not only related to the content. There are also pedagogical aspects associated with the specificities of the discipline, what some would call *didactics*, which is also referred to as *Pedagogical Content Knowledge* (PCK), according to the framework developed by Shulman [10]. Furthermore, the technological competencies also play an important role, as school teaching involves more and more interactions with technology. These technological competencies were included into the *Technological, Pedagogical and Content Knowledge* (TPACK) framework of Mishra and Koehler [7].

In Switzerland, informatics was introduced country-wide as a mandatory discipline for all in 2018. And in the French-speaking part of the country, the curriculum for primary and lower secondary was modified in 2021 to integrate "digital education" as a new domain. This domain encompasses informatics elements as well as the more traditional subdomains of media and use of digital tools, which already existed in the previous curriculum. Because of the political organisation, the implementation of those decisions is going at different pace from one canton to the other. However, the last six years have been particularly challenging for the professionals active in the fields of informatics education, with the drafting of several curricula in informatics and the creation of different teacher education programs.

This article proposes to give a glimpse into primary and secondary teachers' knowledge to teach informatics in this region. In order to grasp information about their profile and their declarative knowledge to teach informatics, a survey was submitted to a number of teachers involved in some way into the teaching of informatics with their pupils.

Our research questions are the following:

RQ1 *What are the main characteristics of teachers teaching informatics in school in terms of their personal, professional and academic profile?*
RQ2 *How can we characterize the knowledge of those teachers to teach informatics through the lens of the TPACK model?*
RQ3 *What kind of similarities and differences can we observe between primary and secondary teachers (again according to the TPACK model)?*

2 Theoretical Framework

Teachers involved into the teaching of a discipline demonstrate a multifaceted form of knowledge, bringing together elements of content, pedagogy and, technology. We refer to the TPCK or TPACK framework [7], as it has been widely used in the field of educational research to characterise the knowledge of teachers. In the context of informatics, the TPACK domains can be described as follows:

1. *Content Knowledge* (CK) refers to the teacher's understanding of the subject matter. This includes facts, concepts, theories, and principles.
2. *Pedagogical Knowledge* (PK) involves the general methods and processes of teaching. This includes understanding how students learn, classroom management, lesson planning, and assessment.
3. *Technological Knowledge* (TK) is the ability to use various technologies effectively. This includes understanding how to operate technology tools and software and the ability to learn and adapt to new technologies.
4. *Pedagogical Content Knowledge* (PCK) represents the blending of content and pedagogy. It involves knowing how to present informatics content in ways that make it understandable and accessible to learners.
5. *Technological Content Knowledge* (TCK) involves understanding how technology and given informatics contents interact. This includes knowing which technologies are best suited for which types of content.
6. *Technological Pedagogical Knowledge* (TPK) is about understanding how teaching and learning change with the use of particular technologies, independently of informatics content. This includes knowing the pedagogical affordances and constraints of various technologies.
7. *Technological Pedagogical Content Knowledge* (TPCK) is the intersection of all three knowledge domains: content, pedagogy, and technology. It represents a teacher's understanding of how to teach content with technology in a pedagogically sound manner.

The TPACK framework is particularly special for informatics because the lines between technological and content knowledge are often blurred: informatics, by its very nature, is deeply intertwined with technology at its core, as it has been shown by [1]. It is very debatable that such or such knowledge aspect is to be classified as closer to content or closer to technological knowledge. Adding the pedagogical component to each combination of T, C, and TC adds subtleties of its own (further discussed in [5]). However, even if the literature about the TPACK model is extended, little research has addressed the adaptation of the model within the context of informatics. [11] built a conceptualisation of TPACK for primary years' informatics, but it covered only the topics of algorithms and programming. [6] studied the effectiveness of a professional development program in Computational Thinking in relation to programming for primary school teachers in Hong Kong, using the dimensions of the TPACK model. But in most of the research conducted on TPACK with informatics teachers, the surveys used generic questions that did not address the specificities of informatics in terms of content and of the special relation between content and technology.

3 Data Collection and Methodology

In this article, we propose a self-reported quantitative evaluation instrument of informatics teachers' knowledge addressing the 7 domains of TPACK. A first version of the survey was built in the context of an Erasmus+ project, the CAI project, in 2020, during which 339 answers were collected across different French-speaking countries in Europe and abroad [5]. Inspired by the TPACK model, the questions of the surveys had not been classified a priori into the different domains of TPACK and this proved quite difficult to relate them properly afterwards. Following that experience, the authors of the present article refined the survey to create a second version, clarifying the TPACK classification of the questions. This version 2 was used to collect the data we present here. The questions related to the TPACK part are discussed later and are shown in full in Appendix A.

To target a variety of teachers, we used different ways of contacting them and sending them our survey. Pre-service and in-service primary teachers involved in teaching a 4-lesson introduction to programming in the context of a STEM project were involved. The survey was sent to the members of the main association of informatics teachers in the country that groups mostly secondary and a few higher-education teachers. At the same time, the survey was distributed to pre-service teachers attending digital education courses or didactics of informatics in the context of teacher education. We had a total of 64 answers. Data was processed and analyzed using the R Statistical Software [8].

We separated the questions into categories: personal, professional and academic profile, representation of informatics, knowledge in informatics teaching according to TPACK. In the next section, we present an analysis of the obtained answers that helps us answer our research questions, and detail some follow-up methodology used when the results made us want to refine our initial analysis.

4 Results and Discussion

4.1 Demographics

Out of 64 respondents, 29 (45%) are females and 35 (55%) males. We have an equal number of primary and upper-secondary teachers (26), with fewer lower-secondary teachers (9) and a few higher-education teachers (3).

Figures 1 and 2 show the distribution of the informatics education and teaching experience, respectively. To depict this better, this distribution was split into females and males (up and down from the middle horizontal line), and into teaching level (horizontally).

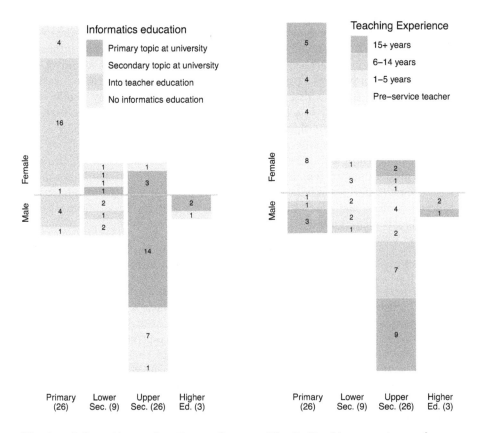

Fig. 1. Informatics education of respondents by gender (above [f] or below [m] the center line) and teaching degree.

Fig. 2. Teaching experience of respondents by gender and teaching degree.

In Fig. 1, the background of each participant has been classified into 4 categories with respect to their education in informatics as an academic discipline: (1) those whose primary field of study at university was informatics; (2) those who studied informatics at a tertiary level but as a secondary topic while having another major; (3) those who had some informatics training during their teacher studies; and (4) those who never had formal informatics education.

In our population, the distribution of genders over the various teaching degrees is far from uniform. Among the primary teachers, there is a large majority of women (81%) while an even larger proportion of upper-secondary teachers are men (85%). Most primary teachers got an education in informatics during their teacher education (77%) and around a fifth of them had no education in informatics at all (19%). Nearly all the upper-secondary teachers had an informatics education at the university (96%), with a distribution of 65% having informatics as their main topic and 31% having it as a second topic.

Lower-secondary teachers are more evenly distributed between genders with 56% of men and 44% of women. And we can observe the same for their informatics education: 22% had it into teacher education while 44% had it at university, but with only one of them as a primary topic. 33% have no informatics education.

Figure 2 shows the teaching experience of our respondents by gender and teaching level. Noteworthy is a twice greater proportion of pre-service teachers at the primary level (8/26) than at the upper-secondary level (4/26). We will come back to this in the analysis later.

This answers RQ1, revealing pronounced gender imbalances, with primary education predominantly female and upper-secondary education largely male, alongside varied informatics education backgrounds, emphasizing the importance of tailored professional development programs to address these discrepancies across different educational tiers.

4.2 Teachers' Degree and Knowledge to Teach Informatics

The major part of the survey consists of assertions related to the knowledge of teachers to teach informatics. The teachers expressed their agreement with each of these assertions on a 5-point Likert scale, ranging from "strongly disagree" (represented with a score of 1) to "strongly agree" (represented with a score of 5). For our analysis, these assertions are mapped to each of the 7 domains of TPACK outline above (although this mapping was by design not explicitly shown to the respondents). Each domain contains between 7 and 10 assertions. The internal consistency of the questions related to each domain was tested with Cronbach's α, which shows results qualified from "good" to "excellent" (CK: 0.94; PK: 0.89; TK: 0.86; PCK: 0.92; TPK: 0.88; TCK: 0.90; TPCK: 0.93).

Here are a few examples of assertions from the survey, with the category into which it is classified followed by the number of questions within the category:

- *CK1: I have sufficient knowledge in the domain "Algorithms and programming".*
- *TK5: I can easily develop my skills in using new computing tools.*
- *TPCK9: I am able to use digital tools to assess my students' knowledge in different domains of informatics.*

For each teacher, we computed the mean of the scores for all the assertions of each domain to get the general score of this teacher on that domain. This provided a 7-dimensional representation of the declarative knowledge of this teacher. We then grouped our respondents according to their teaching level (primary, lower secondary, etc.) and computed the mean and standard deviation of the scores to obtain a global characterisation per teaching level. The resulting whole picture of the knowledge of teachers in the domains of TPACK can be seen in Fig. 3.

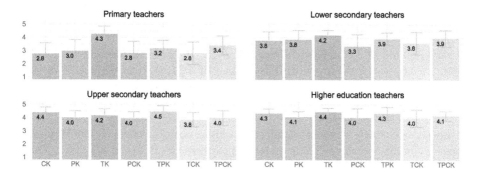

Fig. 3. Knowledge of teachers in the seven domains of TPACK

What Fig. 3 shows us at a glance is that among teachers, primary teachers have the lowest values in most categories; lower-secondary teachers have slightly higher values than them; and upper-secondary teachers as well as higher-education teachers have the highest values, with a very similar profile. The Technological Knowledge (TK) gets the most similar scores between the different profiles of teachers. Primary teachers even outperform upper-secondary teachers on this domain with a score of 4.3 against 4.2.

Taking each teachers' category separately, primary teachers' scores for three domains of TPACK are below the average value of 3, which corresponds to "Neither agree nor disagree" on a 5-point Likert scale (CK: 2.8, PCK: 2.8, TCK: 2.8). These are the domains of knowledge that are rated as the lowest by primary teachers and can be characterised as somehow "negative" as they are under the average value. It's interesting to notice that what is in common between those three domains is the "C", for Content. The knowledge domains that primary teachers declare as the weakest for them have all to do with Content Knowledge, we can then understand that Content Knowledge is perceived by the primary teachers as weak in comparison with others. The domain that particularly stands out from the others is TK with a high score of 4.3, characterizing primary teachers on average slightly higher than the "Agree" level on the assertions about their Technological Knowledge. The PK domain is just on the average with a value of 3, then TPK and TPCK are slightly above the average with 3.2 and 3.4 scores respectively.

We found this relatively low PK result for primary teachers surprising and investigated further. Indeed, primary teachers benefit from a longer training at the University of Teacher Education (180 ECTS) compared to lower-secondary (120 ECTS) and upper-secondary (60 ECTS) teachers—and the PK questions are independent of informatics contents. We hypothesized that the larger proportion of in-service teacher at the primary level (see Fig. 2) could help explain that; however, we were unable to find a statistically significantly different distribution of scores between pre- and in-service primary teachers on the PK score. Our hypothesis is that the primary teachers are more aware of the pedagogical challenges in their classroom, which may exhibit a greater heterogeneity than those in the secondary levels, and are thus more modest in their self-assessment.

For upper-secondary teachers, there is little variation in the average score on each domain of TPACK with high values for all of them, starting with TCK (score of 3.8) and finishing with TPK (score of 4.5). We can deduce from this that upper-secondary teachers' self-efficacy to teach informatics is high. Higher-education teachers have a very similar profile to the upper-secondary teachers in terms of TPACK scores.

Lower-secondary teachers stand in a middle position between primary and upper-secondary teachers. Their scores range from 3.3 (PCK) to 4.2 (TK). They are quite a bit higher than the ones of primary teachers, except for TK, where primary teachers are higher (4.3 versus 4.2). Lower-secondary teachers' scores are all slightly lower than the ones of upper-secondary teachers in all domains, except for TK that has the same score for the two categories of teachers (4.2).

If we compare the profiles of the two lowest categories in terms of knowledge scores, primary and lower-secondary teachers, it is interesting to notice that for both of them, strong points are on TK, TPK and TPCK, three categories where they declare their highest knowledge, and three categories that contain the "T", for Technology. At the same time, the weak points for both of them are on CK, PCK and TCK, three categories where they declare their lowest knowledge, and three categories that contain the "C", for Content.

Standard deviations on each domain for primary teachers and lower-secondary teachers are quite high, while for upper-secondary and higher-education teachers they are low, indicating more variation in all domains of knowledge for primary and lower-secondary teachers.

As a summary for the analysis of Fig. 3, and to provide a part of the answer to RQ2 and RQ3, we can say that primary teachers are the ones who express the lowest level of knowledge, while upper-secondary and higher-education teachers express the highest level of knowledge. Primary and lower-secondary teachers express low self-efficacy in domains related to Content and higher self-efficacy in domains related to Technology, with a wide variation between the individuals. Technological Knowledge stands as the only domain with high scores for all teachers. For teacher education, we can conclude that primary and lower-secondary teachers are mostly in need of education related to the content of informatics and less on technological aspects. It should also be taken into account that there might be a great diversity of profiles in these categories of individuals.

4.3 Distribution of Teachers and Knowledge to Teach Informatics

Establishing teacher profiles using seven dimensions is challenging. We wanted to obtain a better characterisation of a reduced number of typical profiles—at first, independently of the teaching level, gender, or background. We thus performed a reduction of dimensionality followed by a cluster analysis according to the following procedure, using as data the 7 obtained averages on the 7 TPACK domains for each teacher. To this end, we:

1. Performed a Principal Component Analysis (PCA) on our data to estimate the number of principal components or dimensions that we would keep;
2. Executed a Factor Analysis (FA) with the new dimensions to determine the correlation between our original variables and the new dimensions;
3. Computed the coordinates of all our individuals in the new dimensions.

For Step 1, the inspection of the scree plot of the PCA (not shown here for space constraints) indicates that two dimensions seem to be the best choice. The percentage of variance explained by the first two dimensions is high, especially for Dimension 1 (79.05%, and 8.11% for Dimension 2).

Table 1. Loadings for the two factors obtained from the Factor Analysis

Domain of TPACK	Dimension 1	Dimension 2
CK	0.071	0.943
TK	0.177	0.718
PCK	0.706	0.262
PK	0.722	−0.363
TPK	0.803	0.073
TCK	0.534	0.397
TPCK	0.902	0.109

The loadings listed in Table 1 show us that the PK, PCK, TPK, TPCK (and in a more moderate way, TCK) means are correlated with Dimension 1 and that CK and TK variables are strongly correlated with Dimension 2. We now try to better interpret the obtained dimensions.

All the domains of TPACK with high loadings on Dimension 1 contain a pedagogical component (P), except for TCK that has more balanced loadings between Dimensions 1 and 2. This suggests that Dimension 1 is strongly related to pedagogy. At the same time, all the domains with "composed" knowledge have high loadings on Dimension 1, showing that this dimension is related to compound knowledge, which typically appears when teachers deal at the same time with an interrelation of Content, Pedagogical or Technological Knowledge. This kind of interrelated knowledge with a mix of content and pedagogy is what we usually identify as *didactics*. We propose to call this Dimension 1 "Didactical Competencies".

Dimension 2, with strong loadings from CK and TK, suggests a focus on core knowledge areas in content and technology. We propose to call this Dimension 2 "Content and Technology Foundations".

The Factor Analysis gave us a score for each respondent on the two dimensions that shows their level of association with them. We can then plot the distribution of our individuals on these two dimensions. In order to identify groups of teachers among this distribution, we performed a k-means clustering on the scores of our teachers on Dimensions 1 and 2.

To determine the number of clusters we should have, we computed a distance matrix with the scores of teachers and performed an agglomerative hierarchical clustering using Ward's method. Looking at the produced dendrogram (not shown here due to space constraints), we decided to keep six clusters for our analysis as a balanced solution to group our individuals. Using the resulting classification of our individuals into those six clusters, we computed with their scores a means point for each cluster. We used these points as initial centroids and applied a k-means clustering that optimises the assignment of teachers to clusters. As a result, we can plot the distribution of our teachers on the two reduced dimensions of TPACK, "Didactical Competencies" and "Content and Technology Foundations", showing the clusters they belong to and also their teaching level. It is depicted in Fig. 4.

Looking at the position of the different clusters as in Fig. 4, we can interpret their characteristics and propose a name for each of them.

- *Cluster 1—Content Mastery Educators.* High scores in Content and Technology Foundations (y-axis) and moderate scores in Didactical Competencies (x-axis). Teachers in this cluster demonstrate advanced skills in content and technology and competent didactical skills, but for this second dimension not as advanced as those in Cluster 2.
- *Cluster 2—Advanced Informatics Educators.* High scores in both dimensions. Teachers in this group exhibit strong didactical competencies coupled with a solid foundation in content and technology.
- *Cluster 3—Emerging Educators.* Negative scores in both dimensions. This group shows noticeable deficiencies in both didactical competencies as well as content and technology.
- *Cluster 4—Didactics-Focused Educators.* Negative scores in Content and Technology Foundations (y-axis), but more moderate scores in Didactical Competencies (x-axis), with some individuals reaching modest positive scores. Teachers in this group exhibit didactical skills that are developing, but lack advancement in content and technology.
- *Cluster 5—Content-Focused Educators.* Negative scores in Didactical Competencies (x-axis), but more moderate scores in Content and Technology Foundations (y-axis), with some individuals reaching modest positive scores. Teachers in this cluster show relative strength in content and technology but a need for significant improvement in didactical skills.
- *Cluster 6—Novice Educators.* Lowest scores in both dimensions, particularly in Content and Technology Foundations (y-axis). This group is markedly behind in both didactical skills as well as content and technology knowledge.

In Fig. 4, we also represent the teaching level of the teachers. We can see that Clusters 1 (Content Mastery Educators) and 2 (Advanced Informatics Educators), with the highest scores on TPACK, are overwhelmingly populated by

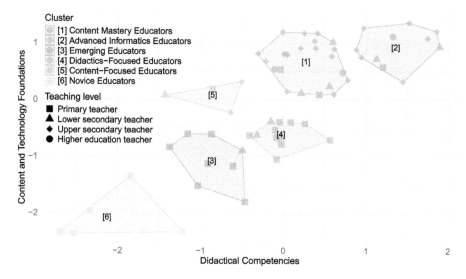

Fig. 4. Distribution of teachers according to the two dimensions of the TPACK Knowledge, with the cluster represented by the colors and the teaching level by the shape of the points.

upper-secondary teachers. The higher-education teachers also belong to these two groups. In contrast, there are only two primary teachers here, one per cluster.

Clusters 3 (Emerging Educators) and 6 (Novice Educators), with the lowest scores on TPACK, are populated almost exclusively by primary teachers, with the exception of one lower primary teacher as one of the individuals with the highest scores in Cluster 3.

Cluster 4 (Didactics-Focused Educators), with medium scores on Didactical Competencies but low scores on Content and Technology Foundations, is composed by a majority of primary teachers with few lower-secondary teachers.

Cluster 5 (Content-Focused Educators), with medium scores on Content and Technology Foundations but low scores on Didactical Competencies, is a small cluster composed of a majority of lower and upper-secondary teachers, with one primary teacher.

Going beyond the teaching level shown here, we were interested to know whether teaching experience was related to the two identified dimensions of the Factor Analysis; i.e., if didactical competencies and/or knowledge in the foundations of content and technology improved along with experience. Our data shows it is not the case, as none of these dimensions reveals significant correlation with the number of years of experience ($\rho_{\text{dim.1}} \approx -0.012$ and $\rho_{\text{dim.2}} \approx 0.002$).

5 Conclusion and Outlook

This study provides insights into the knowledge of teachers to teach informatics across different educational levels in French-speaking Switzerland. Through an analysis utilizing the TPACK framework, we identified specific areas where teachers may require additional support, a dimensionality reduction followed by a clustering analysis revealed distinct teacher profiles, ranging from advanced informatics educators with strong didactical competencies to novice educators with deficiencies in both content and technology knowledge. Our analysis highlighted the significant difference between primary and upper-secondary teachers.

Our takeaways regarding teacher education programs are (a) the need for a stronger focus on the contents of informatics for primary and lower secondary; (b) the need for strong didactical aspects on all levels; and (c) the lack of need for further emphasis on the technological aspects. Additionally, efforts should be made to promote gender diversity in informatics education.

Our research, of course, has limits. We are aware of the fact that a survey can only capture a reduced form of knowledge, self-assessed and declarative, and is not representative of the complete knowledge that teachers have. In further research, we wish to complete our study with observations about the enacted form of knowledge manifested in the classroom to get a broader picture of teachers' knowledge to teach informatics.

Appendix A—Survey Statements

Translated from French into English

CK1: I have sufficient knowledge in the field "Algorithms and programming".
CK2: I have sufficient knowledge in the field "Computer systems and networks".
CK3: I have sufficient knowledge in the field "Data representation".
CK4: I have sufficient knowledge in the field "Digital technologies and society".
CK5: I am able to establish links between informatics concepts from different fields.
CK6: I am constantly reinforcing and enriching my knowledge of informatics.
CK7: I have sufficient knowledge to deal with concepts and subjects related to my discipline (informatics).
CK8: I am able to think and approach my discipline (informatics) as an expert in my field.
TK1: I can easily use a variety of technological tools (computer, tablet, smartphone, beamer, interactive whiteboard, etc.).
TK2: I can effectively use a variety of computer systems (MacOS, Linux, Android, iOS...).
TK3: I can easily use a variety of general-purpose applications (such as word processing, spreadsheet, presentation software, etc.).
TK4: I can easily use a variety of web applications or services (e-mail, search engines, blogs, wikis, forums, social media, etc.).
TK5: I can easily develop my skills in using new computing tools.
TK6: I can solve technical problems with a variety of computer systems and software (PC, computer lab, etc.).
TK7: I can develop programs in professional programming languages (e.g. Java, Python, C/C++, PHP, JavaScript...).
TK8: I can easily manipulate programmable devices (e.g. Arduino, Raspberry...).
PK1: I can organize my teaching (e.g. maintain pedagogical control of my class, choose the appropriate level of difficulty, manage time and space, etc.).

PK2: I can adapt my teaching choices to the heterogeneity of the class.
PK3: I can manage classroom interaction to guide pupils' work.
PK4: I can plan learning activities (e.g. create successive logical sequences).
PK5: I am able to implement activities in my classroom (e.g. investigation, problem solving, collaborative learning, project-based, creativity and innovation activities, etc.).
PK6: I am able to assess my pupils' learning.
PK7: I know effective ways of guiding students' reflection on their own learning.
PK8: I can organize my classroom environment to motivate students to learn.
PK9: I can make links between my classroom practice and educational theories.
PCK1: I can implement effective teaching strategies to support learning in the field "Algorithms and programming".
PCK2: I can implement effective teaching strategies to support learning in the field "Computer systems and networks".
PCK3: I can implement effective teaching strategies to support learning in the field "Data representation".
PCK4: I can implement effective teaching strategies to support learning in the field "Digital technologies and society".
PCK5: I can consider learning difficulties (e.g. pupils' misconceptions) in relation to the concepts-processes of the informatics discipline.
PCK6: I know how to design varied teaching activities in relation with the content (e.g. investigation, problem solving and project-based for informatics).
PCK7: I can implement specific activities to foster student collaboration, creativity and innovation in informatics.
PCK8: I am able to implement interdisciplinary learning activities with informatics (e.g. STEM, STEAM...).
PCK9: I am able to implement unplugged activities for my pupils (activities without computers).
PCK10: I am able to assess my pupils' knowledge of different domains of informatics.
TPK1: I am able to select appropriate digital tools to improve student learning outcomes.
TPK2: I am able to select digital tools that are consistent with my teaching strategies.
TPK3: I am able to help my pupils use digital technology appropriately for learning purposes.
TPK4: I am able to help my pupils use Internet tools to find the information they need for their own learning.
TPK5: I can use specific digital tools in inquiry-based and problem-solving learning activities.
TPK6: I am able to use specific digital tools in collaborative learning activities.
TPK7: I am able to use digital tools to design and organize student assessment.
TPK8: I am able to use educational programming environments (e.g. Scratch, Blockly...) to improve student learning outcomes.
TPK9: I am able to use robotics and automation software and devices to improve student learning outcomes.
TCK1: I know digital tools that are appropriate for approaching the various fields of informatics.
TCK2: I am familiar with digital tools that are suitable for presenting concepts-processes in my subject that are difficult to represent by other means (e.g. simulations of algorithms).
TCK3: I am familiar with digital tools that can enhance students' conceptual understanding.
TCK4: I can choose appropriate digital tools for a progressive implementation of the content.
TCK5: I can identify the functions and working methods of different types of software.
TCK6: I am able to develop projects in educational programming languages (e.g. Scratch, ScratchJr, Blockly, etc.) to tackle informatics content.
TCK7: I am able to use educational robotics to approach informatics content.
TPCK1: I am able to implement investigation, problem-solving and project-based activities in informatics using digital tools.
TPCK2: I am able to implement activities that foster student collaboration, creativity and innovation in informatics using digital tools.
TPCK3: I am able to implement interdisciplinary learning activities with informatics (e.g. STEM, STEAM...) using digital tools.

TPCK4: I am able to implement activities in informatics using various software applications and web services.
TPCK5: I am able to implement teaching strategies that effectively combine digital tools and appropriate pedagogical approaches in the field "Algorithms and Programming".
TPCK6: I am able to implement teaching strategies that effectively combine digital tools and appropriate pedagogical approaches in the field "Computer systems and networks".
TPCK7: I am able to implement teaching strategies that effectively combine digital tools and appropriate pedagogical approaches in the field "Data representation".
TPCK8: I am able to implement teaching strategies that effectively combine digital tools and appropriate pedagogical approaches in the field "Digital technologies and society".
TPCK9: I am able to use digital tools to assess my students' knowledge in different fields of informatics.
TPCK10: I am able to assess the match between teaching strategies, content in informatics and digital tools.

References

1. Angeli, C., Valanides, N., Christodoulou, A.: Theoretical considerations of technological pedagogical content knowledge. In: Handbook of Technological Pedagogical Content Knowledge (TPACK) for Educators, pp. 11–32. Routledge (2016)
2. Bell, T., Andreae, P., Lambert, L.: Computer science in New Zealand high schools. In: Proceedings of the Twelfth Australasian Conference on Computing Education, vol. 103, pp. 15–22 (2010)
3. Brown, N.C.C., Sentance, S., Crick, T., Humphreys, S.: Restart: the resurgence of computer science in UK schools. ACM Trans. Comput. Educ. **14**(2), 9:1–9:22 (2014). https://doi.org/10.1145/2602484
4. Hubwieser, P.: Computer science education in secondary schools - the introduction of a new compulsory subject. ACM Trans. Comput. Educ. **12**(4), 1–41 (2012). https://doi.org/10.1145/2382564.2382568
5. Komis, V., Bachy, S., Goletti, O., Parriaux, G., Rafalska, M., Lavidas, K.: Connaissances du contenu et connaissances technologiques des enseignants en Informatique en milieu francophone. Review of Science, Mathematics and ICT Education (2022)
6. Kong, S.C., Lai, M., Sun, D.: Teacher development in computational thinking: design and learning outcomes of programming concepts, practices and pedagogy. Comput. Educ. **151**(2019), 103872 (2020). https://doi.org/10.1016/j.compedu.2020.103872
7. Mishra, P., Koehler, M.J.: Technological pedagogical content knowledge: a framework for teacher knowledge. Teach. Coll. Rec. **108**(6), 1017–1054 (2006)
8. R Core Team: R: A Language and Environment for Statistical Computing. Vienna, Austria (2024). https://www.R-project.org/
9. Sadler, P.M., Sonnert, G., Coyle, H.P., Cook-Smith, N., Miller, J.L.: The influence of teachers' knowledge on student learning in middle school physical science classrooms. Am. Educ. Res. J. **50**(5), 1020–1049 (2013)
10. Shulman, L.S.: Those who understand: knowledge growth in teaching. Educ. Res. **15**(2), 4–14 (1986). https://doi.org/10.30827/profesorado.v23i3.11230
11. Vivian, R., Falkner, K.: Identifying teachers' technological pedagogical content knowledge for computer science in the primary years. In: ICER 2019 - Proceedings of the 2019 ACM Conference on International Computing Education Research, pp. 147–155 (2019). https://doi.org/10.1145/3291279.3339410

Exploring Transformative Professional Development Within K-12 Computing Education

Sue Sentance[1]( ), Robert Whyte[1,2], and Diana Kirby[1,2]

[1] Raspberry Pi Computing Education Research Centre, University of Cambridge, Cambridge, UK
{ss2600,rw724,dgk21}@cam.ac.uk
[2] Raspberry Pi Foundation, Cambridge, UK

Abstract. Many computing educators find themselves teaching a subject that is relatively new to them, making access to high-quality, effective professional development (PD) essential. However computing education research does not always unpack the approach being taken to PD, which may reflect underpinning values and beliefs about teachers' role in the process. The study reported in this paper set out to explore computing PD opportunities using Kennedy's framework of transformative, malleable and transmissive PD, whereby 'transformative' PD refers to approaches that encourage collaborative inquiry and critical professionalism. In the study, 341 computing teachers in primary and secondary education in the UK and Ireland reported on PD they had considered impactful. Results showed that most teachers highlighted transmissive forms of PD as being impactful, primarily delivery-focused training courses, and only 18 teachers described PD categorised as transformative. Most teachers reported that PD was impactful if it built on their prior knowledge. As it is likely that many PD programs are designed around transmissive approaches to PD, we argue that computing teachers should be supported to engage with a broader range of PD opportunities, particularly those that are focused on inquiry and teacher agency.

Keywords: computing education · K-12 education · teacher education

1 Introduction

Professional development (PD) for in-service computing teachers takes many forms, from short training sessions to formal qualifications undertaken part-time. Within general education PD research, the forms and modalities of PD have long been researched, with meta-analyses highlighting that effective PD is likely to be collaborative and sustained over time [8,15]. Other research has focused on the need for PD to support the development of 'critical professionalism' [4], and the term 'transformative' PD has been coined to describe ways of supporting teacher agency and inquiry [4,17,21].

In the field of computing education[1], the notion of transformative PD is not often discussed (an exception would be [25]). The delivery of PD in the form of workshops and training for teachers is common [20], and often around subject knowledge [11]. Computing is a new subject for many in-service teachers, who are likely to request subject knowledge training. However, there has been criticism of PD that implies a deficit in the teacher, rather than drawing on a teacher's strengths and existing experience [16]. In this paper, we were interested to investigate what PD teachers reported as impactful, and to align that to research on transformative PD. The survey-based study described here involved 341 teachers from the United Kingdom and Ireland, with both qualitative and quantitative analysis conducted on the responses. This represents an initial exploration into the way that we conceptualise PD and its benefits for computing teachers.

The five countries investigated in this study - England, Scotland, Wales, Northern Ireland and the Republic of Ireland - vary greatly in population size, from 56.55 m (England) to 1.9 m (Northern Ireland), and in the way they have implemented computing. Education is a devolved matter in the UK, such that national parliaments and legislatures have responsibility for their respective education systems, the development of curricula and the provision of teacher training. In **England**, Computing has been a mandatory subject for children aged 5–16 since 2014, and an elective subject from age 16 since the 1970s [7]. The National Centre for Computing Education (NCCE) has offered teacher training and resource development in computing since 2018 [29]. **Scotland**'s curriculum was updated in 2016, although computing science has been available as a discrete and elective subject at the secondary level for many years. Pupils have an entitlement from age 3 to 15 to a Broad General Education (BGE) which includes Technologies. In **Wales**, the new 2022 Curriculum for Wales [34] reinforces the societal importance of digital competence as a statutory cross-curricular skill alongside literacy and numeracy for all learners aged 3–16, and the Technocamps project offers training to improve teacher confidence and capability to deliver the curriculum [22]. In **Northern Ireland**, digital skills are included from primary through to upper secondary as part of *Using ICT*. Finally, the **Republic of Ireland** has offered a Leaving Certificate in Computer Science since 2018, with an associated program of PD for teachers.

2 Transformative Professional Development

Teacher PD is an essential part of improving school performance and learner outcomes [2], and a large field of study that has been researched for decades. Recent work has placed an emphasis on the importance of long-term, inquiry or learner-centered structures that support teachers as they collaboratively develop the professional knowledge they need to use in their own context [3]. In computing, PD courses take many different forms, for example, online MOOC-style PD [26, 35], remotely-delivered but asynchronous courses [24], or face-to-face courses

---

[1] Computing is a generic term we use throughout to include computer science (CS), computing science, informatics and other CS-related subjects.

of varying lengths [23]. However, equating PD with 'training' alone risks forgetting many other approaches to professional learning that may impact teachers' confidence and classroom practice. Other approaches to PD that have been explored in the computing PD literature include belonging to a community of practice (CoP) or professional learning network (PLN) [31], working towards accredited qualifications [30], peer coaching [6], co-designing activities [14], and action research [5].

Kennedy [16,17] developed a framework of models of PD using a spectrum from transmissive to transformative PD (see Fig. 1). The first level of PD, transmissive, includes approaches such as training, deficit models and the cascade model, which "attend primarily to occupational aspects of professional learning" [12, p.165]. The second level, 'malleable', includes models such as award-bearing PD and CoPs, indicating that these types or models of PD can be used to different ends depending on the intended (or unintended) purpose [17]. The spectrum indicates an increasing capacity for autonomy and teacher agency in the transformative direction. The third level of PD, 'transformative' is focused on collaborative professional inquiry, defined as:

> "...all models and experiences that include an element of collaborative problem identification and subsequent activity, where the subsequent activity involves inquiring into one's own practice and understanding more about other practice, perhaps through engagement with existing research" [17, p. 693]

Purpose of Model		Examples of models of CPD which may fit within this category
Transmissive		Training models
		Deficit models
	Increasing capacity for professional autonomy and teacher agency	Cascade model
Malleable		Award-bearing models
		Standards-based models
		Coaching/mentoring models
		Community of practice models
Transformative	↓	Collaborative professional inquiry models

Fig. 1. Spectrum of PD models [17]

Other researchers give different descriptions of what constitutes transformative PD. Mockler [21] describes transformative PD as that which aims for the transformation of society, in that teachers learn to support students to think critically. Sachs chooses to categorise PD as *retooling, remodelling, revitalising* and *reimagining* [28], with 'reimagining' described as transformative in its intent and practice; teachers are individually and collectively equipped to act as "shapers, promoters and well-informed critics of reforms" [28, p.160]. In their review of transformative PD, Boylan et al. [4] assert that although transformative PD is yet a small field, its importance lies in its focus on the critical professionalism of the educator. It therefore provides a valuable lens through which to examine computing teachers' reporting of their own PD experiences.

Research in computing PD has already emphasised the importance of PD that is based on inquiry and communities of practice (e.g. [13,27,31]). Although not explicitly labelled as 'transformative', it exemplifies PD that supports teachers as critical professionals. The study in this paper aimed to investigate the extent to which teachers in a specific set of countries accessed these opportunities and found them impactful. Thus, the research questions are framed as follows:

RQ1 What professional development opportunities do computing teachers in the UK and Ireland describe as impactful to their practice?
RQ2 To what extent can teachers' impactful experiences be described as transformative PD?

3 Methodology

The study was conducted via the development, distribution and analysis of a survey, based on **ME**asuring **T**eache**R E**nacted **C**omputing **C**urriculum (METRECC), a validated survey instrument developed by an international Innovation and Technology in Computer Science Education (ITiCSE) working group in 2019 [10]. METRECC was designed to measure aspects of the experiences of computing teachers around the world and since 2019 has been used with teachers in 14 different countries. The METRECC survey is openly available for researchers to use.[2]

3.1 Data Collection

The METRECC survey was localised for UK and Ireland teachers [32]. To answer the RQs, three new questions were added to METRECC as follows:

1. Description of one PD activity that had the greatest impact on one's teaching in the last 12 months (free text).
2. Length of the PD activity (free text).
3. Factors that contributed to the PD being impactful (16 check boxes).

Other questions about PD for teachers included in the survey related to (i) participation in a range of PD types (10) in the last 12 months, (ii) barriers to participation in professional development, and (iii) localised questions for teachers in England, Wales and Ireland about their participation in national initiatives. Because these questions relate to participation and not impact, they are not the focus of this study but are reported elsewhere [18].

---
[2] https://csedresearch.org/resources/evaluation-instruments/tool/?id=185. Data relating to the current study will be made available as supplementary material.

The survey was open to respondents in England, Scotland, Wales, Northern Ireland and Ireland in February and March 2022. Purposive sampling was used to identify computing teachers, using methods including mailing lists, newsletters, blog posts, social media, promotion through school and teacher networks. Snowball sampling was also used with participants encouraged to share the survey with other computing teachers. The whole survey was completed by 512 teachers, with 359 entering responses for the three additional questions. The overall findings are reported elsewhere [32].

3.2 Data Analysis

The data relating to the type of PD found to be impactful was coded using a phronetic iterative approach [33] that drew on Kennedy's framework. The initial intent was to use the nine models from Kennedy's 2014 article (see Fig. 1) deductively when coding. It was clear that we were not able to definitively determine which model we could ascribe so inductive coding was used to develop codes for the PD, which were aligned to Kennedy's models where appropriate, and subsequently assigned to the three top-level areas of transmissive, malleable and transformative. Two of the three researchers worked together to determine the coding scheme over three iterations, until consensus was reached. Length of engagement with PD is also relevant to its effectiveness and potentially transformative nature [8], so the teachers' answer on length was used to further refine the coding. A third researcher then coded a 15% sample of the data with an inter-rater agreement via Cohen's Kappa calculated as $\kappa = 0.86$ indicating strong agreement [19]. The final coding scheme used for analysis is shown in Table 1.

Having allocated all statements to categories and types of PD, we compared them with the following teacher characteristics: experience of teaching CS, age, gender, and qualification level. Teachers also selected factors that supported their description of impactful PD and these were also compared with the types. Descriptive and inferential statistical analysis were used to investigate the relationships between these variables. Specifically, Chi-squared tests for independence were used to compare categorical variables with cellwise residual analysis [1] alongside Kruskal-Wallis tests with Dunn's pairwise comparisons for ranked variables [9].

4 Results

Of the 359 responses to the questions about impactful PD, 341 remained once 'none' or equivalent answers were excluded. Most teachers responding were from England (75.4%) with all other countries represented. Teachers wrote between 1 and 97 words ($M = 9.58$, $SD = 10.76$). The length of the PD described as impactful varied from one hour to a year. Table 1 shows the breakdown of transmissive, malleable and transformative PD against the coding scheme.

Most of the PD reported as impactful was classified as *transmissive* (63.5%). This included 158 (46.5%) instances of training, which ranged from face-to-face training events of several hours to lengthier online courses:

Table 1. Impactful PD categorised by Kennedy's types

Type	Coded	n	%
Transmissive	Training	158	46.5%
	Achievement of certificate	48	14.1%
	Using curriculum resources	8	2.4%
	Training others (cascade)	2	0.6%
	Sub-total	**216**	**63.5%**
Malleable	Self-study	31	9.1%
	Participating in a network/community	29	8.5%
	Accredited qualification	17	5.0%
	Mentoring/observation/coaching activities	14	4.1%
	Attending conference	8	2.4%
	Collaborating within department or school	5	1.5%
	Mentoring others (specifically)	2	0.6%
	Examining for awarding body	1	0.3%
	Sub-total	**107**	**31.5%**
Transformative	Creation of curriculum resources	5	1.5%
	Engagement with research	5	1.5%
	Participation in research projects	4	1.2%
	Leading a network/community	2	0.6%
	Practitioner research or inquiry	2	0.6%
	Sub-total	**18**	**5.3%**

"I have attended online webinars ... which have focused on the teaching of computing with their materials. It has been really useful to get more PD about basics of computer science especially the vocabulary and also ideas for how to start with the youngest pupils."

The type of PD in which teachers have participated is clearly dependent on what is offered. The NCCE [29] has been set up to deliver PD in England, including certified courses, and accounts for many of the experiences that teachers found impactful. Similarly, in the Republic of Ireland, a number of courses and workshops are made available to support the delivery of the new Leaving Certificate and other courses:

"Attending the different CSInc workshops that are held online. Great presenters and the material is delivered with energy that makes you interested."

We distinguished between teachers achieving a certificate (transmissive) and those undertaking accredited qualifications (malleable), using the criteria that achieving a certificate represented participation in a shorter period of training, and a qualification had to be formally assessed and involve some self-directed activity. We noted that a number of teachers were working towards qualifications, including Master's degrees, university-led modules with accreditation, and leadership qualifications that would take months or years to achieve:

"I have just completed an MA Education, this included research on PRIMM."

Also in the malleable category, we included participating in a network (8.5%) and self-study (9.1%) with a number of examples given:

"Sitting and tinkering with micro:bits, MakeCode Arcade has had the greatest impact in the last 12 months."

Only 18 statements were classified in the transformative category, including participating in a research project, engaging with research in another way, or leading a group of teachers in a network. One response refers to participation in a co-creation research activity around culturally responsive teaching in computing:

"A ...PD activity that has greatly helped my teaching is being part of a working group in helping to produce culturally relevant guidelines for the CS curriculum to be used by fellow CS educators. "

Another response from a primary teacher refers to the setting up of a network for other teachers:

"... computing network group set up, to have regular training updates, discussions and share ideas and resources with one another. "

Considering the reasons given for PD being impactful (Table 2), the most common factor given was that it built on prior knowledge ($n = 288$, 84.46%) followed by PD with coherent structure ($n = 221$, 64.81%) and the content being appropriate to teachers' subject teaching needs ($n = 221$, 64.81%). Less than half of the impactful PD activities focused on pedagogy ($n = 163$, 47.80%) or assessment ($n = 106$, 31.09%).

We investigated coded PD types against factors for why PD was impactful using a series of post-hoc Chi-Squared tests. We found significant associations between certain PD types and a range of factors. For transmissive PD experiences, teachers were more likely to state that they had a coherent structure (4.0, $p < .05$) and that they provided opportunities for active learning (3.5, $p < .05$). Conversely, teachers were less likely to suggest that transformative PD experiences had a coherent structure (3.1, $p < .05$) or that they took place over an extended period of time (2.7, $p < .05$). Teachers were more likely to report that participating in professional learning networks provided networking opportunities (4.4, $p < .05$), while self-study PD opportunities were less likely to do so (4.1, $p < .05$). Using curriculum resources and mentoring and coaching activities were more likely to take place in school settings (4.2, $p < .05$ and 3.8, $p < .05$,

Table 2. Number of teachers who selected each factor, ordered by most popular responses

Factors that made PD impactful	n	%
It built on my prior knowledge	288	84.46
It had a coherent structure	221	64.81
It appropriately focused on content needed to teach my subjects	221	64.81
It provided opportunities for active learning	191	56.01
It provided opportunities to practice/apply new ideas and knowledge in my own classroom	185	54.25
It addressed pedagogy	163	47.80
It provided networking opportunities	152	44.57
It took place over an extended period of time (e.g. several weeks or longer)	147	43.11
It provided opportunities for collaborative learning	146	42.82
It adapted to my personal development needs	129	37.83
It addressed assessment of student learning	106	31.09
It focused on innovation in my teaching.	102	29.91
It provided follow-up activities	95	27.86
It took place at my school	33	9.68
It involved most colleagues from my school	11	3.23
None of the above	2	0.59

respectively). Finally, pursuing formal qualifications or certified PD courses was more likely to take place over an extended period of time (5.7, $p < .05$ and 3.3, $p < .05$, respectively); conversely, participating in professional learning networks was less likely to take place over an extended period of time (3.6, $p < .05$).

Finally, as teacher responses were part of a larger survey, we were able to investigate the relationship between impactful PD type and other responses, including age, gender, CS teaching experience, phase of teaching and highest qualification. No significant findings were noted.

5 Discussion

We sought to answer the following questions: *RQ1) What professional development opportunities do computing teachers in the UK and Ireland describe as impactful to their practice?* and *RQ2) To what extent can teachers' impactful experiences be described as transformative PD?*. We were interested to find out whether teachers reporting their experiences of PD were engaging in the kind of PD that scholars have been describing as transformative, for example whether they were engaging in collaborative inquiry [17] or critical professionalism [4].

For RQ1, we found that while teachers described a range of activities, nearly half answered the question by describing a particular training course or workshop. They also found benefits in other activities classified as malleable, including PLNs, engaging with colleagues, working towards qualifications, and mentoring activities. When we investigated whether there was any particular relationship with the other data that we had collected in the rest of the survey, such as the qualifications held by the teachers, the length of time they've been teaching, computing, their age, their gender and the reasons that they had chosen those particular types of PD to report as impactful, we didn't find any significant relationships. Correlations between type of PD and factors that supported their choice were not surprising, apart from the relationship between length and transformative PD, which may have been due to the small sample. Overall, if the type of PD teachers are choosing is not related significantly to those factors it could well be driven by what is being delivered locally. It is encouraging that teachers are finding courses and workshops to be impactful and beneficial to their practice. Further research is needed to investigate the extent to which this type of PD might transform teaching in the longer term.

For RQ2, we identified 18 teacher statements that we could align to the notion of transformative PD as described (e.g. by [17,21,28]). Four teachers participated in research projects run by universities, two had carried out their own practitioner research projects and five had more generally engaged with research; this represents being more inquiring about the subject of computing. As there were only 18 responses that we could code as one of the transformative approaches to PD, the analysis that could be conducted around why these types of PD had impact was limited. Further research is needed to investigate the types of PD that are made available to teachers in each of the five jurisdictions.

In their review of transformational PD, Boylan et al. discuss purpose, agency, sociality and knowledge as four characteristics that can be used in analysis [4]. The development of the sociality aspect of transformative PD can create increased trust between teachers and with communities [4] and we saw evidence of this in the creation of networks and peer engagement, although we aligned with Kennedy in classifying some of this as 'malleable'. In terms of knowledge, being engaged with research can constitute a more critical analysis of pedagogy and curriculum, although we did not see any evidence of engagement with social justice issues. From our data, we were not able to ascertain specific *purposes* of the transformational PD, or to observe the development of teacher agency.

Increasingly, computing is a subject which is seen at the forefront of discussions around social and ethical issues, including privacy, bias, decision-making, and internet safety. As these topics become core elements of curricula, it is important for teachers to engage in inquiry and to develop criticality about the nature of computing education. If we are going to break down barriers and make the subject inclusive for all, then what we teach, what resources we use, what examples we use, and how we assess, are all areas with which teachers can critically engage. Education in some jurisdictions may be situated in a political backdrop that has systemically reduced teacher autonomy [21]; discussion of this issue is beyond the scope of this paper.

Transformative PD may include trying new pedagogy in the classroom, investigating research into subject-specific pedagogy or actively establishing networks to facilitate collaborative inquiry among peers. Such forms of PD may be less easy to scale as they involve experimentation, discussion and reflection, but are important if young people are going to be able to participate in an increasingly technological society, with an understanding of its benefits and risks. Through a transformative teaching profession we can develop "critical, literate, socially aware citizens with a strong sense of their own civic responsibility" [21, p.738].

One limitation of the study was that the questions were added to an already lengthy survey, meaning that teachers' responses were not as detailed as we might have liked. The rationale for such a design was to investigate the relationships between impactful PD and other characteristics; however as reported, there were no significant findings in this regard. Further research involving interviews or focus groups would facilitate a more in-depth analysis and enable exploration of the ways in which teachers perceive PD offered to them and its impact.

6 Conclusion

This paper represents an initial attempt to consider computing PD through the lens of transformative PD, supporting increased teacher agency, autonomy and criticality. Computing is a subject interfacing with societal, ethical and political discourses, and computing education encompasses its impact, as well as the basic principles of the subject. The results from this study indicate that only a small number of computing teachers in the UK and Ireland report finding transformative PD impactful, with the majority reporting that an instance of PD classified as transmissive had the most benefit to their teaching and learning. The results are clearly dependent on the type of PD offered. Given that teachers new to computing are likely regarded as having a deficit in subject knowledge, PD opportunities may be largely restricted to delivery-focused workshops and courses. With a growing interest in transformative PD and the way in which it supports teacher agency and critical teacher professionalism [4], and given that more teachers will have experience of computing teaching as it becomes embedded into the curriculum, we suggest further research is needed to investigate the effectiveness of computing PD that increases autonomy and agency, such as engaging with research and inquiry-focused professional networks.

Acknowledgments. We are very grateful to our collaborators for their work on this project: Irene Bell, Elizabeth Cole, Tom Crick, Nicola Looker and Keith Quille.

References

1. Beasley, T.M., Schumacker, R.E.: Multiple regression approach to analyzing contingency tables: post hoc and planned comparison procedures. J. Exp. Educ. **64**(1), 79–93 (1995)

2. Bolam, R.: Emerging policy trends: some implications for continuing professional development. J. In-Serv. Educ. **26**(2), 267–280 (2000). https://doi.org/10.1080/13674580000200113
3. Borko, H., Jacobs, J., Koellner, K.: Contemporary approaches to teacher professional development. In: Peterson, P., Baker, E., McGaw, B. (eds.) International Encyclopedia of Education (Third Edition), 3rd edn, pp. 548 – 556. Elsevier, Oxford (2010). https://doi.org/10.1016/B978-0-08-044894-7.00654-0
4. Boylan, M., Adams, G., Perry, E., Booth, J.: Re-imagining transformative professional learning for critical teacher professionalism: a conceptual review. Prof. Dev. Educ. 1–19 (2023)
5. Brandes, O., Armoni, M.: Using action research to distill research-based segments of pedagogical content knowledge of k-12 computer science teachers. In: Proceedings of the 2019 ACM Conference on Innovation and Technology in Computer Science Education, pp. 485–491 (2019)
6. Cateté, V., Alvarez, L., Isvik, A., Milliken, A., Hill, M., Barnes, T.: Aligning theory and practice in teacher professional development for computer science. In: Proceedings of the 20th Koli Calling International Conference on Computing Education Research, pp. 1–11 (2020)
7. Clark, M.A.C., Boyle, R.D.: Computer science in english high schools: we lost the S, now the C is going. In: Mittermeir, R.T. (ed.) ISSEP 2006. LNCS, vol. 4226, pp. 83–93. Springer, Heidelberg (2006). https://doi.org/10.1007/11915355_8
8. Cordingley, P., Bell, M., Holdich, K., Hawkins, M., Crisp, P.: Understanding what enables high-quality professional learning. Technical report, Centre for the Use of Research and Evidence in Education (CUREE) (2013)
9. Elliott, A.C., Hynan, L.S.: A SAS® macro implementation of a multiple comparison post hoc test for a Kruskal-Wallis analysis. Comput. Methods Programs Biomed. **102**(1), 75–80 (2011)
10. Falkner, K., et al.: An international study piloting the MEasuring TeacheR Enacted Computing Curriculum (METRECC) instrument. In: Proceedings of the Working Group Reports on Innovation and Technology in Computer Science Education, Aberdeen Scotland UK, pp. 111–142. ACM (2019). https://doi.org/10.1145/3344429.3372505
11. Fincher, S.A., Kolikant, Y.B.D., Falkner, K.: Teacher learning and professional development. In: Fincher, S.A., Robins, A.V. (eds.) The Cambridge Handbook of Computing Education Research, pp. 727–748. Cambridge Handbooks in Psychology, Cambridge University Press (2019). https://doi.org/10.1017/9781108654555.026
12. Fraser, C., Kennedy, A., Reid, L., McKinney, L.: Teachers' continuing professional development: contested concepts, understanding and models. J. In-Serv. Educ. **33**(22), 153–169 (2007)
13. Goode, J., Margolis, J., Chapman, G.: Curriculum is not enough: the educational theory and research foundation of the exploring computer science professional development model. In: Proceedings of the 45th ACM Technical Symposium on Computer Science Education, Atlanta, Georgia, USA, pp. 493–498. ACM (2014)
14. Grover, S., Cateté, V., Barnes, T., Hill, M., Ledeczi, A., Broll, B.: First principles to design for online, synchronous high school CS teacher training and curriculum co-design. In: Proceedings of the 20th Koli Calling International Conference on Computing Education Research, pp. 1–5 (2020)
15. Guskey, T., Yoon, K.: What works in professional development? Phi Delta Kappan **90**, 495–500 (2009). https://doi.org/10.1177/003172170909000709

16. Kennedy, A.: Models of continuing professional development: a framework for analysis. J. In-Serv. Educ. **31**(2), 235–250 (2005)
17. Kennedy, A.: Understanding continuing professional development: the need for theory to impact on policy and practice. Prof. Dev. Educ. **40**(5), 688–697 (2014). https://doi.org/10.1080/19415257.2014.955122
18. Kirby, D.: UK and Ireland Computing Teachers' Survey: Results Published. Blog post. Raspberry Pi Computing Education Research Centre, University of Cambridge (2023). https://computingeducationresearch.org/uk-and-ireland-computing-teachers-survey-results-published
19. McHugh, M.L.: Interrater reliability: the kappa statistic. Biochemia Medica **22**(3), 276–282 (2012)
20. Menekse, M.: Computer science teacher professional development in the United States: a review of studies published between 2004 and 2014. Comput. Sci. Educ. **25**(4), 325–350 (2015). https://doi.org/10.1080/08993408.2015.1111645
21. Mockler, N.: Trans/forming teachers: new professional learning and transformative teacher professionalism. J. In-Serv. Educ. **31**(4), 733–746 (2005)
22. Moller, F., Crick, T.: A university-based model for supporting computer science curriculum reform. J. Comput. Educ. **5**(4), 415–434 (2018). https://doi.org/10.1007/s40692-018-0117-x
23. Mouza, C., Codding, D., Pollock, L.: Investigating the impact of research-based professional development on teacher learning and classroom practice: findings from computer science education. Comput. Educ. **186**, 104530 (2022)
24. Mouza, C., Mead, H., Alkhateeb, B., Pollock, L.: A virtual professional development program for computer science education during covid-19. TechTrends **66**(3), 436–449 (2022)
25. Nakajima, T.M., Goode, J.: Transformative learning for computer science teachers: examining how educators learn e-textiles in professional development. Teach. Teach. Educ. **85**, 148–159 (2019). https://doi.org/10.1016/j.tate.2019.05.004
26. Qian, Y., Hambrusch, S., Yadav, A., Gretter, S.: Who needs what: recommendations for designing effective online professional development for computer science teachers. J. Res. Technol. Educ. **50**(2), 164–181 (2018)
27. Ryoo, J., Goode, J., Margolis, J.: It takes a village: supporting inquiry-and equity-oriented computer science pedagogy through a professional learning community. Comput. Sci. Educ. **25**(4), 351–370 (2015)
28. Sachs, J.: Metaphors for continuing teacher professional development: skilling or emancipating teachers. In: Mockler, N., Sachs, J. (eds.) Rethinking Educational Practice Through Reflexive Inquiry, pp. 153–168. Springer, Dordrecht (2011). https://doi.org/10.1007/978-94-007-0805-1_11
29. Sentance, S.: Moving to mainstream: developing computing for all. In: Proceedings of the 14th Workshop in Primary and Secondary Computing Education, WiPSCE 2019, pp. 1–2. Association for Computing Machinery, New York (2019). https://doi.org/10.1145/3361721.3362117
30. Sentance, S., Csizmadia, A.: Professional recognition matters: certification for in-service computer science teachers. In: Proceedings of the 2017 ACM SIGCSE Technical Symposium on Computer Science Education, SIGCSE 2017, pp. 537–542. ACM (2017). https://doi.org/10.1145/3017680.3017752
31. Sentance, S., Humphreys, S.: Understanding professional learning for computing teachers from the perspective of situated learning. Comput. Sci. Educ. **28**(4), 345–370 (2018)

32. Sentance, S., Kirby, D., Quille, K., Cole, E., Crick, T., Looker, N.: Computing in school in the UK & Ireland: a comparative study. In: Proceedings of the 2022 Conference on United Kingdom & Ireland Computing Education Research, pp. 1–7. Association for Computing Machinery, New York (2022). https://doi.org/10.1145/3555009.3555015
33. Tracy, S.J.: Qualitative Research Methods: Collecting Evidence, Crafting Analysis, Communicating Impact. Wiley, Hoboken (2019)
34. Welsh Government: Curriculum for Wales 2022 (2020). https://hwb.gov.wales/curriculum-for-wales
35. Yurkofsky, M.M., Blum-Smith, S., Brennan, K.: Expanding outcomes: exploring varied conceptions of teacher learning in an online professional development experience. Teach. Teach. Educ. **82**, 1–13 (2019)

Teachers' Motivation to Engage with Students in a Computer Science and Computational Thinking Challenge: Does Motivation Conform to a 'One-Size-Fits-All' Model?

Lidia Feklistova[1]($\boxtimes$) 📷, Tatjana Jevsikova[2] 📷, Bence Gaál[3] 📷, and Zsuzsa Pluhár[3] 📷

[1] Institute of Computer Science, University of Tartu, Tartu, Estonia
lidia.feklistova@ut.ee
[2] Institute of Data Science and Digital Technologies, Vilnius University, Vilnius, Lithuania
tatjana.jevsikova@mif.vu.lt
[3] Faculty of Informatics, Eötvös Loránd University, Budapest, Hungary
gaalbence@inf.elte.hu, pluharzs@ik.elte.hu

Abstract. The international Bebras challenge (BC) aims to raise the students' interest in computer science (CS) and contribute to their problem-solving and computational thinking (CT) skills development. Through solving short conceptual tasks that are close to real-life context, students obtain the essential literacy needed to be successful in the modern world. Although the initiative has been running for about 20 years, teachers' motivation to engage with students in this challenge remains underexplored. This study employs self-determination theory as a theoretical framework and the work tasks motivation scale for teachers as an instrument. Data collected from 334 teachers across Estonia, Hungary, and Lithuania were analyzed. The results showed teachers' motivation most significantly stemmed from intrinsic motivation and identified regulation. There were no significant differences in all types of motivation between male and female teachers or teachers with different years of teaching experience. However, teachers who were more experienced in engaging in the BC demonstrated higher levels of almost all types of motivation. Mature teachers were more externally motivated than their younger colleagues. Teachers who used the Bebras tasks in their lessons had a higher level of intrinsic motivation and identified regulation than those who did not use these tasks. Teachers teaching various subjects showed different levels of identified regulation. The study provides implications for teachers, school administration, and the BC organization.

Keywords: teacher motivation · self-determination theory · Bebras · computational thinking

1 Introduction

Teachers' work includes teaching, collaborating with parents, administrative tasks, organizing competitions, etc. Effective task performance requires motivation, defined as one's activation and intention to engage in activities [1]. Despite its importance, motivation has been under-researched as a multifaceted construct from teachers' perspectives [2], and there is no consensus on the impact of teachers' background characteristics on their motivation. While motivation for mandatory tasks has been studied [3, 4], voluntary activities need further exploration.

This study examines teachers' voluntary engagement in the Bebras challenge (BC), aimed at enhancing students' interest in computer science (CS) and developing their problem-solving and computational thinking (CT) skills through working on concept-based tasks. Although the BC has been active for about 20 years [5], research has primarily focused on students [6, 7], with limited attention to teachers' motivation.

The study aims to explore teachers' motivation to engage with their students in the BC, considering various motivation types and background characteristics (e.g., age, gender, professional seniority). Given that the Bebras tasks integrate real-life contexts rather than simply focusing on pure CS, it is important to understand the motivation of teachers across different subjects to use these tasks.

There are different theories and frameworks with unique insights into motivation and from different perspectives [8]. The current study is framed by the most widely accepted self-determination theory.

1.1 Self-determination Theory

Self-determination theory is conceptualized as an approach to one's motivation and personality that concerns individual inner resources for personality development and behavior [1]. According to the theory, there are several types of motivation that result in different situational responses. Amotivation is related to a disinclination to do anything or an unwillingness to engage in any activity [1] because activity results are not valued [9] or are not expected to be reached [10]. An intrinsically motivated person engages in an activity because of enthusiasm, personal interests, deeply held values, and enjoys the activity itself. Extrinsic motivation refers to engagement in activity to get positive outcomes or avoid negative ones. One's behavior is caused by external sources or conditions. Extrinsic motivation is a multifaceted construct that encompasses qualitatively different regulation types. External regulation refers to behavior that is carried out as a reaction to an external call to receive an external reward or avoid punishment. Introjected regulation refers to behavior caused by external demands and rules that are taken into account but are not fully accepted as one's own. People engage in activity to receive an internal reward or avoid failure, guilt or self-criticism. Identified regulation refers to behavior that occurs when the activity is accepted or done as personally important and voluntarily, not under the influence of external pressure. Integrated regulation refers to behavior that occurs when requirements and rules are fully absorbed by the person and are incorporated into one's other values and needs [1]. However, some researchers argue that integrated regulation is hardly statistically separable from identified regulation and intrinsic motivation [11, 12], and consider it separately shows little added value [13].

1.2 Teachers' Motivation

Teachers have different motivations for teaching [14–16], class preparation, evaluation of students [3, 14], professional development [4], etc. Without a doubt, teachers' motivation has an impact on students' motivation for learning [15, 16]. An ideal teacher is one who has a high level of identified regulation and intrinsic motivation, and a low level of external and introjected regulations [17]. Intrinsically motivated teachers are more competent and more productive in teaching, demonstrate a higher level of job satisfaction [15], more frequently engage in non-teaching tasks such as performance of administrative tasks, work on projects, and participation in different activities [18].

Although the teaching profession is dominated by females [19] who are more motivated to teachers' work [20] and to spend their time on non-professional volunteering activities [21], some studies indicate no statistical difference between male and female teachers in motivation [22, 23]. However, in some studies, the motivation of male teachers is higher than that of female teachers [24].

There are several studies on the relationship between gender and different types of motivation but the results are still contradictory. Some studies indicated no significant difference between male and female teachers in intrinsic motivation [25, 26], identified, introjected, and external regulations [14, 26]. Others found that female teachers were more intrinsically motivated to perform their tasks [27] and had lower levels of identified [3], introjected, and external regulations [28] than their male colleagues. Regarding engaging in complementary tasks (e.g., involvement in extracurricular activities), male teachers are more externally motivated than female colleagues, but all other types of motivation are not dependent on the teachers' gender [14].

Teachers from different age groups do not differ in external regulation, but older (52 +) teachers have higher levels of introjected regulation and amotivation, while younger teachers report better intrinsic motivation and identified regulation [3]. Less experienced teachers are more motivated than their more experienced colleagues [22, 24]. Interestingly, intrinsic motivation varies depending on professional seniority [27].

Prior research suggests that teachers tend to be more intrinsically motivated to teach their subjects but extrinsic motivation also matters [29, 30]. While comparing teachers of core (e.g., language, math) and general (e.g., art, music, sports) subjects, no significant differences in all types of regulation and intrinsic motivation were found [26].

1.3 The Bebras Challenge and the Contest Management System

The Bebras challenge is a global voluntary initiative started in 2004 in Lithuania. It aims to raise the students' interest in CS and support the development of their problem-solving and CT skills by solving short conceptual tasks that are close to real-life contexts. Each year, member countries add tasks to the international database from where national organizers pick tasks for their national challenges [5, 31]. The BC targets 6–18-year-old students who are divided into six age groups, and each group has its own set of tasks [32]. The tasks cover at least one CS concept, are wrapped with an attractive story, and, if possible, based on real-life context. To solve tasks, students apply CT skills like logical thinking, algorithmic design, and pattern recognition [5].

The challenge has been the focus of several studies. Researchers analyzed the effects of using the Bebras tasks on the development of CT skills [7], the difficulty level of tasks [33], performance by girls and boys [6], etc. However, to the best of our knowledge, no study has yet explored what motivates teachers to engage in the BC.

In the academic year 2023/2024, some countries, including Estonia and Hungary, used the Finnish virtual learning environment, ViLLE, to deliver the BC. The environment allows the creation of different types of tasks, provides automatic assessment and immediate feedback for the students, and learning analytics tools for the teachers [34].

The Bebras Lodge, developed by the Vilnius University team, is a tool to create different types of interactive tasks with SVG support. The developed tasks can be exported to other environments. In Lithuania, this system serves as a contest management system to run the BC, and provides data analytics tools. From fall 2021 onwards it is also supported by ViLLE.

1.4 Research Questions

Reviewing scientific literature, several gaps were detected. Thus, to contribute to the field, this study explores the role of teachers' different types of motivation to engage in the BC and the use of these tasks in lessons. Also, the relationship between teachers' motivation and their background characteristics is studied. To achieve this aim, the following research questions are posed:

RQ1: What types of motivation dominate among teachers engaged with students in the Bebras challenge?
RQ2: Are there any differences in teachers' background characteristics within different types of motivation?
RQ3: How does teachers' motivation to use the Bebras tasks in their lessons differ?

2 Methodology

2.1 Instruments

Data was collected using a questionnaire created by the BC team. In the first part, teachers indicated their gender, selected from the interval data provided their belonging to a certain age group, years of professional seniority, and years of engagement in the BC. In the open question, teachers were asked to write subjects they teach.

In the second part, teachers' motivation was measured with the validated The Work Tasks Motivation Scale for Teachers [14]. This part of the questionnaire started with the question, "Why do you engage in the Bebras challenge?" and was followed by 15 items measuring different types of motivation: intrinsic motivation, identified regulation, introjected regulation, external regulation, and amotivation (three items per each type of motivation). Unlike the original scale, we opted for a 5-point Likert scale, where value 5 referred to "strongly agree" and 1 referred to "strongly disagree". For the current study, we changed the word "task" used in the original version of the scale to "the Bebras challenge" which suited better to the context of the study.

The third part had binary question where teachers had to indicate whether they use the BC tasks in the lessons (e.g., in class activities, as part of homework). At the final stage of preparing the questionnaire, it was translated into Estonian, Hungarian, Lithuanian, and Russian languages.

2.2 Data Analysis

IBM SPSS 28 software package and Python libraries (pandas, matplotlib, likert_plot) were used for the statistical analysis and data visualization.

Descriptive statistics were used to calculate percentage, median, etc. Quantitative data normality has been checked using the Shapiro-Wilk test. The test indicated that the data was not normally distributed. Therefore, non-parametric tests with the significance level set to $\alpha = 0.05$ were utilized. The Mann–Whitney U test was used for pairwise comparisons between two independent samples (e.g., gender groups). The Kruskal–Wallis H test was used to determine the existence of differences between more than two independent groups (e.g., teachers of different age groups). Although analyzed data was not normally distributed, Cronbach's alpha could be applied to such data [35] to measure the internal consistency of the used questionnaire and its reliability. Calculated Cronbach's alpha was equal to 0.80 for the overall reliability. The reliability of subconstructs (based on different types of motivation) was as follows: intrinsic motivation (0.83), identified regulation (0.76), introjected regulation (0.88), external regulation (0.69), and amotivation (0.83). All Cronbach's alphas for scale and its subscales were sufficient and acceptable [36].

This study did not analyze each of the 15 items separately. It was focused on the types of motivation, i.e., we calculated the mean of each of the 5 types of motivation based on three items belonging to the corresponding type (Appendix 1). In the questionnaire, teachers wrote the subjects they taught. For the analysis, three groups of subjects were formed by the authors of this study: "only CS" (teachers teach subjects only in the CS field, i.e. informatics, robotics, programming lessons, etc.), "natural sciences and CS" (besides CS subjects, teachers also teach mathematics, physics, chemistry, biology or geography) and "other subjects" (besides CS subjects, teachers also teach languages, history, ethics or work as primary school teachers).

2.3 Participants and Procedure

This cross-country study involved teachers from Estonia, Hungary, and Lithuania. In total, responses from 334 teachers were received, 78% of whom were females. In our sample 32 females and 6 males were from Estonia, 103 females and 35 males from Hungary, 124 females and 34 males in Lithuania. The overrepresentation of females is far from being a bias in the sample since significant dominance of female teachers is common in this field [19] and studied countries.

Regarding background characteristics of participants (Fig. 1), about half of them belonged to the 46–55 age group, about three quarters had 15 + years of working experience as teachers, about one-third have been engaged in the BC with their students for 10 + years, and slightly less than a half of them were teaching only CS subjects.

In all three countries, after the national BC, the organizers sent an email with a link to the questionnaire. In Estonia, the email was sent to all 148 school teachers who voluntarily registered themselves as coordinators of the BC in their school for the academic year 2023/2024. In Hungary, the email was sent to all registered teachers (512), and in Lithuania to all teachers who participated in the BC (243). The email contained information about the study purpose and the link to the online questionnaire (in the ViLLE

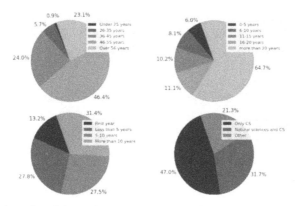

Fig. 1. Distribution of participants by age groups (top left), professional seniority (top right), years of engagement in the challenge (bottom left), and category of subjects taught (bottom right)

environment for Estonia and Hungary, and in the Bebras Lodge for Lithuania). Participation in this study was voluntary. Teachers were not required to enter their names or any other identifying codes and were asked to complete the questionnaire over approximately two weeks in December 2023. The response rates were 26% in Estonia, 27% in Hungary, 65% in Lithuania but were still acceptable for surveys with small samples [37].

3 Results

3.1 Dominating Types of Motivation Among Teachers

In this study, we explored five types of motivation: intrinsic motivation, identified, introjected, external regulations, and amotivation (Fig. 2).

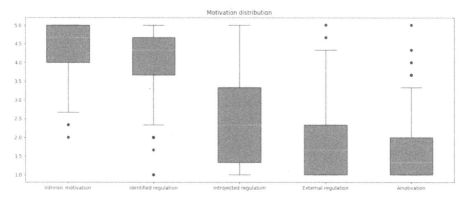

Fig. 2. Distributions of levels of different types of motivation among studied teachers

For intrinsic motivation, the median is close to the upper end of the scale (4.7), with mean score of participants ranging from 2 to 5. Exploring questionnaire intrinsic motivation items separately it was noticed that 98% of teachers (strongly) agreed that they engage in the BC because they find it interesting to do (Appendix 1, Fig. A1.A). The mean score of identified regulation ranges from 1 to 5 with the median 4.3. The vast majority of teachers (87%) (strongly) agreed that they they find the BC important for the academic success of students (Appendix 1, Fig. A1.B). Results on introjected regulation present a complex scenario with the median dropping to the middle of the scale (2.3) and mean score ranging from 1 to 5. The majority of respondents indicated that they engage in the BC not because they would feel bad about not organizing such challenges (60%), or guilty (54%) (Appendix 1, Fig. A1.C). External regulation is at a lower median (1.7), with mean score ranging from 1 to 5. Only 30% of teachers (strongly) agreed that engagement in the BC is the demand of their work. Most teachers (91%) (strongly) disagreed that they were engaged in the BC because of being paid for it (Appendix 1, Fig. A1.D). The median for the amotivation is low (1.3) and 90% of teachers (strongly) disagree about not seeing the reason for this activity (Appendix 1, Fig. A1.E). However, four upper outliers reaching the values of 3.6–5 were detected (Fig. 2).

3.2 Differences in Types of Motivation According to Teachers' Background Characteristics

In this study, we focused on the following teachers' background characteristics: gender, age, professional seniority, and years of engagement with students in the Bebras challenge (Appendix 2).

No significant differences were found in any type of motivation either between female and male teachers (Mann-Whitney test, $p > 0.05$) or between teachers' groups with different years of teaching experience (Kruskal-Wallis test, $p > 0.05$).

Teachers of different age groups differed in terms of external regulation (Kruskal-Wallis $H = 9.56, p = 0.049$). Although the level of external regulation in a group of mature teachers (55 +) was the highest compared to other age groups, pairwise comparison with the Mann-Whitney U tests revealed a difference only with the age group of 36–45 ($Z = -2.698, p = 0.007$) and a tendency to be higher in comparison to the age group of 26–35 ($Z = -1.824, p = 0.068$). In addition, mature teachers had a higher level of introjected regulation than teachers aged 26–35 ($Z = -2.318, p = 0.02$). In other pairwise comparisons, no significant differences were found ($p > 0.05$).

Regarding motivation among teachers' groups with different years of engagement in the BC, the Kruskal-Wallis H test did not indicate any difference in terms of intrinsic motivation, but differences between studied groups were significant in identified ($H = 8.810; p = 0.032$), introjected ($H = 37.221; p < 0.001$), external regulation ($H = 33.090; p < 0.001$) and amotivation ($H = 10.709; p = 0.013$) (Fig. 3).

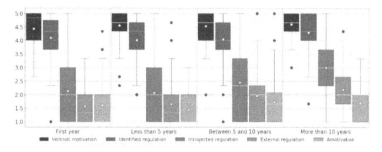

Fig. 3. Motivation levels distributed by the years of engaging in the Bebras challenge

Pairwise comparison with the Mann-Whitney U test has revealed significantly higher levels of identified, introjected, external regulations, and amotivation in the most experienced group compared to the "less than 5 years" group (respectively, $Z = -2.609$, $p = 0.009$; $Z = -5.760$, $p < 0.001$; $Z = -5.023$, $p < 0.001$; $Z = -3.103$, $p = 0.002$). The level of identified, introjected and external regulation was also significantly higher in the most experienced group compared to the "5–10 years" group (respectively, $Z = -2.500$, $p = 0.012$; $Z = -3.341$, $p < 0.001$; $Z = -2.145$, $p = 0.032$). The most experienced in engaging in the challenge teachers had significantly higher levels of introjected ($Z = -4.035$, $p < 0.001$) and external regulations ($Z = -4.457$, $p < 0.001$) than the least experienced group. External regulation was significantly higher in the "5–10 years" group compared to teachers involved in the challenge for the first time ($Z = -2.483$, $p = 0.013$). Groups " < 5 years" and "5–10 years" differed significantly in the levels of introjected ($Z = -2.181$, $p = 0.029$), external regulations ($Z = -2.630$, $p = 0.009$), and amotivation ($Z = -2.325$, $p = 0.02$) with higher levels for more experienced group. In other pairwise comparisons, no significant differences were found.

3.3 Differences in Motivation According to the Usage During the Lessons

About half of all studied teachers use the Bebras tasks in their lessons, i.e. 49% of teachers who teach only CS subjects use these tasks in their lessons; 52.6% of natural sciences and CS teachers, and 58.5% of other subjects teachers.

The only significant difference between groups of teachers representing different subjects was found in terms of identified regulation (Kruskal-Wallis $H = 7.926$, $p = 0.019$) (Appendix 2). Pairwise comparison with the Mann-Whitney U test indicated that teachers from the group "Other subjects" had a higher level of identified regulation than the teachers from the group "Natural sciences and CS" ($Z = -2.798$, $p = 0.007$). No significant differences were found in other pairs of groups ($p > 0.05$).

Regarding the use of the Bebras tasks in the lessons, teachers formed two groups: those who used the tasks and those who did not use them. The comparison with the Mann-Whitney U test indicated that teachers who used tasks in their lessons were more intrinsically motivated and had a higher level of identified regulation than their colleagues who did not use these tasks (respectively, $Z = -2.583$, $p = 0.01$ and $Z = -4.786$, $p < 0.001$). In all other types of motivation, the differences were not significant. When focusing only on those teachers who used the tasks in their lessons, the same tendency of higher levels of intrinsic motivation and identified regulation was noticed (Table 1).

Table 1. Levels of motivation types for teachers using the Bebras tasks in their lessons (N = 174)

Motivation type	Min	Max	Mean	Median	SD
Intrinsic motivation	2.00	5.00	4.61	5.00	0.53
Identified regulation	1.67	5.00	4.30	4.33	0.66
Introjected regulation	1.00	5.00	2.59	2.67	1.16
External regulation	1.00	5.00	1.89	1.67	0.84
Amotivation regulation	1.00	5.00	1.61	1.33	0.69

The level of intrinsic motivation is similarly high for all teachers' groups with different years of engagement in the BC. Differences were found in identified (Kruskal–Wallis $H = 11.121$, $p = 0.011$) and introjected regulation (Kruskal–Wallis $H = 14.542$, $p = 0.002$) with the highest levels of these kinds of motivation for teachers having more than 10 years of experience with the BC.

4 Discussion and Conclusions

In this cross-country research, 334 teachers participated with female teachers making up 78% of the sample. Previous findings also highlight the dominance of females in the profession [19]. Most teachers were 46 or older and had over 15 years of teaching experience, underscoring the need to attract younger teachers to engage with their students in the BC. Notably, one-sixth of the study participants were new to the BC.

About half of the respondents exclusively teach CS, while many integrate CS with other subjects, enhancing students' CT skills. Intrinsic motivation and identified regulation were the primary drivers for teachers' engagement in the BC, reflecting personal interest and academic recognition without external pressure. Domination of these types of motivation among schoolteachers was also found in the study by de Wal et al. [17]. High intrinsic motivation correlates with better teaching performance and student outcomes [15, 16, 18]. In this study, a low level of amotivation can be considered as a meaningful result since teachers who are amotivated tend to do their duties in an automatic manner without investing enough energy in students' development [38].

No significant gender differences in motivation types were found, consistent with previous studies [14]. However, mature teachers (55 +) exhibited higher external and introjected regulation than younger colleagues, indicating pressure to participate despite recognizing the educational value. This contrasts with studies where less experienced teachers showed more motivation [22, 24].

Teachers with over 10 years in the BC showed higher identified regulation, indicating long-term commitment and task importance. However, they also exhibited higher amotivation levels, raising concerns about future engagement. We observed an intriguing nuance that the level of external regulation among teachers with prior experience in engaging in the challenge was significantly higher the more experienced in engaging in the challenge teacher was. Nearly half of the teachers used the Bebras tasks across various subjects, reflecting their integration into diverse curricula and indicating higher intrinsic motivation and identified regulation.

This study's limitations include the voluntary nature of participation and potential cultural differences affecting motivation. Future research should explore motivational variations across countries and reasons behind task usage in lessons.

Overall, this study focused on teachers' motivation to engage in the BC, a voluntary activity that attracted teachers with high intrinsic and identified motivation, indicating a genuine interest and personal commitment. While external pressure was generally low, some teachers displayed amotivation, suggesting a need for clearer communication about the challenge's relevance. Gender and years of professional seniority did not significantly affect motivation, but mature and experienced teachers showed higher introjected and external regulations. Long-term participants showed signs of amotivation, indicating a need for new motivational factors.

The study found that the Bebras tasks, designed to improve students' CS knowledge and develop problem-solving and CT skills, are actively used across different subjects, driven by teachers' personal interest and desire to support students' academic success. These findings contribute to the literature on teacher motivation in complementary tasks and have practical implications for teacher engagement in international challenges aimed at enhancing students' CS and CT skills.

Appendix 1. Teachers' Answers Per Each Item

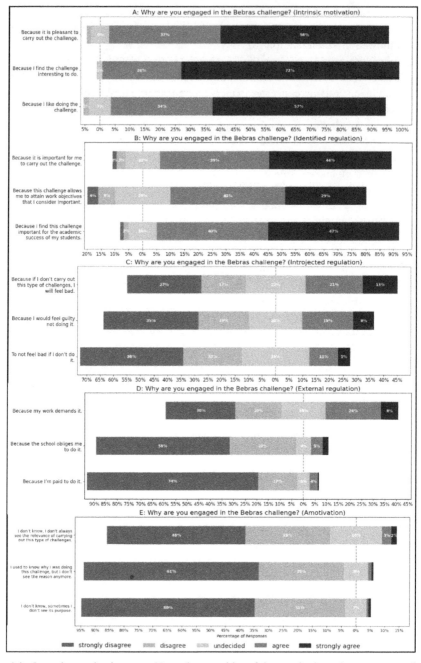

Fig. A1. Items by motivation type. Note: the two sides of the x-axis show the percentage distribution of the negative and positive groups, with the neutral group halved. If no percentage label is shown, the percentage of respondents is less than 2%.

Appendix 2. Differences Between Groups

Group	N	Intrinsic	Identified	Introjected	External	Amotivation
Gender						
Male	75	167.51	154.53	172.07	158.83	154.19
Female	259	167.50	171.25	166.18	170.01	171.35
U test		9711.5	8740.0	9369.5	9062.0	8714.5
Z		−0.001	−1.339	−0.471	−0.899	−1.425
Sig. (2-tailed)		0.999	0.181	0.638	0.369	0.154
Age						
<= 25	3	92.17	95.00	80.67	100.83	111.00
26–35	19	158.92	138.53	125.42	151.03	159.61
36–45	80	176.89	175.03	159.96	148.76	177.95
46–55	155	166.06	168.15	171.01	169.30	165.78
55 +	77	165.69	168.34	182.03	190.02	164.25
H test		3.170	4.011	8.653	9.560	2.461
Sig		0.530	0.404	0.070	0.049*	0.652
Experience in engaging in the Bebras challenge						
First year	44	159.02	168.01	139.88	130.31	154.69
< 5 years	93	169.81	154.32	133.88	136.65	145.26
5–10 years	92	164.82	155.54	164.85	174.10	177.48
> 10 years	105	171.36	189.44	211.18	204.63	183.82
H test		0.715	8.810	37.221	33.090	10.709
Sig		0.870	0.032*	< 0.001**	< 0.001**	0.013*
Professional seniority						
0–5 years	20	177.53	157.65	154.60	143.45	171.60
6–10 years	27	131.09	163.24	166.43	166.78	175.46
11–15 years	34	180.96	184.43	156.03	149.12	164.88
16–20 years	37	175.96	155.92	155.99	169.03	165.00
> 20 years	216	167.56	168.26	172.61	172.45	166.97
H test		5.669	1.903	2.013	3.157	0.305
Sig		0.225	0.754	0.733	0.532	0.989

(*continued*)

(continued)

Group	N	Intrinsic	Identified	Introjected	External	Amotivation
Subject categories						
CS only	157	169.03	169.93	178.06	176.21	168.96
Natural Sciences + CS	112	163.11	150.18	160.77	158.28	168.71
Other	65	171.38	191.47	153.58	162.36	161.88
H test		0.426	7.926	3.855	2.569	0.302
Sig		0.808	0.019*	0.145	0.277	0.860
Bebras task usage in the lessons						
Do not use	160	154.14	141.49	157.77	168.42	168.44
Use	174	179.79	191.41	176.45	166.66	166.64
U test		11782	9759	12363	13773	13770
Z		−2.583	−4.786	−1.785	−0.170	−0.179
Sig. (2-tailed)		0.010*	<0.001**	0.074	0.865	0.858

*significant at 0.05 level; ** significant at 0.01 level

References

1. Ryan, R.M., Deci, E.L.: Self-determination theory and the facilitation of intrinsic motivation, social development, and well-being. Am. Psychol. **55**(1), 68–78 (2000). https://doi.org/10.1037/0003-066X.55.1.68
2. Kumari, J., Kumar, J.: Influence of motivation on teachers' job performance. Humanit. Soc. Sci. Commun. **10**, 1–11 (2023). https://doi.org/10.1057/s41599-023-01662-6
3. Criado-Del Rey, J., Portela-Pino, I., Domínguez-Alonso, J., Pino-Juste, M.: Assessment of teacher motivation, psychometric properties of the work tasks motivation scale for teachers (WTMST) in Spanish teachers. Educ. Sci. **14**(3), 1–15 (2024). https://doi.org/10.3390/educsci14030212
4. Proudfoot, K.: Introjected regulation in teachers' professional development motivations. Teach. Teach. **28**(8), 1021–1034 (2022). https://doi.org/10.1080/13540602.2022.2144816
5. Dagienė, V., Stupurienė, G.: Bebras – a sustainable community building model for the concept based learning of informatics and computational thinking. Inf. Educ. **15**(1), 25–44 (2016). https://doi.org/10.15388/infedu.2016.02
6. Hubwieser, P., Hubwieser, E., Graswald, D.: How to attract the girls: gender-specific performance and motivation in the Bebras challenge. In: Brodnik, A., Tort, F. (eds.) ISSEP 2016. LNCS, vol. 9973, pp. 40–52. Springer, Cham (2016). https://doi.org/10.1007/978-3-319-46747-4_4
7. Zapata-Cáceres, M., Marcelino, P., El-Hamamsy, L., Martín-Barroso, E.: A Bebras computational thinking (ABC-thinking) program for primary school: evaluation using the competent computational thinking test. Educ. Inf. Technol. (2024). https://doi.org/10.1007/s10639-023-12441-w
8. Irvine, J.: A framework for comparing theories related to motivation in education. Res. Higher Educ. J. **35**, 1–30 (2018)

9. Ryan, R.M., Plant, R.W., O'Malley, S.: Initial motivations for alcohol treatment: Relations with patient characteristics, treatment involvement and dropout. Addict. Behav. **20**(3), 279–297 (1995). https://doi.org/10.1016/0306-4603(94)00072-7
10. Seligman, M.E.P.: Helplessness. Freeman, San Francisco (1975)
11. Gagné, M., Forest, J., Vansteenkiste, M., Crevier-Braud, L., Van den Broeck, A., et al.: The multidimensional work motivation scale: Validation evidence in seven languages and nine countries. Eur. J. Work Organ. Psychol. **24**(2), 178–196 (2015). https://doi.org/10.1080/1359432X.2013.877892
12. Howard, J.L., Gagné, M., Bureau, J.S.: Testing a continuum structure of self- determined motivation: a meta-analysis. Psychol. Bull. **143**(12), 1346–1377 (2017). https://doi.org/10.1037/bul0000125
13. Van den Broeck, A., Howard, J.L., Van Vaerenbergh, Y., Leroy, H., Gagné, M.: Beyond intrinsic and extrinsic motivation: a meta-analysis on self-determination theory's multidimensional conceptualization of work motivation. Organ. Psychol. Rev. **11**(3), 240–273 (2021). https://doi.org/10.1177/20413866211006173
14. Fernet, C., Senécal, C., Guay, F., Marsh, H., Dowson, M.: The work tasks motivation scale for teachers (WTMST). J. Career Assess. **16**(2), 256–279 (2008). https://doi.org/10.1177/1069072707305764
15. Uysal, D.: A review on teachers' and teacher candidates' intrinsic motivation: self-determination theory perspective. Lang. Teach. Educ. Res. **6**(2), 176–198 (2023). https://doi.org/10.35207/later.1331081
16. Zou, H., Yao, J., Zhang, Y., Huang, X.: The influence of teachers' intrinsic motivation on students' intrinsic motivation: the mediating role of teachers' motivating style and teacher-student relationships. Psychol. Sch. **61**(1), 272–286 (2023). https://doi.org/10.1002/pits.23050
17. de Wal, J.J., den Brok, P.J., Hooijer, J.G., Martens, R.L., van den Beemt, A.: Teachers' engagement in professional learning: exploring motivational profiles. Learn. Individ. Differ. **36**, 27–36 (2014). https://doi.org/10.1016/j.lindif.2014.08.001
18. Christodoulidis, T., Tzioumakis, Y.S., Gorozidis, G.S., Papaioannou, A.G.: Teachers' self-determined motivation in relation to non-teaching work tasks. Eur. J. Educ. Stud. **9**(12), 309–331 (2022). https://doi.org/10.46827/ejes.v9i12.4596
19. ElAtia, S., Gomez, L.N., Corsi, E.: If teaching is a female dominated profession, why are so few leading the profession? J. Res. Leadersh. Educ. **19**(1), 102–121 (2024). https://doi.org/10.1177/19427751221137926
20. Al-Salameh, E.M.J.: Teacher motivation: a study of work motivation of the primary stage teachers in Jordan. Am. J. Appl. Psychol. **3**(3), 57–61 (2014). https://doi.org/10.11648/j.ajap.20140303.12
21. Müller, K., Alliata, R., Benninghoff, F.: Attracting and retaining teachers. Educ. Manag. Adm. Leadersh. **37**(5), 574–599 (2009). https://doi.org/10.1177/1741143209339651
22. Gehlawat, M., Gupta, M.: Job satisfaction and work motivation of secondary school teachers in relation to some demographic variables: a comparative study. Educationia Confab **2**(1), 10–19 (2013)
23. Jaafar, N.F.A., Salim, S.S.S.: Teachers motivation towards job performance appraisal among secondary school teachers. Int. J. Acad. Res. Bus. Soc. Sci. **9**(7), 646–653 (2019). https://doi.org/10.6007/IJARBSS/v9-i7/6155
24. Triyanto, R.D.H.: Teacher motivation based on gender, tenure and level of education. New Educ. Rev. **45**, 199–209 (2016). https://doi.org/10.15804/tner.2016.45.3.16
25. Wanakacha, C.K., Aloka, P.J.O., Nyaswa, P.: Gender differences in motivation and teacher performance in core functions in Kenyan secondary schools. Acad. J. Interdisc. Stud. **7**(1), 89–95 (2018). https://doi.org/10.2478/ajis-2018-0009

26. Xie, Z., Zhang, L.F., Deng, M.: Self-efficacy and work motivation among inclusive education teachers in China. Int. J. Disabil. Dev. Educ. **71**(2), 236–250 (2022). https://doi.org/10.1080/1034912X.2022.2094900
27. Bukhari, S.G.A.S., Jamali, S.G., Larik, A.R., Chang, M.S.: Fostering intrinsic motivation among teachers: importance of work environment and individual differences. Int. J. Sch. Educ. Psychol. **11**(1), 1–19 (2023). https://doi.org/10.1080/21683603.2021.1925182
28. Nie, Y., Chua, B.L., Yeung, A.S., Ryan, R.M., Chan, W.Y.: The importance of autonomy support and the mediating role of work motivation for well-being: Testing self-determination theory in a Chinese work organisation. Int. J. Psychol. **50**(4), 245–255 (2014). https://doi.org/10.1002/ijop.12110
29. Alibakhshi, G., Nezakatgoo, B., Popescu, M.: Construction and validation of Iranian EFL teachers' teaching motivation scale. Cogent Educ. **6**(1), 1–18 (2019). https://doi.org/10.1080/2331186X.2019.1585311
30. Martin, N.D., Baker, S.N., Haynes, M., Warner, J.R.: The motivation to teach computer science (MTCS) scale: development, validation, and implications for use. Comput. Sci. Educ. **34**(2), 310–327 (2023). https://doi.org/10.1080/08993408.2023.2182561
31. Dagienė, V., Futschek, G., Stupurienė, G.: Creativity in solving short tasks for learning computational thinking. Constructivist Found. **14**(3), 382–396 (2019)
32. Pluhár, Zs., Kaarto, H., Parviainen, M., Garcha, S., Shah, V., et al.: Bebras challenge in a learning analytics enriched environment: Hungarian and Indian cases. In: Bollin, A., Futschek, G. (eds.). ISSEP 2022. LNCS, vol. 13488, pp. 40–53. Springer, Cham (2022). https://doi.org/10.1007/978-3-031-15851-3_4
33. van der Vegt, W., Schrijvers, E.: Analysing task difficulty in a Bebras contest using cuttle. Olympiads Inf. **13**, 145–156 (2019). https://doi.org/10.15388/ioi.2019.09
34. Laakso, M.J., Kaila, E., Rajala, T.: ViLLE – collaborative education tool: designing and utilizing an exercise-based learning environment. Educ. Inf. Technol. **23**, 1655–1676 (2018). https://doi.org/10.1007/s10639-017-9659-1
35. Sheng, Y., Sheng, Z.: Is coefficient alpha robust to non-normal data? Front. Psychol. **3**, 1–13 (2012). https://doi.org/10.3389/fpsyg.2012.00034
36. Taber, K.S.: The use of Cronbach's alpha when developing and reporting research instruments in science education. Res. Sci. Educ. **48**, 1273–1296 (2018). https://doi.org/10.1007/s11165-016-9602-2
37. Fosnacht, K., Sarraf, S., Howe, E., Peck, L.K.: How important are high response rates for college surveys? Rev. High. Educ. **40**(2), 245–265 (2017). https://doi.org/10.1353/rhe.2017.0003
38. Abós, Á., Haerens, L., Sevil, J., Aelterman, N., García-González, L.: Teachers' motivation in relation to their psychological functioning and interpersonal style: a variable - and person-centered approach. Teach. Teach. Educ. **74**, 21–34 (2018). https://doi.org/10.1016/j.tate.2018.04.010

Analyzing Teachers' Diagnostic and Intervention Processes in Debugging Using Video Vignettes

Heike Wachter(✉) and Tilman Michaeli

Technical University of Munich, Arcisstraße 21, 80333 Munich, Germany
{heike.wachter,tilman.michaeli}@tum.de

Abstract. Providing individualized support to students during debugging is a huge challenge for teachers in K-12 computing education. In these everyday assessment situations, they often have little time to gather relevant information to diagnose the student's problem and respond with an appropriate intervention. Thus, diagnostic and intervention processes in debugging are essential for teachers. Despite the importance, there is a lack of research on this topic and its possible implications for the classroom. Therefore, this paper aims to provide insights into teachers' diagnostic and intervention processes in debugging. In this qualitative study, we investigate situation-specific aspects teachers consider for diagnosing error situations and interventions they apply in a specific debugging-related situation using video vignettes. To this end, scripted video vignettes depicting a typical classroom debugging situation were presented to experienced teachers, who reported their observations in open-ended questionnaires. The data were then analyzed using qualitative content analysis. The results show a wide range of different aspects used in diagnostic processes and in proposed interventions. Furthermore, our results indicate that teachers rarely address motivational and emotional aspects of debugging in their interventions. These findings contribute to a better understanding of teachers' diagnostic and intervention processes and how they can be fostered in teacher education.

Keywords: debugging · K-12 · computing education · diagnostic and intervention process · video vignettes

1 Introduction

Debugging – that is, finding and fixing errors in program code – is an important and unavoidable part of programming [29]. However, for novice programmers, finding and fixing errors is a huge challenge [3] and a barrier to learning programming. In K-12 computing education, students often rely on the teacher for support [3]. In consequence, teachers tend to rush from student to student, trying to get them to solve the problem on their own in a short period of time [25]. Thus, for teachers in K-12 classrooms, individual support for students in debugging is a major challenge as well: On the one hand, the teachers want to support the students so they don't feel neglected. Still, on the other hand, the teachers also want the students to try to debug their program themselves rather than having the solution dictated to them or even typed out for them.

While supporting a student, the teachers go through a multi-step diagnostic and intervention process (cf. [17,18]). First, the teacher must identify the problem and why the student is stuck. Based on this diagnosis, the teacher has to consider a suitable intervention. The assistance should be minimal to foster the student's self-reliance [17]. Finally, the teacher carries out the intervention and evaluates whether the student was able to solve the problem successfully.

Diagnostic and intervention skills are considered as a core element of teachers' PCK and professional competence [1]. However, pre-service teachers often experience difficulties practicing diagnostic and intervention processes in their first years of teaching [5]. Therefore, the development of diagnostic and intervention skills plays a central role in successful teaching and should be fostered in teacher education [4].

However, there is little scientific evidence on teachers' diagnostic and intervention processes in debugging. Detailed information about the processes and how they can be fostered is necessary to promote diagnostic and intervention processes in teacher education. Therefore, the present work aims to gain insights into the processes using video vignettes. Thus, we investigate situation-specific aspects that teachers consider in their diagnosis and their proposed intervention to understand teachers' diagnostic and intervention processes and how they can be fostered.

2 Background and Related Work

Diagnostic Process. In the daily teaching practice, teachers are often confronted with spontaneous assessment situations in which they need to gather information about their students' learning prerequisites, processes, and outcomes [5]. The diagnostic process is defined as the assessment of different situations in which knowledge is applied to solve problems and make decisions [11]. Typically, diagnostic processes focus on identifying aspects or characteristic expressions of individuals [1]. Thus, diagnostic processes in teaching mean the assessment of relevant aspects for student learning [2]. Therefore, teachers need to recognize students' different learning needs, abilities, interests, and motivations [36].

Diagnostic skills are an essential element of teachers' professionalism [1] and also referred to as a key competence [18], as a successful diagnostic process enables teachers to provide individual support to their students and to adapt their teaching to students' needs [36].

In debugging situations, teachers must recognize and assess relevant situation-specific aspects to identify the problem and make a diagnosis. Doing so, they build on knowledge about typical errors, misconceptions, and other problems in introductory programming [30]. They have to understand why the student made an error and cannot solve it independently. A lack of content knowledge, interest, or knowledge of debugging strategies [13,25] could be the reason. Further, motivational and emotional aspects can be crucial in students' debugging processes [16]. Based on this diagnosis, teachers can anticipate various possibilities of support, taking the student's ability and level of knowledge into account [15].

Intervention Process. The results of diagnostic processes can be used to determine subsequent measures, so-called *interventions* [33]. An intervention is a minimal interference in the student's problem-solving process, which enables the student to overcome a barrier in the learning process and continue working independently [20]. In addition, suitable interventions do not focus only on problem-solving but consider the cognitive, motivational, and emotional aspects of learning. [33]. With the help of appropriate interventions, high student achievement can be attained [37]. Therefore, teachers need an extensive repository of interventions [17] and the skill to choose the right intervention for each situation.

In debugging, the teacher implements an intervention based on the previous diagnosis to help the student overcome the difficulties in finding and fixing the error. When deciding on a suitable intervention, the teacher has to consider the student's learning level [15] and how much support is necessary, as the assistance should be minimal to foster the student's self-reliance [17]. Further, there is evidence of features for suitable interventions [17]. In line with current research on intervention features (cf. [33]), debugging interventions must be effective and efficient. The aim is to ensure that students not only grasp the necessary concepts to work independently but also receive timely assistance with minimal time and effort, allowing teachers to attend to the needs of all students equitably.

Investigating Diagnostic and Intervention Processes in Debugging.
Teachers' diagnostic and intervention skills are rarely investigated in computing education. Looking at debugging, existing research focuses on the skills needed for debugging and how these can be taught to students in the classroom. Various studies investigate the debugging behavior of novices, providing evidence on novices' typical errors or difficulties [27], helpful methods and approaches that can support learners in debugging [26], and skills and knowledge needed for effective debugging [25].

However, in contrast to automated approaches to diagnostics and feedback in programming [7], there is little evidence on how teachers diagnose and intervene in class. Tsan et al. [35] investigated teachers' PCK in debugging after a training with Scratch. They concluded that teachers often supported their students with code-level solutions when encountering incorrect code. Furthermore, some preliminary evidence exists on teachers' interventions when supporting students in the K-12 classroom [13]. Concerning student-teacher interaction for debugging, Nixon et al. [28] analyzed two teachers' approaches to support students facing uncertainties in engaging with physical computing systems. They observed strategies the teachers applied in these situations, such as asking questions, articulating the problem, or giving directions. Similarly, Hennessy Elliott et al. [12] analyzed the pedagogical approach of a middle school teacher supporting her students in learning to debug physical computing systems. In particular, they identified pedagogical possibilities used by the teacher for supporting students, such as emphasizing a systematic process that prepares students for potential problems, affective responses to students' frustration and joy, or positioning themselves as learners alongside their students during programming and debugging. In summary, there is only very limited evidence of teachers' diagnostic and intervention processes (and their connection) in debugging.

Video Vignettes. Video vignettes are a common and effective approach for evidence-based teacher education [9, 32] and investigating diagnostic and intervention processes [5]. As specific teaching-learning behaviors are often difficult to observe in natural classroom settings [32], researchers have developed scripted video vignettes [5] to facilitate observation of these aspects. Such video vignettes have the advantage that they offer *representational scaffolding* in contrast to the complex situation in the classroom [8]. Furthermore, they can be viewed multiple times and with different emphases, which helps foster pre-service teachers' PCK [10]. Video vignettes are particularly used in other educational sciences such as maths [34], physics [19], or biology.

3 Methodology

This work investigates situation-specific aspects teachers consider and assess when diagnosing students' debugging problems and the intervention they would suggest in this situation. Therefore, we address the following research questions:

- **RQ1:** *Which situation-specific aspects do teachers consider when diagnosing students' problems?*
- **RQ2:** *Which interventions do teachers propose based on their diagnosis?*

Video Vignettes. We employed a video vignette approach with questionnaires to answer the research questions. To this end, we presented teachers with scripted video vignettes showing typical teaching situations. This allows us to investigate teachers' diagnostic and intervention processes in a particular situation as video vignettes simulate typical classroom situations realistically [9]. In contrast to screenshots and program files where only information from the code is available, the teacher has all the situational aspects available for diagnostic purposes that they would have in an actual classroom situation. In addition, unlike field observations, this approach makes the data collected more comparable, as all participants responded to the same situations.

We used four scripted video vignettes showing typical debugging situations for a pair of students in the classroom. The particular situations are derived from literature on common novice problems and behaviors and from practical experience (see [38]). All vignettes have a duration between 3 and 4 min. The behavior, communication, and content of the screen (see Fig. 1) of two students working together and struggling with a particular error are presented. The content of the vignettes is described below.

In *video vignette 1* (*V1*), two students program a ball in the Java development environment Greenfoot. However, their program contains a syntax error and thus can not be executed. The students identify the incorrect class and try to fix the error independently. But they insert the missing bracket in the wrong place. As a result, the semicolon is missing as a closing argument, and Greenfoot returns an error. In *video vignette 2* (*V2*), the students get multiple error messages caused by an erroneous library import. The incorrectly integrated library leads to an error and two subsequent errors when calling the library functions. They switch between the errors and read the error messages but do not understand them. *Video vignette 3* (*V3*) shows how the students create an object ball and receive a null pointer exception. They do not understand the error message and try to close the window several times. Finally, in *video vignette 4* (*V4*), the students try to implement a boost function for the ball and receive another null pointer exception. The students are unsure about how to proceed since the object exists.

Fig. 1. Screenshot of Vignette 1

We asked teachers participating in the study to rate the authenticity of the teaching situations shown in the video vignettes. Based on the statement, "The video vignette shows an authentic teaching situation," teachers used a 5-point Likert scale ranging from 1 (Strongly Disagree) to 5 (Strongly Agree) for rating.

For all video vignettes, we received confirmation of predominantly realistic classroom situations (mean: 3,86, median: 4).

Data Collection and Analysis. Data was collected in the context of three professional development workshops on debugging with K-12 computer science teachers in Germany. We collected the data at the beginning of the workshops to prevent data bias and to ensure validity. For each vignette, the student's behavior was presented twice, with a five-minute gap in between to take notes. Afterward, the participants had time to complete the questionnaire.

A total of 23 teachers participated in the study. We did not pre-select them, so we had one teacher with little experience in Java programming. However, most of the teachers had advanced knowledge of Java programming and at least five years of teaching experience in grades 7 to 12. Given time constraints, not every vignette was used in all three workshops. In summary, we received 15 completed questionnaires for V1 and V3, 14 for V2, and 13 for V4.

In this workshop setting, we considered questionnaires with an open response format most appropriate for data collection, addressing the limited time available but still enabling open response options. The questionnaire was structured as follows: In the first question, the teachers were asked to describe which aspects of the students' behavior they noticed in the video. The second question deals with why the students cannot solve the problem on their own. The teachers should give their diagnosis and briefly explain how they came to this conclusion. Finally, in question 3, the teachers were asked to explain how they would react as teachers in the respective teaching situation. The questions 1 and 2 refers to RQ 1 and question 3 to RQ2.

To analyze the data, we conducted a qualitative content analysis according to Mayring [23] with inductive category formation. The analysis was software-supported with MAXQDA. Before data analysis, we cleaned the data set of empty and meaningless responses. Then, a category system was developed inductively for the remaining answers. Therefore, each new code was checked to determine whether it could be classified in an existing category or, if not, a new category was created. If, on the other hand, a new coding fits into more than one category, the concerned categories were too specific. They were then combined into a new category with an appropriate name. The first author mainly carried out the coding. For reliability testing, a second researcher independently coded 10% of the data. The categories created intuitively in this way largely corresponded to the first author's categories. If there was a discrepancy, both researchers decided which category name best reflected the content. The intercoder reliability showed a match of 70% (Cohen's Kappa coefficient: 0.70) [24].

4 Results

RQ1: Which situation-specific aspects do teachers consider when diagnosing students' problems?

First, we analyzed the aspects the teachers noted for diagnosing students' problems. Thus, we developed a category system with aspects considered in the teachers' diagnostic process. These categories are described below.

Content Knowledge: Commonly, teachers identified a lack of content knowledge and its application in a particular situation as reasons for the students' struggling. For example, teachers noted a "lack of syntactic knowledge", "lack of basic understanding", or "terms and meaning seem unclear".

Problem-Solving Strategies: In addition, teachers identified aspects concerning problem-solving strategies as one of the reasons why students could not solve the problem independently. Many teachers described the students' approach as "trial and error using hints from the program" or "changing the code without much reflection (trial and error)". Especially in the context of dealing with error messages, the teachers noted the student's lack of any systematic approach to cope with them. One teacher described this as "they lack the experience to 'interpret' the error messages".

Emotion: An emotion describes the expression of feelings, such as joy or anger. Some teachers mentioned students' emotional reactions when dealing with debugging problems. For example, in vignette 4, the teachers recognized the students' joy at their progress ("joy of students about own success"). They also mentioned their frustration when the following error occurred ("error is recognized and generates strong emotional reaction (frustration)").

Motivation: Motivation is the process of setting and pursuing goals and is often influenced by emotions. Teachers noted motivational aspects regarding the students' debugging in the video vignettes. They mentioned that students were initially keen to fix the error but quickly gave up. One teacher described the initial motivation as a "visible desire to find a solution". More teachers mentioned the students' resignation, for example, "giving up quickly" or "the students call the teacher immediately to get help". Some teachers concluded that this lack of motivation was why the students could not solve the problem. For example, they mentioned "because they do not try" or "only half-hearted participating (one student)" as reasons.

Comparing the teachers diagnosis, we found a large variance in the teachers' responses. Teachers perceived different situation-specific aspects when viewing a vignette. Thus, different diagnoses were made for the same debugging situation. Many teachers focused on aspects of content knowledge and debugging strategies during the monitoring. In contrast, motivational and emotional aspects were mentioned only occasionally.

RQ2: Which interventions do teachers propose based on their diagnosis?

Analyzing the teachers' answers on the interventions they would apply in the specific debugging situation, we categorized the interventions as follows:

Asking Questions: One kind of intervention teachers noted, in our data, was to use questions to lead students. We can distinguish between two types of questions: questions at the beginning of the interaction with the student that might serve to quickly gather information about the current problem while still leading the students, for example, "Where does what error occur?" or "What do you want the code to do?". The other type of questions our data reveals are several consecutive questions. We suppose these series of questions were used to guide the student in finding and fixing the error. Therefore, the teachers proposed a series of questions that build on each other to guide the students toward solving the problem. An example of this was for Vignette 2: "What are libraries? Why do we need them? How can we use libraries? What are the consequences of not loading libraries? Were there really three errors?". This type of intervention was mentioned by many teachers regardless of the situation presented in the vignette.

Giving Hints: Another frequently mentioned intervention is giving hints to students on how to solve problems. Teachers use hints, for example, to help students isolate an error: "give hints, where the wrong parenthesis belong to" or "suggest what the problem could be (typical errors)". To solve the problem, hints on programming concepts or keywords in the code are suggested ("remember the keyword new!").

Explain: Another type of intervention we identified is to explain concepts or procedures. Teachers reported that they would explain necessary concepts such as imports ("explain what imports are for") or clarify procedures ("explain to students that an object 'ball' must first be created") to support students. Sometimes, these are illustrated with examples ("make students aware of the correct syntax by giving an example").

Problem-Solving Together: Furthermore, many teachers proposed a collaborative approach to supporting students. For example, they noted down "executing the code step by step to understand the logic" together with the students so that they could understand where the error occurred. Some teachers also suggested teaching students a systematic approach to debugging by doing it together, such as "let the students mark structural units in the code → does each structure have everything required?".

Encourage Independence: Some teachers considered it essential to encourage students' independence. One teacher, e.g., noted: "encourage them to find their own solutions". Furthermore, teachers proposed to "encourage students to use some of the existing solutions" or strategies they already know. Another approach in this category was to "let them analyze the error message" and "look up commands individually" or to "let students refer to syntax (look it up)".

Discuss in Class: Some teachers suggested discussing errors that occur for the first time or affect a large number of students in the class: "discussion in the class when an error occurs for the first time".

For all vignettes, we found that the teachers often did not suggest only one type of intervention in a particular debugging situation but combined different approaches. For example, for the syntax problem in vignette 1, one teacher noted down to first give a hint about where the missing parenthesis should go and then explain why the compiler does not show the correct location for the parenthesis. A closer look at the chosen interventions reveals that teachers primarily focus on aspects regarding content knowledge and problem-solving strategies. Regarding content knowledge teachers suggested: "referring students to syntax", "looking up commands one by one", "explaining import procedure", and "explaining the structure of a control condition". In terms of problem-solving strategies, teachers suggested, for example, "discussing a systematic approach", "letting the students explain the procedure and encouraging them to use some of the solutions already available", and "making suggestions about what could be the reason (typical errors)" or drawing attention to program features ("pointing out the red wave"). At the same time, motivational and emotional aspects that impact self-directed learning are rarely considered within the interventions. For example, in video vignette 3, the students try to solve the error independently and persist for a long time. Most teachers did not note this aspect as part of their diagnosis, and no teacher mentioned praising them for their effort in their intervention. Considering the intervention chosen in the context of the situation presented and the diagnosis made, we find that only some teachers chose interventions tailored to the situation and diagnosis. In one case, for example, the teacher noted in his diagnosis, "The students show a lack of prior knowledge. They cannot categorize the terms." and his suggested intervention was to "run the program step by step to understand the logic". Furthermore, many teachers chose rather general intervention strategies that work in different situations, e.g., "discuss systematic approach" or "analyze error message together", regardless of their diagnosis.

5 Discussion

To gain insights into teachers' diagnostic and intervention processes in debugging, we investigated them through video vignettes. The teachers rated the authenticity of the video vignettes with an average acceptance value of 3.86 and median of 4 on a 5-level Likert scale (1: "strongly disagree", 5: "strongly agree"). Thus, we assume the video vignettes reflect the teachers' practical experience and authentically resemble typical classroom situations.

Our results show a large variance in the considered situation-specific aspects and the resulting diagnosis among the teachers. Thus, teachers made different diagnoses for the same video vignette. We were surprised by these results, and we can't exactly explain where the differences came from. Possible reasons for the differences could be different backgrounds, different experiences, or different qualifications of the teachers. Which should be investigated in future work.

Furthermore, our data indicates that teachers often focused on aspects of content knowledge and problem-solving strategies but rarely noted motivational and emotional aspects. Content knowledge and problem-solving strategies address central components of programming and debugging skills [31] and thus are essential to consider. However, there is evidence that motivational and emotional aspects are particularly important for supporting students in debugging. Debugging can be seen as a productive failure [14] and thus involves an interplay between emotion, motivation, and learning [22]. Various studies investigated students' emotional reactions toward debugging (e.g., [6,16]). They found that emotional reactions, especially negative ones, impact students' performance, and self-efficacy [21]. Thus, we consider motivation and emotion essential aspects for teaching to consider while diagnosing and intervening. Hennessy Elliott et al., e.g., present a teaching approach in debugging, considering these aspects [12].

The intensity of support in teachers' proposed interventions also varied considerably between teachers. Some focused on promoting students' independence and suggested only minimal assistance. Others proposed actively accompanying the students' solution process by discussing the code. These results are in line with [25]. The differences in the suggested intervention may originate from the video vignette situation and the respective representational scaffolding. In the actual teaching practice, interventions are also heavily dependent on the available time for one particular student, as one teacher noted: "Depending on the time available: general advice if there is much time, more specific advice the less time is available."

One perspective to analyze teachers' proposed intervention can be whether they focused primarily on fostering students' process or the product [12]. While the former aims to support the student's debugging process in the longer term with its intervention, the latter is primarily concerned with helping the student solve the current problem and achieve an executable program. In our data, we found both dimensions. For example, one teacher suggested "reading and understanding the code with the students (taking it apart)". This collaborative approach helps the student to understand the error and how to deal with it - so the focus is on the process. Another teacher suggested giving the students a hint that "the semicolon and the bracket are arranged incorrectly". Here, the focus of the proposed intervention is on solving the problem quickly and, therefore, on the product. Overall, we saw a focus on the product for most suggested interventions in our data.

Limitations. A possible limitation of this study is the difference between the video vignettes and the actual classroom situations. Participants have much more time to focus on individual cases and see a much longer extract of the students working on their problem (about 3–4 min) as possible in the teaching practice. In addition, video vignettes miss the teacher-student relationship. Usually, teachers know their students and their characteristics. These may influence the diagnosis as well as their proposed interventions. However, the representational scaffolding provided by this approach allows detailed insights into the participants' processes. Moreover, teachers rated the situations presented in the video vignettes as authentic.

A methodological limitation could be that we used questionnaires with an open-ended response format to conduct the study. Interviews could have provided a deeper insight into the diagnostic and intervention process due to their interactive nature and the possibility of asking follow-up questions. Therefore, building on these results, we plan to extend the study with interviews.

6 Conclusion and Future Work

This paper provides findings on teachers' diagnostic and intervention processes in debugging. To this end, we presented scripted video vignettes to teachers showing specific situations with students struggling with debugging. This allowed us to analyze how teachers diagnose particular problem situations and what interventions they suggest to support their students in these situations.

Our results show a large variance in the situation-specific aspects considered for the diagnosis, and different diagnoses for the same situation. Furthermore, our data indicates that teachers often base their diagnoses on aspects related to content knowledge and problem-solving strategies, while motivational and emotional factors are only rarely considered.

The interventions suggested by the teachers to deal with the problem situation provide insights into the teachers' intervention repertoires and the selection of an intervention for a particular diagnosis. As with the diagnosis, our data shows that teachers rarely considered motivational and emotional aspects in their interventions. Furthermore, the data indicates that many teachers chose interventions that work in different situations; only some teachers chose interventions tailored to the situation and diagnosis.

Despite their importance in teachers' daily practice, diagnostic and intervention skills (not only for debugging) have received very limited attention within computing education. We believe that it is essential to foster such skills in teacher education and professional development. To this end, our findings contribute to our understanding of teachers' diagnostic and intervention processes in debugging and provide valuable implications. In particular, we consider it crucial to emphasize the importance of emotional and affective components in diagnosing and intervening in the classroom. Similarly, our findings highlight the importance of striking a balance between helping students get unstuck (product focus) and promoting their autonomy in debugging by providing appropriate strategies (process focus). In general, the apparent disparity and variety of diagnoses and interventions we found in our data points to the complexity of this process – which, in turn, underscores the need for supporting teachers.

In future work, we aim to investigate the quality of teachers' diagnostic and intervention processes. Furthermore, we want to evaluate the effectiveness of a video vignette approach for fostering diagnostic and intervention skills in debugging in teacher education.

References

1. Aufschnaiter, C.V., et al.: Diagnostic competence: theoretical considerations concerning a central construct of teacher education. ZfPäd **61**(5), 738–758 (2015)
2. Binder, K., et al.: Diagnostic skills of mathematics teachers in the COACTIV study. In: Leuders, T., Philipp, K., Leuders, J. (eds.) Diagnostic Competence of Mathematics Teachers, pp. 33–53. Springer, Cham (2018). https://doi.org/10.1007/978-3-319-66327-2_2
3. Carver, S.M., Klahr, D.: Assessing children's logo debugging skills with a formal model. JECR **2**(4), 487–525 (1986)
4. Chernikova, O., et al.: Simulation-based learning in higher education: a meta-analysis. Rev. Educ. Res. **90**(4), 499–541 (2020)
5. Codreanu, E., et al.: Between authenticity and cognitive demand: finding a balance in designing a video-based simulation in the context of mathematics teacher education. Teach. Teach. Educ. **95**, 103146 (2020)
6. Dahn, M., DeLiema, D.: Dynamics of emotion, problem solving, and identity: portraits of three girl coders. Comput. Sci. Educ. **30**(3), 362–389 (2020)

7. Danielsiek, H., et al.: Undergraduate teaching assistants in computer science: teaching-related beliefs, tasks, and competences. In: EDUCON, pp. 718–725 (2017)
8. Fischer, F., et al.: Representational scaffolding in digital simulations-learning professional practices in higher education. ILS **123**(11/12), 645–665 (2022)
9. Gamoran Sherin, M., Van Es, E.A.: Effects of video club participation on teachers' professional vision. J. Teach. Educ. **60**(1), 20–37 (2009)
10. Gaudin, C., Chaliès, S.: Video viewing in teacher education and professional development: a literature review. Educ. Res. Rev. **16**, 41–67 (2015)
11. Heitzmann, N., et al.: Facilitating diagnostic competences in simulations in higher education: a framework and a research agenda. FLR **7**(4), 1–24 (2019)
12. Hennessy Elliott, C., et al.: Toward a debugging pedagogy: helping students learn to get unstuck with physical computing systems. ILS **124**(1/2), 1–24 (2023)
13. Hennig, H., Michaeli, T.: Investigating teachers' diagnostic and intervention skills in debugging. In: Proceedings of the 17th WIPSCE. ACM (2022)
14. Kafai, Y.B., et al.: Rethinking debugging as productive failure for CS education. In: 50th ACM TS SIGCSE, pp. 169–170 (2019)
15. Karst, K., Dotzel, S., Dickhäuser, O.: Comparing global judgments and specific judgments of teachers about students' knowledge: is the whole the sum of its parts? Teach. Teach. Educ. **76**, 194–203 (2018)
16. Kinnunen, P., Simon, B.: Experiencing programming assignments in CS1: the emotional toll. In: Proceedings of the Sixth ICER, pp. 77–86 (2010)
17. Klock, H., Siller, H.S.: Measuring an aspect of adaptive intervention competence in mathematical modelling processes. In: CERME11 (2019)
18. Klug, J., et al.: Diagnostic competence of teachers: a process model that accounts for diagnosing learning behavior tested by means of a case scenario. TATE **30**, 38–46 (2013)
19. Krumphals, I., et al.: Fostering pre-service physics teachers' diagnostic skills and readiness through video vignettes and micro-teaching sessions: an exploratory single-case study. Book of Extended Abstracts, p. 364 (2023)
20. Leiss, D.: Adaptive teacher interventions in mathematical modelling-empirical findings of a comparative laboratory and classroom study. JMD **31**, 197–226 (2010)
21. Lishinski, A., et al.: Students' emotional reactions to programming projects in introduction to programming: measurement approach and influence on learning outcomes. In: ACM ICER, pp. 30–38 (2017)
22. Litts, B.K., et al.: Perceptions of productive failure in design projects: high school students' challenges in making electronic textiles. In: Singapore: ISLS. ISLS (2016)
23. Mayring, P.: Qualitative content analysis: theoretical foundation, basic procedures and software solution. SSOAR, Klagenfurt (2014)
24. McHugh: Interrater reliability: the kappa statistic. Biochemia Medica **22** (2012)
25. Michaeli, T., et al.: Current status and perspectives of debugging in the K12 classroom: a qualitative study. In: EDUCON, pp. 1030–1038. IEEE (2019)
26. Michaeli, T., et al.: Improving debugging skills in the classroom: the effects of teaching a systematic debugging process. In: WIPSCE, pp. 1–7 (2019)
27. Michaeli, T., et al.: Investigating students' preexisting debugging traits: a real world escape room study. In: Koli Calling 2020. ACM (2020)
28. Nixon, J., et al.: Teachers' learning to support students during science inquiry: managing student uncertainty in a debugging context. In: ICLS, pp. 601–608 (2023)
29. Perscheid, M., et al.: Studying the advancement in debugging practice of professional software developers. Software Qual. J. **25**(1), 83–110 (2017)
30. Qian, Y., et al.: Students' misconceptions and other difficulties in introductory programming: a literature review. TOCE **18**(1), 1–24 (2017)

31. Robins, A., Rountree, J., Rountree, N.: Learning and teaching programming: a review and discussion. Comput. Sci. Educ. **13**(2), 137–172 (2003)
32. Seidel, T., et al.: Developing scripted video cases for teacher education: creating evidence-based practice representations using mock ups. In: Frontiers in Education (2022)
33. Severing, E., Weiß, R.: Quality development in research on vocational education, vol. 12. W. Bertelsmann Verlag (2013)
34. Sommerhoff, D., et al.: Pre-service teachers' learning of diagnostic skills in a video-based simulation: effects of conceptual vs. interconnecting prompts on judgment accuracy and the diagnostic process. Learn. Instr. **83** (2023)
35. Tsan, J., et al.: An analysis of middle grade teachers' debugging pedagogical content knowledge. In: ITiCSE, pp. 533–539. ACM (2022)
36. Vogt, F., Rogalla, M.: Developing adaptive teaching competency through coaching. Teach. Teach. Educ. **25**(8), 1051–1060 (2009)
37. Weinert, F.E., Schrader, F.W., Helmke, A.: Quality of instruction and achievement outcomes. Int. J. Educ. Res. **13**(8), 895–914 (1989)
38. Zoppke, T., Michaeli, T., Romeike, R.: Individuelle Unterstützung beim Debuggen – Video-Vignetten für die Lehrkräftebildung. In: INFOS 2023 (2023)

Role-Playing of Misconceptions in Teacher Training: Enhancing Pre-service Teachers' Understanding of Students' Programming Processes

Martin Weinert[✉] and Hendrik Krone

TU Dortmund University, Dortmund, Germany
{martin.weinert,hendrik.krone}@cs.tu-dortmund.de

Abstract. To teach programming effectively, instructors must possess diagnostic skills and the ability to provide individualized interventions. This requires a deep understanding of students' mental models and common misconceptions in programming, along with the capacity to assist students in refining their mental models where necessary.

In our approach, we utilize videos depicting secondary school students' programming processes to train pre-service teachers in diagnostic skills. While these videos facilitate initial diagnoses, they alone cannot confirm them. Therefore, a complementary method is essential to teach diagnostic conversations and interventions effectively.

To address this need, we developed tasks that aim at these skills by incorporating role-playing of students with misconceptions. Our research focused on evaluating pre-service teachers' engagement with these tasks and their reported outcomes.

Our findings reveal that it is hard for them to get into the mind of a student who holds misconceptions. They also report that trying to do so is useful for understanding students' thought processes.

The results suggest that role-playing tasks can foster the transition from theoretical knowledge about mental models to the practical ability to simulate their effects. In this way, our tasks contribute to bridging the gap between theory and practice in teacher training.

Keywords: Teacher Training · Diagnostic Skills · Mental Models · Misconceptions · Programming

1 Introduction

To ensure that our students learn computer science topics effectively, we need to equip our teachers with the necessary skills to help each and every student to reach his or her individual learning goals. This requires the teachers to be able to first asses their students' mental models and then help to refine them if necessary. Regarding the topic of programming, teachers' knowledge of misconceptions and their diagnostic skills are important precursors of effective teaching [9,16]. These topics should therefore be adequately taught to pre-service teachers.

Videos of programming students are one way of learning about misconceptions [3], and this helps the pre-service teachers to apply their knowledge about misconceptions and develop first diagnostic skill. However, neither does this involve direct interaction with the presented cases nor can the cases be resolved with certainty.

To counter these problems we developed tasks in which the pre-service teachers come up with cases themselves and role-play students as well as interviewers. Hazzan et al. argue that pre-service teachers should *wear different hats* in training [8]. Our tasks directly implement this idea by requiring the pre-service teachers to sometimes view cases from the perspective of a student and sometimes from the perspective of a teacher/interviewer. Role-playing has already been employed in educational settings [2,10,12] and has positive effects on understanding other people [7]. We employed role-playing in a course for pre-service teachers and focused on the following research questions:

RQ1 How do pre-service teachers conduct diagnostic interviews in a role-playing situation?
RQ2 How do pre-service teachers experience tasks about role-playing students with misconceptions?
RQ3 How should role-playing tasks be designed to support the pre-service teachers effectively?

To answer these questions, we have conducted a series of design experiments [6] in which we evaluated how pre-service teachers interact with a role-playing task. We collected the conversations from the role-playing sessions and reports from the pre-service teachers about the tasks and analyzed them in a qualitative process.

We found that pre-service teachers very rarely manage to induce cognitive conflicts during role-playing. Sometimes this comes from constructed responses that deny the cognitive conflict and hinder further progress of a conversation. We derived guidelines for role-playing tasks that should alleviate the difficulties of the pre-service teachers.

2 Theoretical Background

2.1 Conceptual Change and Cognitive Conflicts

Mental models and misconceptions tend to be held strongly by the people who have constructed them. Students usually do not change their conceptions unless in actual need of further development. Therefore, it is assumed that they need to be presented with cognitive conflicts in order to abandon their ideas about a concept and construct new ones [14].

The need for cognitive conflicts has been studied in different areas [13]. Fumador et al. have shown that in maths the effect of cognitive conflicts is higher than conventional teaching [4]. It should also be noted that the use of cognitive conflicts might have a negative effect on certain populations [18]. Nonetheless, cognitive conflicts have proven to be a useful tool for teachers. Pre-service teachers should therefore get the opportunity to develop their skills in introducing cognitive conflicts.

2.2 Role-Playing

Role-playing is an activity in which the participants impersonate fictitious actors. It is a collaborative activity in which the imagined actors interact in some way. The actors can be people in real-world(-like) settings or non-human parts of systems in general.

Role-playing has been used as a teaching method in different subjects [2,7,12]. It has especially been used in computer science [1,10]. Role-playing concepts can also be incorporated into courses [17] and therefore could be used in teacher training.

An important aspect of role-playing is *perspective-taking* [7]. This means to actively consider another persons viewpoint [5], which might be different to the own one. An important mechanism of role-playing is the possibility to experiment [7]. Since role-players are part of an imagined world, they can observe the reactions that their behavior produces. This mechanism of experimentation allows them to build and develop mental models of the played out situation.

Role-playing is therefore a special form of what Hazzan et al. call *wearing different hats* [8]. According to them, it is important for teachers to be able to switch their point of view to see situations from different perspectives. This includes the viewpoint of a student, which might be trained by imagining how he or she might react in certain situations.

3 Methods

3.1 Course and Task Structure

The presented tasks are part of a course on diagnosis and individualized assistance. The pre-service teachers first learn about misconceptions and mental models in general. Afterwards they also learn about programming misconceptions. Then they analyze videos of programming students and try to diagnose misconceptions and other mental models (Fig. 1).

In the presented unit, the pre-service teachers first analyze a diagnostic interview from Hazzan et al. [8] This interview consists of a programming task, the solution a student produced and a transcript of a conversation of that student with an interviewer. Afterwards, they construct similar cases themselves. To do that, they first select a programming task and produce a correct solution for it. Then they select a misconception (or multiple ones) and produce a flawed solution to the previously selected programming task.

During the role-playing session, each case is presented as a learning station. The pre-service teachers move freely between the stations and interact with

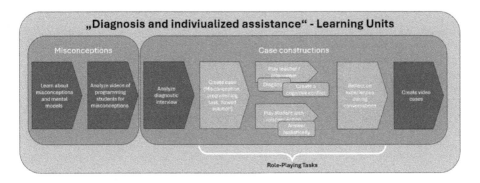

Fig. 1. Course and task structure

them. If they are at the station of a fellow pre-service teacher, they play the role of a teacher or interviewer. They pretend to meet the student, who created the flawed solution from the visited station. A conversation can be started (or continued) by writing a question or statement on an index card and leaving it at the station. From time to time the pre-service teachers return to their own stations and switch roles to play the student from their own case. In this role they reply to the questions at their station by coming up with an answer the student might have given. This answer is also written on an index card and connected to the question. In this manner multiple asynchronous conversations are played out.

The students have different goals when playing out the two roles: In the role of a teacher/interviewer, they first try to diagnose the misconception that was included in the case. Afterwards, they try to create a cognitive conflict in the student. In the role of the student, they try to answer the proposed questions realistically. This means that they have to stick to their misconceptions, unless presented with absolute necessity for change.

After the role-playing session, the pre-service teachers reflect on their experiences during the tasks. Their ideas and conclusions for future practice are collected and discussed. During the whole unit, the instructor mainly acts as a moderator and provides guidance during the role-playing sessions and group discussions.

3.2 Example of Data

To better understand the role-playing task, we present an example of a case and the resulting conversations of the role-playing session.

Task and Solution of a Student. Figure 2 shows an example task and a proposed flawed solution. (An overview of addressed misconceptions can be found attached, in Table 5 in Appendix A) The task requires moving the first number of an array to the last position and shifting the remaining numbers one position

```
1     //Task:
2     //Write a method to move the first number of an array
3     //(of data type int) to the last position, with all
4     //further numbers moving one position forward.
5
6     //Solution:
7     public void method(int[] arr) {
8         for (int i = 0; i < arr.length; i++) {
9             i = i + 1;
10            i + 1 = i;
11        }
12    }
```

Fig. 2. Example task and a solution of a student that holds multiple misconceptions

forward in the process. The pre-service teacher tried to create a setting where the student holds multiple misconceptions:

1. **Problem:** In line 9/10, the student performs a swap incorrectly. In line 9 i is overwritten with the value of $i + 1$. In line 10, the previous value of i is supposed to be saved in $i + 1$.
   Misconception: The student believes that line 9 and 10 are executed simultaneously [15].
2. **Problem:** In line 9 and 10 the index i is manipulated without accessing the array itself.
   Misconception: The student believes that the array is manipulated by working with the index alone.

Example of the Role-Playing Conversation. An example of the role-playing session's result is shown in Fig. 3. This case resulted in two conversations that were created in parallel. These conversations are sequences of questions and answers. In very rare cases conversations also branched and/or merged.

3.3 Evaluation

The role-playing tasks were evaluated in multiple ways, to include different perspectives into the analysis. In this section we discuss how the data was evaluated.

Data from three consecutive years was included in our investigation. A total of 27 pre-service teachers participated in the role-playing tasks. The tasks were implemented in a course on diagnosis and individualized assistance, which is a mandatory course in teacher training during the bachelor phase.

Pre-service Teachers' Reports. The course in which the tasks were given had to be completed with a portfolio, consisting of two parts: A reflective report on the personal learning processes during the different units of the course and a

Speaker	Text
T	Where is the variable i + 1 initialized?
S	In the line with i + 1 = i
T	Then why did you write int i = 0 first and then you can write i + 1 = i?
S	Because the i = 0 is in the head of the for-loop
T	What happens if you execute this?
S	In the array, i and i + 1 are swapped
T	What happens here if i = i + 1 and i + 1 = i are written in one block in a for loop?

(a) Learning environment with movable walls on which the discussions took place using index cards

(b) Transcribed and translated conversations from a case

Fig. 3. Examples of conversations in the role-playing session

video analysis. The content of the report on the learning processes was not graded to encourage the pre-service teachers to not only report good outcomes but also problems with the units. In this report they had to focus on three topics: How they worked on the units, what aspects of the tasks made them achieve learning outcomes, and what aspects did not help. A part of these reflections was a report on the learning processes during the role-playing tasks.

The central conclusions from these reports were collected, grouped according to the units and reviewed. This collection was separated from the overall grading process of the portfolios.

Simulated Conversations. To understand what the pre-service teachers did during the simulated conversations, the questions and answers were collected. They were analyzed in a process based on qualitative content analysis [11]. Two researchers (the authors of this article) worked on the material in a three step process. The process consisted of a first sighting, the structured encoding and finally a clarification of inconsistencies. In the first step, the researchers reviewed the material in an unstructured way to develop initial category systems for the questions and answers. In the second step, they coded the material and further developed the category system. After coding the researchers compared their results and discussed discrepancies without trying to convince the other researcher. After that they either kept or changed their choice. Finally, agreements and disagreements were counted to find the inter-coder reliability.

The corresponding figures are shown in Sect. 3.3. The agreement was already very high (see [11]) before the discussion process, and stayed so afterwards (Table 1).

Table 1. Overview over coding values

Value	Absolute	Relative
Coding units	259	100 %
Agreements before discussion	247	95.4%
Agreements after discussion	254	98.1%

During the coding process the two coders also collected hypotheses that came up while analyzing the material. These hypotheses were discussed and checked for plausibility afterwards.

4 Results

4.1 Category System

The qualitative analysis resulted in two category systems: One for the teachers' questions and one for the students' answers. These two category systems are presented here.

Categories for Teachers' Questions: Table 2 shows the category system that emerged from the analysis of questions asked in the role of a teacher.

Table 2. System of categories that emerged from the analysis of teachers' questions

Code	Name	Example
gD	General diagnostic question	What does the console show at the println(...)?
sD	Specific diagnostic question	When do you think will line 6 (what's inside the else) be executed?
Cc	Conflict construction	Would the program still work if you would name the variables differently? E.g. 'int' or 'maximum'?
E	Explanation	Look up what the '=' was used for, before and how we defined if-statements.
T	Task	Please try to repeat the task in your own words.
W	Wrong	What is the function of public Exercise()? *[The referenced code was part of the task itself]*

The first three codes (gD, sD, Cc) refer to the types of questions that were expected mainly, since they refer to the two phases of diagnostic conversations.

Questions that were intended to get more information about the student's concepts in general were coded as *general diagnostic questions (gD)*. In contrast, *specific diagnostic questions (sD)* showed that the student's problem was found or a certain misconception was identified. Questions that intended to induce a cognitive conflict were coded as *conflict constructions (Cc)*. Some pre-service teachers did not try to induce cognitive conflicts, but rather provided *explanations (E)*. A question or statement asking the student to repeat the *task (T)* is closely related to a general diagnostic question. Finally, some contributions were plainly *wrong (W)* or unrelated to misunderstandings of the case.

Categories for Students' Answers: Table 3 shows the category system that emerged from the analysis of answers given in the role of a student.

Table 3. System of categories that emerged from the analysis of students' answers

Code	Name	Example
R	Realistic	x is the number that you get. For example, when you get 5 then x should go from 1 to 5 and these numbers should be shown
C	Constructed	It depends

The answers produced by the pre-service teachers while playing the role of students were categorized as *realistic (R)* or *constructed (C)*. An answer that might be encountered in actual practice or was close enough to that was encoded as *realistic (R)*. Answers that tried to avoid a cognitive conflict in an unrealistic way or included Knowledge that the student would probably not have were coded as *constructed (C)*.

4.2 Quantitative Aspects

Table 4. Distributions of codings for questions (left) and answers (right)

Code	Quantity	%
gD (General Diagnosis)	25	17.9
sD (Specific Diagnosis)	75	53.6
Cc (Conflict construction)	19	13.6
E (Explanation)	10	7.1
T (Task)	8	5.7
W (Wrong)	3	2.1
Total	140	100

Code	Quantity	%
R (Realistic)	99	86.8
C (Constructed)	15	13.2
Total	114	100

To get an impression of the distribution of conversation contents, we present the numbers of encodings. Table 4 shows overviews of the quantities of question and answer types.

When in the role of a teacher/interviewer, the pre-service teachers often performed a general diagnosis or asked for a repetition of the task. Both are critical, because they imply that the pre-service teachers do not have an idea what the problem might be. They usually should be able to get an idea of the misconception from the case itself. However in nearly every fourth instance (23.6%, $gD + T$) they seem to have no specific starting point, as they resort to a general diagnosis or task repetition.

Another critical aspect is that only few attempts were made to lead to a cognitive conflict. This number was expected to be higher in comparison to the specific diagnoses.

Also critical is that there was a significant amount of attempts (7.1%) to fix the problem by providing an explanation. In the setting of the role-playing task this only makes sense after a cognitive conflict has been reached. However, not only was this accomplished in very few instances, the explanations were also not related to these situations. Explanations were sometimes even given as a first statement in a conversation.

A positive observation was that the pre-service teachers usually gave realistic answers, when in the role of a student.

4.3 Qualitative Aspects

After the coding phase, different phenomena and hypotheses were discussed.

The first phenomenon was that the pre-service teachers seem to not introduce new scenarios when trying to create a cognitive conflict. This was noticed, when the course instructor's contributions were examined. They were not included in the analysis itself, but were kept in the material as context for the pre-service teachers' replies. It was apparent that the instructor tried to induce cognitive conflicts by introducing different situations, for example by proposing different values for variables in the student's program. In contrast, the pre-service teachers tended to try directing attention to specific parts of the original situation. Remaining in the original situation made it hard to actually reach a cognitive conflict.

A second phenomenon was that conversations could not be continued after a constructed answer. Constructed answers denied the accomplishment of a cognitive conflict and forced the conversation to stay in a phase that was actually finished.

Another observation was that some cases resulted in very few and short conversations. We noticed that these cases featured tasks that implied a very specific solution. These tasks are unsuitable for actual practice in school.

4.4 Pre-service Teachers' Reports

In their reports, the pre-service teachers reported on their learning progress during the units in the course. They reported on different effects they experienced. We focus on what they reported about the role-playing tasks.

In general they rate the tasks as difficult, but at the same time useful and motivating. They state different experiences that might explain why they perceived the tasks in these ways.

The pre-service teachers report that the task required them to apply the previously learned concepts. They had to integrate their knowledge about misconceptions, appropriate tasks and useful diagnostic questions. This might lead to a positive impression because they needed to apply that knowledge for the first time. Such an integration of multiple concepts might also lead to a high congnitive load, which would explain the perceived difficulty.

They also report that they had to *think a misconception through* for the first time, which leads to a deeper understanding. Apparently they did not do this when learning about misconceptions. This implies that learning about a misconception does not immediately involve thinking about its role or consequences in practice.

Another report is that it was necessary to think differently about tasks. It was new for the pre-service teachers to anticipate what might go wrong when working on a task. They had to shift their perspective from the teacher's view of a task to the student's view.

An important effect they noticed comes from the difficulty of getting into the mind of a student. Because thinking in this way stands in contrast to the usual thought process, it is hard to apply it consistently. This leads to the misconception appearing in some parts of a program but being absent in others.

5 Discussion

We presented a unit that aims to help pre-service teachers acquire diagnostic and assistive skills. The tasks proved to be helpful, but challenging (RQ2). The perceived difficulty might come from the requirement of integrating different concepts into one case at the same time. It might also come from the pre-service teachers having little experience with creating tasks for students.

The main usefulness of our tasks comes from trying to get into the mind of a learner. Learning about misconceptions from literature is good to get a first idea. However, it does not directly lead to a deep understanding of the inner workings of a misconception. Pre-service teachers tend to focus on how the misconception is wrong rather than on how it works (RQ1). Our role-playing tasks shift that perspective, because they require the pre-service teachers to imagine what a student might say. For this they need to think about the knowledge the student has rather than the lack thereof.

The constructed answers might have come up because the pre-service teachers were instructed to stick to their misconceptions, which is an integral part of the task. However, it might sometimes be seen as a game, where the acted out student tries his or her best to avoid accepting a cognitive conflict. Therefore, it might be useful to relax this rule or clarify when it would be right to confirm a cognitive conflict. This might be accomplished by asking the pre-service teachers to come up with situations or requirements for abandoning the misconception. Through this they might get an idea of when it would be appropriate to acknowledge a cognitive conflict.

The *constructedness* of the tasks might be rooted in the lack of experience with task development. It might be useful to do an additional round of case creation to get an initial idea of how to create realistic tasks.

The pre-service teachers also tend not to propose new scenarios (RQ1). A reason for that might be that it is not clear to them that this might be useful to reduce the situation's complexity and focus on certain aspects. They might think that it is best to stay in the situation at hand and navigate inside it. An alternative explanation might be that they still are in an early phase of understanding of the case. In that case they are just still in the process of collecting information to come up with a first hypothesis. To clarify this, it might be useful to analyse the conversations together with the pre-service teachers and give direct feedback on the conversations.

In summary, we have found evidence that role-playing tasks can help pre-service teachers interconnect their theoretical knowledge about misconceptions and prepare it for application in practice. To help other educators in providing their students with this opportunity, we close this article with guidelines for role-playing tasks that we derived from our findings and plan to implement in future courses (RQ3). We also plan on testing and refining them in the future.

6 Guidelines for Implementation of Role-Playing Tasks

1. Implement the presented role-playing tasks: Give the role-playing tasks to pre-service teachers in a course to provide them with the opportunity to role-play as students with a misconception.

2. Include a first round of case construction: Let the pre-service teachers construct cases that are not used in the role-playing task, first. Discuss these tasks with the group and give feedback to prevent overly constructed cases.

3. Ask for definitions of misconceptions: Make the pre-service teachers write down the misconceptions that they included in their cases. They should phrase how the student thinks and avoid only stating problems.

4. Encourage acceptance of cognitive conflicts: Pre-service teachers should try to realistically and in a fair way judge whether a cognitive conflict is reached. They should be aware that their task is not to stick to their misconceptions under all circumstances. The pre-service teachers should be made aware that the situation should not be regarded as a game, since the person playing the student decides the outcome.

5. Analyze conversations afterwards and highlight good practice: Discuss the general experiences of the pre-service teachers and analyze the conversations with them. Work out good practices and possible hindrances for successful conversations.

A Addressed Misconceptions in Constructed Cases

Table 5. Misconceptions addressed by pre-service teachers in the cases they created for the role-playing sessions. (Some cases featured multiple misconceptions)

Misconception	Number of uses
Syntax	
Wrong direction of assignment	4
Assignment increments value instead of overwriting it	2
Omitting sign with variable name makes value positive	1
Function calls allow extra arguments	1
Array access through index alone (i instead of $a[i]$)	1
Variable declaration in wrong scope	1
Confusion of assignment operator with comparison operator	1
Variables	
Swap of values without helper variable or other preservation	2
Variable name determines its content	1
Variable as stack	1
Variable holds formula (with automatic update)	1
Variable values are only evaluated once the variable is used	1
Variable values can only be used when previously printed	1
Conditionals	
Conditional is executed immediately when condition is true	1
Execution is terminated after a conditional finishes	1
Conditional selects appropriate case even if it is missing	1
Program terminates if condition of conditional is false	1
else branch of conditional is always executed	1
Machine model	
Simultaneous execution of multiple instructions	1
All loops are executed in parallel	1
Division of integer by double yields double (in Java)	1
Assignment copies array in Java (deep copy)	1
String in *print* instruction in executed as regular instruction	1
Miscellaneous	
Misinterpretation of task	1
Bubblesort runs in a single pass	1
Wrong application of De Morgan's laws	1
Use of single variable for multiple purposes at once	1

References

1. Börstler, J.: Improving CRC-card role-play with role-play diagrams. In: Companion to the 20th Annual ACM SIGPLAN Conference on Object-Oriented Programming, Systems, Languages, and Applications (2005)
2. Cook, A.S., Dow, S.P., Hammer, J.: Towards designing technology for classroom role-play. In: Proceedings of the Annual Symposium on Computer-Human Interaction in Play (2017)
3. Fischer, J., Romahn, N., Weinert, M.: Fostering reflection in CS teacher education. A video-based approach to unveiling, analyzing and teaching novices' programming processes. In: Kori, K., Laanpere, M. (eds.) Proceedings of the International Conference on Informatics in School: Situation, Evaluation and Perspectives. CEUR Workshop Proceedings, vol. 2755, pp. 128–139. CEUR-WS.org (2020)
4. Fumador, E., Agyei, D.: Students' errors and misconceptions in algebra: exploring the impact of remedy using diagnostic conflict and conventional teaching approaches. Int. J. Educ. Learn. Dev. **6**(10) (2018)
5. Galinsky, A.D., Moskowitz, G.B.: Perspective-taking: decreasing stereotype expression, stereotype accessibility, and in-group favoritism. J. Pers. Soc. Psychol. **78**(4) (2000)
6. Gravemeijer, K., Cobb, P.: Design research from a learning design perspective. In: Educational Design Research (2006)
7. Hammer, J., To, A., Schrier, K., Bowman, S.L., Kaufman, G.: Learning and Role-Playing Games, pp. 283–299. Routledge, New York (2018)
8. Hazzan, O., Lapidot, T., Ragonis, N.: Guide to Teaching Computer Science: An Activity-Based Approach. Springer, London (2014). https://doi.org/10.1007/978-1-4471-6630-6
9. Kennedy, C., Kraemer, E.T.: Qualitative observations of student reasoning: coding in the wild. In: Proceedings of the 2019 ACM Conference on Innovation and Technology in Computer Science Education (2019)
10. Leverington, M., Yüksel, M., Robinson, M.: Using role play for an upper level CS course. J. Comput. Sci. Coll. **24**(4), 259–266 (2009)
11. Mayring, P.: Qualitative content analysis: theoretical foundation, basic procedures and software solutions. Klagenfurt (2014)
12. Nakamura, T., Taguchi, E., Hirose, D., Masahiro, I., Takashima, A.: Role-play training for project management education using a mentor agent. In: 2011 IEEE/WIC/ACM International Conferences on Web Intelligence and Intelligent Agent Technology (2011)
13. Pacaci, C., Ustun, U., Ozdemir, O.F.: Effectiveness of conceptual change strategies in science education: a meta-analysis. J. Res. Sci. Teach. **61**(6), 1263–1325 (2023)
14. Posner, G.J., Strike, K.A., Hewson, P.W., Gertzog, W.A.: Accommodation of a scientific conception: toward a theory of conceptual change. Sci. Educ. **66**(2), 211–227 (1982)
15. Qian, Y., Lehman, J.: Students' misconceptions and other difficulties in introductory programming: a literature review. ACM Trans. Comput. Educ. **18**(1), 1–24 (2017)
16. Sadler, P.M., Sonnert, G., Coyle, H.P., Cook-Smith, N., Miller, J.L.: The influence of teachers' knowledge on student learning in middle school physical science classrooms. Am. Educ. Res. J. **50**(5), 1020–1049 (2013)

17. Sheldon, L.: The Multiplayer Classroom: Designing Coursework as a Game. CRC Press, Boca Raton (2020)
18. Zohar, A., Aharon-Kravetsky, S.: Exploring the effects of cognitive conflict and direct teaching for students of different academic levels. J. Res. Sci. Teach. **42**(7), 829–855 (2005)

Author Index

A
Angermann, Tatjana 61

B
Bergner, Nadine 73
Bollin, Andreas 61
Brugger, Katharina 61

C
Chen, Jia-Yi 18

D
Dobiáš, Václav 99
Dolezal, Dominik 3

F
Feklistova, Lidia 152

G
Gaál, Bence 152
Grgurina, Nataša 30

H
Horváth, Győző 111

J
Jemetz, Michael 3
Jevsikova, Tatjana 152

K
Kastner-Hauler, Oliver 85
Kirby, Diana 139
Komis, Vassilis 125
Krone, Hendrik 180

L
Lavicza, Zsolt 85
Lee, Greg 18
Leonhardt, Thiemo 73

M
Marx, Erik 73
Michaeli, Tilman 167
Mößlacher, Corinna 61
Motschnig, Renate 3

P
Parriaux, Gabriel 125
Pellet, Jean-Philippe 125
Pluhár, Zsuzsa 152

S
Sabitzer, Barbara 85
Sentance, Sue 139
Šimandl, Václav 99
Sysło, Maciej M. 44

T
Tengler, Karin 85
Tolboom, Jos 30

V
Vaníček, Jiří 99

W
Wachter, Heike 167
Weinert, Martin 180
Whyte, Robert 139
Witt, Clemens 73
Wu, Yi-Ling 18

© The Editor(s) (if applicable) and The Author(s), under exclusive license to Springer Nature Switzerland AG 2025
Zs. Pluhár and B. Gaál (Eds.): ISSEP 2024, LNCS 15228, p. 195, 2025.
https://doi.org/10.1007/978-3-031-73474-8

Printed in the USA
CPSIA information can be obtained
at www.ICGtesting.com
CBHW051921201024
16144CB00007B/160

9 783031 734731